The Forgotten Sage

The Forgotten Sage

Rabbi Joshua ben Hananiah and the Birth of Judaism as We Know It

Maurice D. Harris

Foreword by
Leonard Gordon

CASCADE *Books* • Eugene, Oregon

THE FORGOTTEN SAGE
Rabbi Joshua ben Hananiah and the Birth of Judaism as We Know It

Copyright © 2019 Maurice D. Harris. All rights reserved. Except for brief quotations in critical publications or reviews, no part of this book may be reproduced in any manner without prior written permission from the publisher. Write: Permissions, Wipf and Stock Publishers, 199 W. 8th Ave., Suite 3, Eugene, OR 97401.

Cascade Books
An Imprint of Wipf and Stock Publishers
199 W. 8th Ave., Suite 3
Eugene, OR 97401

www.wipfandstock.com

PAPERBACK ISBN: 978-1-4982-0076-9
HARDCOVER ISBN: 978-1-4982-8651-0
EBOOK ISBN: 978-1-4982-0077-6

Cataloguing-in-Publication data:

Names: Harris, Maurice D., author | Gordon, Leonard David, foreword writer
Title: The forgotten sage : Rabbi Joshua ben Hananiah and the birth of Judaism as we know it / Maurice Harris, with a foreword by Leonard Gordon.
Description: Eugene, OR: Cascade Books, 2019 | Includes bibliographical references.
Identifiers: ISBN 978-1-4982-0076-9 (paperback) | ISBN 978-1-4982-8651-0 (hardcover) | ISBN 978-1-4982-0077-6 (ebook)
Subjects: LCSH: Joshua ben Hananiah—1st century. | Rabbinical literature | Jewish legends | Jews—History | Judaism—Essence, genius, nature. | Judaism—History—Talmudic period, 10–425.
Classification: BM502.3 H377 2019 (paperback) | BM502.3 (ebook)

Manufactured in the U.S.A.   05/23/19

Scripture quotations marked (NIV) are taken from the HOLY BIBLE, NEW INTERNATIONAL VERSION®. NIV®. Copyright©1973, 1978, 1984 by International Bible Society. Used by permission of Zondervan. All rights reserved.

OJPS translation © 1917 Jewish Publication Society.

For Bob and Glenda Crabbe -
May their memories be a blessing.

Contents

Foreword by Rabbi Leonard Gordon | ix
Preface | xi
Acknowledgments | xiii
Abbreviations | xv
Introduction | xvii

1 **Setting the Stage** | 1
2 **The Rabbis Also Have a Resurrection Story** | 13
3 **After the Holocaust** | 27
4 **Clash of the Early Rabbinic Titans—Part I** | 40
5 **Clash of the Early Rabbinic Titans—Part II** | 59
6 **Boom!** | 74
7 **Eliezer's Gaze Burns Everything It Touches** | 88
8 **Diplomacy, War, and Passing the Torch** | 113
9 **Don't Trust This Book—It Could Be Wrong** | 138
10 **Why This Rabbi Matters Now** | 150
11 **About Joshua Podro** | 157

Bibliography | 161

Foreword

We all know Abraham and Sarah and we all know Moses, Miriam, and Aaron, but few of us know the names and stories of the leaders who recreated Judaism after the Temple was destroyed by Rome in 70 C.E. Their task was monumental: a religion and a nation that had been focused on the Temple in Jerusalem and that had been led by hereditary priests and kings, would now need to reimagine itself. The physical center of Jewish life would now be in the verdant north of Israel, the Galilee, and not the rocky, often dry hills of Judea. As worship and learning replaced sacrifice, the religious center of the people's lives would be the synagogue and the house of study. And the central symbol of the Jewish people would be the Torah scroll, God as manifest on earth through text, in place of the menorah, shofar, and firepan that were symbols of the Temple and its grandeur.

Rabbi Maurice Harris, a teacher and author with a distinctive capacity for rendering the complex accessible in his books on Moses and the book of Leviticus, now turns his attention to the central question of Jewish survival. He brings to the project his experience as a congregational leader and a thinker devoted to building vibrant Jewish communal institutions in the pluralistic American environment. Ultimately, *The Forgotten Sage* asks what resources does our past have as we try to reimagine Judaism today? Like the rabbis of the second century C.E., we are a community living in the aftermath of catastrophe. Within the living memory of some, our American Jewish community is a post-traumatic community living in relative comfort in a place removed from, and connected to, the place where just seventy years ago European Jewry was almost extinguished. Like our ancestors living in the Galilee after the Jewish center in Judea was destroyed, we know that an older way of life needs to be both recalled and reimagined. What will that work of memory and reconstruction look

Foreword

like? The work of the first generations of rabbis is a distant mirror that can inform our own conversations.

In order to give his story a narrative focus, Rabbi Harris looks at the traditions around Rabbi Joshua ben Hananiah. Joshua was a figure who bridges two eras in the history of Judaism. A Levite whose family would have had vivid memory of the Temple worship, he became a leading sage in the era of rebuilding, someone who studied, we are told, with Rabban Yohanan ben Zakkai, the figure most often credited with saving the young rabbinic class as the Romans prepared to destroy the holy city.

The stories of the early rabbis are complex and their relationship to history remains subject to scholarly debate. Rabbi Harris's goal is not to decide what actually happened, probably an impossible task. Instead, he gives us a portrait of how the rabbis imagine this fruitful and creative period in Jewish history. The sources he draws on were close enough to the events described to more or less accurately reflect the earliest layer of Jewish thought on the death and resurrection of Judaism and Jewish life. In this book, you will learn about the relationship between the early rabbis and the leadership of Rome, and the complex relationships among the rabbis themselves. The rabbis needed to not only figure out how to do God's will in a radically new environment, they also needed to learn how to debate the Jewish future without destroying one another. Their commitment to compromise speaks directly to our day when those who argue about matters of religion and state often seem incapable of finding common ground.

When the Temple was destroyed it was not clear if Judaism and the Jewish people would survive. For hundreds of years small groups of rabbis, masters and their disciples, moved around the Galilee thinking and debating, preserving the past and building the institutions that would ensure the Jewish future. The success of their conversations is evidenced both in the dominance of rabbis, synagogues, and houses of study in the medieval and early modern eras, and in the way rabbinic Judaism continues to inform the outlines of Jewish life today. As our generation considers the rebirth of Judaism in the aftermath of the Shoah, I can think of no more important stories for our generation to consider and learn from than those gathered in this book.

Rabbi Leonard Gordon, D.Min.

Preface

"Moses delivered Israel from Egyptian bondage, making free men out of slaves, giving them a new religious dispensation, eradicating the rebels, and keeping the remainder in the wilderness until they were strong and disciplined enough to invade and hold Canaan. David's heroic adventures as a guerrilla leader, his eventual defeat of the Philistines, his restoration of Israelite independence, have equally glorified his name as a national deliverer. Ezra and Nehemiah won deserved praise for bringing back the remnant of Israel from Babylonian captivity and rebuilding the ruined walls of Jerusalem. . . . In desperate fighting against enormous odds, the Maccabee brothers prevented the Seleucids from Hellenizing Israel.

. . . Yet, if I were asked to name a national deliverer of Israel who performed the most difficult and thankless task of all, and showed the greatest faithfulness, I should unhesitatingly name Rabbi Joshua ben Hananiah, the poor Levite nail maker who judged Israel, saved her from complete demoralization in a most unhappy phase of her history, and conditioned her to survive even worse ordeals during the next eighteen centuries."[1]

—from Robert Graves's foreword to Joshua Podro's *The Last Pharisee: The Life and Times of Rabbi Joshua Ben Hananyah— A First Century Idealist* (1959)

---

1. Podro, *The Last Pharisee*, 7.

Acknowledgments

In the fall of 1999, I took my first courses in Rabbinic Civilization and Talmud. I was in my second year of studies at the Reconstructionist Rabbinical College (RRC) just outside of Philadelphia, and I had so much to learn. It was my good luck that RRC had just hired Rabbi Leonard Gordon, D.Min., to teach the year-long required course, "Rabbinic Civilization." I was equally fortunate to begin what would be multiple semesters of Talmud study with Rabbi Sarra Lev, Ph.D.

These classes quickly became the ones I looked forward to the most. Few teachers can tell a story, and then raise questions to mine and undermine that same story, with the clarity, humor, and precision of Rabbi Gordon. In Rabbi Lev's class, I broke my head over and over again against the pivots, turns, bumps, and sudden twists of Talmud. My study partner and I would attempt to diagram the *sugya* (a distinct section of Talmud) that we were studying, only to end up with drawings of incomprehensibly nested flow charts that could have doubled as science-fiction engineering schematics. With focus, patience, support, and high expectations, Rabbi Lev helped me learn to love the workout that is Talmud study. I could not possibly have set out to write a book like this without the educational foundation I gained thanks to these two brilliant and big-hearted teachers.

During the five years I worked on this book, many people read drafts of chapters and offered valuable feedback. I'm especially grateful in this regard to Rabbi Rena Blumenthal, Naomi Malka, Meagan Prince, and Bryan Schwartzman.

There were several synagogues that gave me the opportunity to give talks and lead adult education programs on elements of this book while it was a work in progress. In particular, I would like to thank Joel Rosenblit of Temple Beth Sholom in Salem, Oregon for giving me the chance to teach there. Thank you to Jackie Land and the members of Oseh Shalom

Acknowledgments

congregation in Laurel, Maryland for the chance to give a talk based on parts of the book, and similarly, thank you to the members of Or Shalom Jewish Community in San Francisco.

In 2015, I took part in a writers' workshop sponsored by the Collegeville Institute called "Writing Spirit, Writing Faith," led by the amazing Mary Lane Potter. Apart from Mary, I was the only Jewish person in this group of thoughtful and talented writers, many of whom are clergy in different Christian denominations. I learned so much from everyone in the group. Thank you to Helen Cepero, Deborah Core, Dena Ratliff Dyer, Christina Kukuk, Martha Postlethwait, Sarah Torna Roberts, Amy Seymour, Shirley Showalter, Richard Finley Ward, and Barbara Wheeler-Bride.

Thank you to Dr. David Brodsky and Rachael Burgess for letting me bounce ideas off them. Rabbi Alan LaPayover, Director of the RRC Library, was a constant and helpful resource.

Dr. Elsie Stern and Rabbi Mira Wasserman, Ph.D., both faculty members at RRC, helped me with questions about biblical and rabbinic texts, respectively.

Thank you to Jeremy Stone, the grandson of Joshua Podro, for sending me a photo of his grandfather, whose 1959 book about Rabbi Joshua ben Hananiah, *The Last Pharisee*, inspired me to move forward with this project at a critical juncture.

Thank you to my wife, Melissa Crabbe, for listening to hours and hours of my thoughts and questions about the issues involved in this book, and for sharing her incisive insights. I'm also grateful to my children, Clarice and Hunter, for their enduring encouragement and love.

The wonderful people at Wipf & Stock have my eternal thanks. In particular, I'd like to thank my editor, Robin Parry, and to thank James Stock for his encouragement and for treating me to many cups of very strong coffee at Theo's café.

This is my third Jewish studies book, and I am indebted to all the amazing teachers at the Reconstructionist Rabbinical College, as well as to the rabbis and thought leaders throughout the Reconstructionist movement of Judaism, for the tools and methods that have shaped me as a rabbi, as a Jew, and as a human being.

Finally, I thank the Source of Life for the gift of life and the joy of writing.

Abbreviations

Avot. R. Nat.	Avot d'Rabbi Natan
b.	Babylonian Talmud
Bekh.	Bekhorot
Ber.	Berakhot
B. Metz.	Bava Metzia
Deut. Rab.	Deuteronomy Rabbah
Ed.	Eduyyot
Eruv.	Eruvin
Exod. Rab.	Exodus Rabbah
Gen. Rab.	Genesis Rabbah
Git.	Gittin
Hag.	Hagigah
Hor.	Horayot
Hul.	Hullin
Ketub.	Ketubbot
Lam. Rab.	Lamentations Rabbah
Lev. Rab.	Leviticus Rabbah
m.	Mishnah
Meg.	Megillah
Mek.	Mekhilta
Midr. Tanh.	Midrash Tanhuma
Ned.	Nedarim
NIV	New International Version
Num. Rab.	Numbers Rabbah

Abbreviations

OJPS	Jewish Publication Society 1917 translation
Pesah.	Pesachim
Qoh. Rab.	Ecclesiastes Rabbah
Rosh Hash.	Rosh Hashanah
Ruth Rab.	Ruth Rabbah
Sanh.	Sanhedrin
Shabb.	Shabbat
t.	Tosefta
Ta'an.	Ta'anit
y.	Jerusalem Talmud
Yad.	Yadayim

Introduction

How did Judaism get its love of debate? Its openness to multiple viewpoints? How did Judaism come to so vigorously embrace questioning, including questioning God? What led Judaism to include within its religious "personality" a deep skepticism towards popular messianic figures (including, but not limited to, Jesus), yet an unflagging optimistic belief in a better future for humanity, in a messianic era to come?

How did Jews successfully cope with the collective trauma of their national destruction and forced exile by the Romans roughly two thousand years ago, without disintegrating as a people? Or without veering off into extreme responses to collective trauma (like asceticism), or without becoming eternally and dysfunctionally angry?[2]

What led to the rabbinic tradition's general distrust and suspicion of war as a viable response to oppression—an attitude that some have described as a rabbinic tendency towards "pragmatic pacifism?"[3] (I know, some people are thinking, "Pragmatic *pacifism*? But what about the Israeli army?" It's complicated, but for now suffice it to say that for the better part of two thousand years this was the tendency of the rabbinic tradition.) At the same time that Jews tended to distrust military responses to oppression

---

2. In 1990, the Dalai Lama received a group of Jewish religious leaders in Dharamsala to ask them similar questions. He was interested in learning things that might help the Tibetan people survive their own exile and domination. Some of this historic gathering is described in Rodger Kamenetz's 1994 book, *The Jew in the Lotus: A Poet's Rediscovery of Jewish Identity in India*.

3. Rabbi Maurice Lamm, in a 1978 essay on Jewish law and conscientious objection, wrote, "It must be affirmed that Judaism rejected total pacifism, but that it believed strongly in pragmatic pacifism as a higher morally more noteworthy religious position." I saw Lamm's quote in an online article by Rabbi Michael Broyde (https://www.myjewishlearning.com/article/pacifism-in-jewish-law/).

Introduction

and injustice, how did they become a people known for sticking up for the underdog and the unwanted?

Also, how did Jews find a way to remain a united people, despite being spread thin across so many countries, and how did they manage to do this without developing a centralized religious authority structure, like a pope or caliph, to serve as the binding glue uniting them despite their geographical dispersion? It seems a bit counter-intuitive that Jews would not have developed a centralized religious authority structure, given that Judaism's holiest sacred text, the Torah, is *very* authoritarian. The whole Torah is based on the assertion of God's absolute authority and the requirement that Jews submit to that authority.

To combine these many questions into one question: how did a lot of the things that people most admire about Judaism get started, and who were the people who helped set the religion on a path that led to Judaism manifesting these qualities? (Sorry, I realize that that was actually two questions. In Judaism it's really hard to limit yourself to just one question.)

Well, the answer is complicated. Many people, from biblical times to the present, contributed to the development of Judaism as we recognize it today. The stories of the heroes of the Hebrew Bible, from Abraham and Sarah to Moses, David, Esther, and Ezra, certainly helped shape the faith. And while we don't know whether many of these biblical figures actually lived or to what degree the stories about them reflect actual events, we do know that the stories, poems, and laws written by the ancient Israelites gave birth to many of the best religious ideas of Judaism.

The Jews of the biblical period absolutely deserve their due credit for their immense influences on the religion Judaism would evolve to become, but the Jews who really set the religion on the path to develop the character traits I described above were post-biblical. They were the ancient rabbis. They're the ones who drew on biblical elements in ways that helped bring us the kind of Judaism that questions and doubts, that resists allowing any one rabbi or dogmatic belief to assume too much authority. In her book *Slayers of Moses*, Susan A. Handelman writes that "the relentless skepticism of the rabbis manifested in the constant search for alternative explanations, an intense scrutiny of the most seemingly insignificant and mundane details, and the dialectical twists and turns of Rabbinic thought."[4]

---

4. Handelman, *Slayers of Moses*, 28.

Introduction

Although there were many ancient rabbis[5] who contributed to Judaism developing along these lines, it wasn't inevitable that Judaism would take on these characteristics. Throughout the pre-rabbinic and early rabbinic eras (roughly 175 B.C.E.–220 C.E.),[6] there was a lot of internal conflict within the Jewish community. And in the aftermath of the Roman destruction of Jerusalem and the exile of the Jews (70 C.E.), those conflicts grew more urgent. In that climate of trauma, crisis, and desperation for survival, different rabbis pushed hard for divergent visions of what Judaism would look like.

There were ancient rabbis who would have led Judaism to become more doctrinal and less open to debate; more militant and less reluctant to take up arms against oppressors; more intolerant of other faiths; more hierarchical in its religious leadership; and more focused on adhering strictly to the ideas of the past than on using creative interpretive methods to revitalize and renew the religion in each generation. The fact that Judaism *didn't* ultimately go those routes was largely due to the struggles and teachings of multiple rabbis across many generations.

Rabbinic literature doesn't give us a unified or coherent story about how rabbinic Judaism formed and took on its characteristics. But it does include a series of stories that feature one rabbi in particular whose decisions and teachings may have created a "tipping point" that set Judaism firmly on its course towards becoming the decentralized, multi-opinionated, exile-surviving, other-religion-respecting, pragmatic-yet-altruistic, wounded-yet-hopeful religion that we recognize in our time. Strangely, the vast majority of Jews today have never heard of him. And outside the Jewish world, he is utterly unknown. His name was Joshua ben Hananiah, and this book is about him, and the rabbis of his generation.

* * *

5. By "ancient rabbis" I mean the scholars and rabbis who lived and taught roughly during the years 100 B.C.E. to 550 C.E.

6. To be more precise, if we go back in time to 200 B.C.E., we're probably talking about a proto-rabbinic era, in which the Pharisees as a movement were developing the interpretive, ritual, and communal patterns that would come to characterize much of the rabbinic movement. It's impossible to point to a specific year when it makes sense to stop talking about the Pharisaic movement and start talking about the early rabbis. Ironically, the earliest written records we have that use the term "rabbi" are in the New Testament. Suffice it to say, by the time we get to the life and times of Jesus, there are already rabbis and Pharisees in the Judean religious landscape, and by the time we get to 200 C.E., there are plenty of rabbis, but Pharisees are only referred to in rabbinic literature in the past tense.

Introduction

He was physically ugly, unselfish, and poor. He made his living as a nail maker, or possibly a charcoal maker—one story tells of there being a lot of soot on the walls of his modest home. He was a young man during the last years of the Second Temple (the "Second Temple" was the Temple that stood in Jerusalem at the time of the Roman conquest), and legend has it that he even sang in the Temple choir.[7]

When anti-Roman Jewish militants, known as the "Zealots," launched a military revolt against the Roman occupation of Judea in 66 C.E., Joshua was a young sage under the tutelage of the most revered rabbi in Jerusalem, Yohanan ben Zakkai. Yohanan was deeply opposed to the Zealots. After the war with Rome intensified, the Romans cut off all supplies to the city. When the situation in besieged Jerusalem became hopeless, Joshua helped smuggle his master out of the city so he could attempt to negotiate for some remnant of Judaism to survive the imminent Roman destruction.

After the Romans devastated Jerusalem and burned down the Second Temple, they exiled large numbers of the surviving Jews to other parts of their empire, many as slaves. Rabbi Joshua was among the survivors who were allowed to stay behind, and from this point forward he became a kind of Jew we very much recognize in the post-Holocaust era: the shattered survivor of national catastrophe on a scale of horror for which there are no words. He was a trauma survivor tasked with trying to help a crushed and now scattered people survive and rebuild.

---

7. *b. Arakh.* 11b. Joshua was the descendant of Levites, the Israelite tribe from which came the priests as well as various Jewish families eligible to perform different kinds of Temple-service.

1

Setting the Stage

One of my goals with this book is to make the stories surrounding Rabbi Joshua and the early rabbis accessible to a wide, general readership. The chapters that follow this one focus in depth on a series of stories about Joshua and other key early rabbis found in the major works of ancient rabbinic literature, especially the Talmud and various collections of Midrash. In my experience as an adult educator in the Jewish community, and as a guest teacher in churches and interfaith learning settings, I've found that, because most people aren't familiar with the world of rabbinic literature, it's really helpful for me to start with a sweeping big picture of the stories I plan to discuss, and then come back to focus on each important part of that big picture and bore into the juicy details.

So, in this chapter you'll find: a very quick recap of the mythic story arc of the Hebrew Bible, an overview of the early rabbinic story that precedes Rabbi Joshua's lifetime, and then a quick encapsulation of the drama of the early rabbis in the era that Joshua lived (roughly 50 C.E. to 130 C.E.). If you're already well-acquainted with any or all of these things, you might want to skip parts of this chapter.

Before we dive in, a quick word for readers who aren't familiar with how the word "myth" is used in scholarly writing about religion. In this book, I use the words *myth* and *mythic* to refer to stories that intend to express timeless cosmic meaning and serve to orient people in the world. When I use these words, I don't mean them in the casual way they get used in modern English to mean "lies," as in, "oh, that's just a big *myth*!" While I don't believe that the mythic stories of any religion should be taken literally, I also don't mean to diminish the insights and truths found within sacred stories by using the word "myth." Okay, now onward!

The "Back Story" to the Story of the Early Rabbis (or the Story of the Hebrew Bible in a Nutshell)

Most Jews, Christians, and Muslims know at least the highlights of the great mythic foundation story of the Torah (Genesis–Deuteronomy). In case you need a quick recap, here's one:

> God creates the world; Abraham becomes the first monotheist and moves with his family to the land of Canaan; God promises Abraham that his descendants will inherit Canaan (the Promised Land); Abraham's offspring, the Hebrews, end up in Egypt, where they multiply greatly and a paranoid Pharaoh enslaves them; God sends Moses to liberate them; after ten nasty plagues and the splitting of the Sea of Reeds, the Hebrews are free; at Mount Sinai God gives them the Ten Commandments; Moses leads the Hebrews' through the desert for forty years en route to the Promised Land; on the eve of the Hebrews' arrival at the edge of the Promised Land, Moses gives his farewell address to the people and dies, unable to cross over the Jordan River with them.

This famous story is the mythic bedrock of Judaism, and it's a crucial part of the foundation of Christianity and Islam.

The Torah only includes the first five books of the Hebrew Bible (or Old Testament for Christians). The rest of the books of the Hebrew Bible tell a lengthy and dramatic post-Moses story that begins with Moses's successor, Joshua, leading the Israelites in conquest of the Promised Land.

Following Joshua's successful conquest of Canaan, the Hebrew Bible goes on to describe roughly eight centuries of Israelite civilization in that territory, beginning with several semi-anarchic, early generations of Israelite society. The books of Joshua and Judges describe the adventures and misadventures of the loosely confederated Israelite tribes during this era of decentralized government and ad hoc leadership.

Then comes the legendary rule of Israel's most famous kings, Saul, David, and Solomon. We read about the building of Solomon's Temple in Jerusalem (a.k.a. the First Temple), around 957 B.C.E., and we hear descriptions

Setting the Stage

of the gifts and sacrifices the Israelites would bring to the Temple priests at the appointed sacred times.

The epic story of the Hebrew Bible goes on to tell about the exploits of many generations of Israelite monarchs who followed—some faithful to God's teachings, and some... not so much. In addition to kings and priests, this story also features charismatic messengers of God known as prophets. Some of the prophets are seers of what is to come, some are ardent social justice advocates, some counsel kings, some work miracles, some are poets, some re-frame God's laws—and some are combinations of much of the above. Often, the prophets warn the powerful and the weak alike when they have strayed from God's ways.

In its last episodes, the Hebrew Bible describes the Babylonian empire's horrific destruction of the First Temple in Jerusalem (around 586 B.C.E.) and the exile of the privileged classes of ancient Israel to Babylon (as in, "by the waters of Babylon, we lay down and wept for thee, Zion."[1]) The greatest prophets of this era, such as Jeremiah and Ezekiel, counsel the Jews that God has brought this misfortune upon them due to their failure to follow God's laws (particularly those pesky ones about not worshipping idols and not exploiting the poor). But they also comfort the Jews by telling them that one day God will redeem them from their exile and defeat, and that by repenting sincerely they can help bring about national redemption.

The biblical story finally ends on a hopeful note.[2] The Babylonians get taken over by the neighboring Persians (around 540 B.C.E.). Then, we learn that the Persian king, Cyrus—a more enlightened sort of emperor than his Babylonian predecessors—decides to authorize the return of the Babylonian Jewish exiles and the rebuilding of the Jerusalem Temple. It all comes to a close in the books of Ezra and Nehemiah as hope and renewal have been restored. Construction of the Second Temple begins (about 515 B.C.E.) and a new generation of Jewish leaders starts re-teaching the common Israelites the laws and customs of the Torah.

* * *

After the conclusion of the epic saga of the Hebrew Bible, the official mythic stories of Judaism and Christianity diverge sharply. Christian tradition

---

1. Ps 137:1.

2. Well, sort of. The book that Jewish tradition treats as the chronologically final book of the prophets, Malachi, paints a portrait of a restored Israelite nation repeating some of the same moral and spiritual mistakes that led to calamity in previous eras.

begins its next round of sacred storytelling about five centuries after the Second Temple had been rebuilt. At this point, some two thousand years ago, the Roman Empire was dominating the region and had come to occupy the Jews' homeland. Christian scriptures go on to tell one of the most famous stories in the world: the story of the life, teachings, death, and resurrection of Jesus.

Following those events, the Christian mythic story[3] goes on to focus on the teachings, insights, and organizing activities of key followers of Jesus, most famously Paul. The sacred stories about the earliest centuries in the life of the community of Christ are filled with tales of cruel Roman persecutions as well as the spread of Christianity. Martyrs and missionaries, house churches and internal church debates fill out the arc of early Christianity's great mythic story.

Unbeknownst to many people, there is also another round of ancient Jewish mythic storytelling that is foundational to Judaism—an epic saga that takes place during roughly the same timespan as the early Christian mythic story that I just described above. This is the story of the early rabbis, and the Joshua who is the central character of this book is one of the leading figures of that story. This story can be found mainly within the rabbinic sacred writings known as Midrash and Talmud. In this book, we'll jump into that story sometime after it begins and jump out sometime before it ends, with the events bookending Rabbi Joshua's life framing the telling.

Setting the Scene

Let's set the scene by looking at the situation in the Holy Land around 30 B.C.E., about eighty years before Joshua ben Hananiah was born. For three decades now, the Roman Empire has occupied and ruled the country. Rome's appointed king, the infamous Herod the Great, is in power. The native Jews are deeply divided socially, politically, economically, and religiously. Political unrest, uncertainty, and factionalism abound.

In Jerusalem, Herod is busy enlarging the Second Temple in a massive construction project designed to make it one of the jewels of the Roman

---

3. I realize that I'm oversimplifying a lot here, and that some would rightly point out that there were multiple "Christian mythic stories" in conversation and sometimes in competition with each other during the first centuries of Christianity's development. For the moment, I'm trying to make some broad and general points to frame the chapters that are to follow.

Empire. An iron-fisted client king of the Romans, Herod imposed heavy taxes on the Jewish peasantry to help pay for his audacious building projects. As a pair of scholars of the period, Richard A. Horsley and John S. Hanson, put it:

> So that the ruthless Herod could pay for the many building projects arising out of his passionate devotion to Hellenistic civilization, he had to force maximum economic exploitation of both the land and the people he ruled. The burden, of course, weighed heavily on the peasantry, and the disaffected were many. But Herod maintained stringent political and social control . . .[4]

The Jewish priests and the Jerusalemite upper classes—referred to in both the New Testament and rabbinic literature as the Sadducees—are for the most part politically aligned with their Roman overlords and their power structure. In the rabbinic worldview, the Sadducees don't come up a lot by name, though the Temple priesthood and its rituals are discussed a lot. In parts of early rabbinic literature, the Sadducees are depicted arguing over ritual laws with another Jewish faction, the Pharisees,[5] but overall, it's a bit challenging to say that the Sadducees have a clear profile that emerges out of the early rabbinic texts.[6] For simplicity's sake, let's go with the general depiction of the Sadducees as the privileged officialdom of the Temple: outwardly pious, wealthy, well-connected, and in the eyes of many of their Jewish critics, thoroughly corrupt.[7] Ordinary Jews rely on them for the upkeep of the Temple and for their role in facilitating their ritual offerings to God at the proper times, but many have come to resent and distrust them.

Here's how Horsley and Hanson describe the atmosphere:

---

4. Horsley and Hanson, *Bandits, Prophets, and Messiahs*, 33.

5. m. Yad. 4.6–8.

6. There's much more early rabbinic material to work with if, instead of looking for explicit references to the Sadducees, we look at how the early rabbis discussed the Temple priesthood. But we can't necessarily assume that whenever the early rabbis talked about priests they were talking about Sadducees. There were different classes of priests—not all priests were among the elites running the Temple. Moreover, the early rabbis' attitudes towards the priests are very complicated, and we have to bear in mind that whatever criticisms some of them may have had about some of the priests, as a group the early rabbis were devastated by destruction of the Temple and the sudden end of the priests' entire system of religious authority and practice.

7. Herod the Great intensified the loyalty of the Sadducees by purging out some of this aristocratic, priestly class and replacing them with hand-picked people loyal to himself. See Horsley and Hanson, *Bandits, Prophets, and Messiahs*, 32.

The high priestly families, Herodians, and much of the wealthy aristocracy, of course, were engaged in mutually beneficial collaboration with the Roman imperial system in maintaining control. . . . Such practices by the high priestly families and the Herodians clearly exacerbated the disintegration of the social order, which they, supposedly, were responsible for maintaining.

The Roman governors, however, also contributed to the heightening of tensions. . . . [T]hey became steadily more repressive and intransigent. Right up to the end . . . the [Jewish] people continued to appeal and protest their condition and treatment, while their ostensible leaders, high priests and nobility alike, sat idly by or collaborated in their oppression.[8]

During this era, some intensely anti-Roman militant factions emerge. These underground movements are both religious and nationalist, and many of those involved come to think of themselves as the Maccabees of their time. (The Maccabees, famous from the Hanukkah story, had, against all odds, defeated a major occupying army about a century-and-a-half earlier.) Rabbinic literature will come to refer to these groups as the Zealots.

The Zealots' goal: ending the Roman occupation of Judea once and for all. Their methods: guerrilla warfare and coercion of the local Jewish population to join ranks with their cause. Their targets: Roman officials and soldiers, as well as suspected Jewish collaborators. Think of the IRA in Northern Ireland during the worst of the "Troubles," or any other modern militant liberation movement that bitterly resents the injustice of being oppressed and has committed its people (whether they like it or not) to fighting the enemy, down to the last person if necessary. Among the Zealots there is also an ultra-fanatical faction called the Sicarii, who actively seek out and murder suspected Jewish collaborators. Carrying distinctive knives in their belts, they are feared by one and all.

Next let's meet the Pharisees, the forerunners of the early rabbis.[9] The Pharisees are probably the most widely respected religious movement among the common Jews.[10] They offer a semi-official alternative to the patrician Saducean priestly classes. Their approach to Judaism includes

8. Horsley and Hanson, *Bandits, Prophets, and Messiahs*, 42–43.

9. For a more in-depth exploration of the historical relationship between the Pharisees and the early rabbis, see Shaye Cohen's essay, "The Significance of Yavneh: Pharisees, Rabbis, and the End of Jewish Sectarianism."

10. Richard A. Horsley and John S. Hanson write, "Under Herod's oppressive regime the Pharisees retained some prestige among the general populace, for they did not hesitate to oppose the king." See Horsley and Hanson, *Bandits, Prophets, and Messiahs*, 32.

Setting the Stage

intensive Torah study, interpretive debate, and rigorous personal observance of the commandments. Their movement, functioning as both a compliment to the official priesthood and a populist rival to it, combines conservation of tradition with imaginative religious innovation.

Up and down the length of the land, their sages operate academies that study the Torah and promote a companion set of oral Jewish legal teachings derived from their own particular methods of interpreting the Torah and its laws. Leading Pharisees also participate in the prime religious legal court in Jerusalem, called the Sanhedrin.

The Pharisaic sages come from all walks of Jewish life—as opposed to the elitist, hereditary Temple priesthood. Their movement is a meritocracy—an all-male club, to be sure, but a meritocracy. Torah learning, interpretive skill, piety, and good character are the criteria for becoming a sage. (Coming from a family of great sages doesn't hurt, but it's not a prerequisite.) Among the Pharisees you'll find rich men and poor laborers, born Jews and converts, scions of prominent families and sons of anonymous peasants. A number of priests join them as well. As one scholar of the rabbinic movement described their ranks, "Here were wealthy landowners and halfstarved artisans, ambitious careerists and self-denying saints, ardent patriots and cosmopolitan internationalists, uncouth peasants and polished townsmen."[11]

Their overall attitude towards the Roman occupation is that it is a terrible thing that has to be endured, because attempting to fight the Romans would be suicidal. And so, they encourage a pragmatically pacifistic and cautious approach towards Roman rule. They seek to preserve and protect the Temple and the free practice of Judaism, while preventing the overspread of Roman polytheism.[12] The twentieth-century scholar Louis Finkelstein describes Pharisaism as "the paradoxical combination of . . . idealism and practical common sense . . . ."[13] In contrast to the New Testament's

---

11. Finkelstein, *Akiba: Scholar, Saint and Martyr*, 76.

12. Matthew LaGrone writes that the Pharisees were willing to "[exchange] any claim to political authority for the preservation of religious autonomy." LaGrone, "Judaism and Religious Freedom in the Rabbinic Period (70 CE–1000 CE)."

13. Finkelstein, *Akiba: Scholar, Saint and Martyr*, 14.

frequent portrayal of them as hypocritical baddies,[14] the Pharisees are the good guys in this story.[15]

At this time among the Jews a number of apocalyptic and messianic groups are growing in popularity too. Interpreting the corruption, uncertainty, and rapid social change consuming Judea as a sign of the end of civilization itself, these groups preach that a final battle between the forces of good and evil is imminent. Interestingly, a pair of devastating earthquakes in ancient Israel, one in 31 B.C.E. and another six decades later in 33 C.E., combined with the appearance of Halley's comet in 12 B.C.E., may have contributed to the sense these groups had that Divine and cataclysmic wrath was beginning to be unleashed upon humankind.[16]

Some of these apocalyptic groups openly question the legitimacy of the Temple priesthood.[17] Unlike the Zealots, however, their hearts are not moved to form guerilla bands in the hopes of somehow driving out the Romans by force. No, they are certain that the material world is now corrupt to the core, and that God's direct intervention is coming soon to set things right. One of these groups, the Essenes, withdraws entirely from Jerusalem and takes to the caves near the Dead Sea, forming a closed community of the pious awaiting the return of God's anointed redeemer and the final battle of history.

Given where Judea is located—at the meeting place of Africa, Asia, and Europe—it is a major crossroads of trade and culture. Roman occupation has brought many varieties of Greek philosophy as well as Mediterranean and even South Asian religious ideas into the city squares and dining halls of the area. By this time, many Jews are opting for a more

---

14. The twentieth-century scholar Morris Adler wrote: "The identification of Pharisaism with formal legalism, smugness, self-righteousness, hypocrisy, rigorous observance in the total absence of any inwardness, goes back to the New Testament." Adler, *The World of the Talmud*, 13.

15. For the most part. It's more complicated than that. There are, as it happens, Talmudic passages that seem to criticize some of the Pharisees as well, e.g., b. Sotah 22b. As I said, it's complicated, but for the purpose of understanding the overarching sweep of the mythic story we're examining here, I'm going with calling the Pharisees the good guys.

16. For more on how these earthquakes and astronomical events may have influenced people at the time, see Roller, *The Building Program of Herod the Great*.

17. One of the major religious objections groups like the Essenes had towards the official priesthood of the Second Temple involved the replacement of the traditional family line of high priests with a different family line. This change was illegitimate in the eyes of the Essenes, and it symbolized the corruption of the Jerusalem religious establishment in their eyes. See Horsley and Hanson, *Bandits, Prophets, and Messiahs*, 24–25.

Setting the Stage

cosmopolitan worldview than that of any of the factions I've just described above. Some are assimilationists, or just aren't sure what to make of their rapidly changing world. After all, in 30 B.C.E. there are more philosophical and theological options available than ever before in Judea. The wide reach of Roman rule is flowing ideas from distant lands through Judea like water in the new Roman aqueducts. Many of the Jews who do identify as Pharisees, Sadducees, or one of the other parties, read and write Greek, the international language of the time, and are in constant dialog with Greek and Roman ideas.

Finally, let's return briefly to the political situation of this era. For a sense of just how uncertain and volatile things were throughout the early rabbinic period, consider that there were several Jewish popular revolts against Roman authority during this time. In 4 B.C.E., when Herod the Great died, popular rebellions against the regime broke out in every region of the country.[18] After quelling these revolts, the Romans re-organized their governance strategy, sub-dividing the Holy Land and appointing Herod's sons to serve as rulers over smaller territories. By 6 C.E., the Romans changed tactics again regarding the territory that included Jerusalem and began appointing Roman governors to rule the area directly (Pontius Pilate was one of them).

As with Herod the Great's rule before, under direct Roman rule heavy taxes on the Jewish peasantry remained a constant source of resentment, and when those taxes took the form of Jews having to pay direct tribute to Rome, as required of subjects of territories governed directly by Roman officials, Jewish political and religious resentments intensified.[19] Throughout the next several decades, the Romans had to quell several popular Jewish revolts of different scales.

This is the world that Joshua ben Hananiah was born into, probably around the year 50 C.E. By the time he was sixteen, his nation would be at war with Rome. A few years later, he would witness and survive the Roman destruction of the Second Temple and of his city, Jerusalem.

* * *

We're almost ready now to jump into some of the stories that rabbinic literature about this era presents. But first, this is a good moment to introduce

---

18. Horsley and Hanson, *Bandits, Prophets, and Messiahs*, 33–34.
19. Horsley and Hanson, *Bandits, Prophets, and Messiahs*, 33–36.

an important Hebrew term—the word "halakhah." *Halakhah* literally means "the way" or "the path," but its meaning in rabbinic Judaism is "the complete body of rules and practices that Jews are bound to follow, including biblical commandments, commandments instituted by the rabbis, and binding customs,"[20]—in other words, Jewish law. From here on out, I'll be using the term *halakhah* most of the time to refer to Jewish law.

Also, this is a good time to say a word about the nature of rabbinic literature.[21] The stories I'll be highlighting about Rabbi Joshua and some of his contemporaries don't appear as a coherent narrative in any one book. Rabbinic literature is vast, and it toggles back and forth—sometimes abruptly—between multiple literary genres (legal arguments, stories, category lists, ritual instructions, and more). This book is particularly focused on rabbinic stories, which appear in the Talmud, in Midrash, and in other categories of literature that we'll encounter in the pages ahead.

The great works of rabbinic literature began as oral traditions that were, at different junctures in history, written down, edited, and collected in different parts of the world. Some of these stories are more than two thousand years old, but some may not have taken the written form we have them in until even as late as eight hundred years ago.

The stories we find in rabbinic literature are, like the stories of the Hebrew Bible, mythic in nature. We don't know which parts, if any, of these stories actually took place. We can't be certain whether the stories we find in rabbinic literature are windows into the actual time periods they claim as their settings, or whether they are windows into the religious beliefs and visions of later generations of Jewish editors and rabbis.

For example, one of the most important elements of many of the stories we will explore in this book is a small coastal town called Yavneh, located a bit south of present-day Tel Aviv. There is an entire mini-world of early rabbinic stories set in this town. As it happens, historical and archeological evidence does not seem to support that a major Jewish historical chapter took place there.[22] In contrast, there is an abundance of evidence

---

20. Rich, "Halakhah."

21. Susan A. Handelman offers this helpful definition of rabbinic literature: "In general terms, we can define 'Rabbinic' as the literature and attitudes that began to be formed in the time of the Second Temple roughly from the 4th century B.C.E. onwards and that predominated after the destruction of the Second Temple in 70 C.E. until the redaction of the Babylonian Talmud in approximately the 6th century C.E." Handelman, *Slayers of Moses*, 31.

22. For an overview of scholarly skepticism about whether there really was a major

that the early rabbis developed academies and led synagogues robustly in another part of the Holy Land—the Galilee—thus presenting us with the possibility that Yavneh may have existed more in the rabbinic imagination than in fact. My interest is not in uncovering the actual history of the early rabbinic period; it is in entering the mythic imaginative world of rabbinic literature, which has a lot to offer us in our own spiritual and moral lives in our troubled times.

Finally, one last advanced warning for readers who are new to rabbinic literature. It can be maddeningly non-linear. For example, the Talmud's running narrative sometimes shifts suddenly from detailed legal arguments to folk tales and legends, and nested sub-topics sprout up everywhere. If that wasn't complicated enough, there are two different Talmuds, the Babylonian Talmud and the Jerusalem Talmud, and sometimes they offer very different tellings of the same stories.

As others have noted, rabbinic literature offers us a foreshadowing of postmodern ideas about the difficulties involved in being certain about just which accounts to believe, just what the "true story" is. As we comb through the thousands of pages of rabbinic texts and collect stories (and bits of stories) about the major rabbis, we sometimes find contradictory accounts of the same anecdote. At times those conflicting accounts occur within a single work of rabbinic literature, and in other cases we find them in rabbinic writings that were developed in lands far apart from one another and in different historical periods. The many recorded memories of a figure like Joshua ben Hananiah are layered into narratives that, in some cases, may have taken centuries to arrive at the form we find on the pages we've got today.

Sometimes these variations are minor. In one place we may read that a rabbi said something lasted for seven years and in another text he said seventy. But sometimes the variations are big and meaningful. In one rabbinic text it could be Joshua who said something specific, but in another it's someone else. In one version of a story the narrator has included additional comments by rabbis of later generations, while in another text we may just get a simple version of the core narrative, or even a different set of comments by a different bunch of later rabbis. It's hard, with rabbinic literature, to be sure about whose perspective(s) are framing the story we're reading and which context(s) are the ones in play.

---

early rabbinic center at Yavneh, see Barbara Thiede's 2018 essay, "Is Modern Rabbinic Judaism Based on a Myth?"

And yet, it is possible to follow the roughly coherent storylines that sketch out some of the most vivid personalities among the ancient rabbis. You just have to accept the degree of uncertainty, as well as the multiplicity of voices and versions, that come with the storylines. I wondered for a while about calling the book you are holding in your hands *The (Book) of Joshua*, but I could never have called it *The Book of Joshua*. There is no such book in rabbinic literature—at best, there is a "book" or a (book) to be inferred, to be stitched and taped together out of some prominent storylines and recurring themes. And given that rabbinic literature tends to offer up alternative and even contrary versions of so many of its stories, the portrait of Joshua that you'll find in the coming chapters is subject to doubt (and we'll explore some of those doubts in chapter 9, "Don't Trust This Book—It Could Be Wrong").

So, having said all of that, and despite the important caveats and disclaimers, let's begin exploring some of the rabbinic stories about Joshua ben Hananiah. Though he remains a generally unknown figure, his Judaism is a Judaism that most Jews today recognize, and many non-Jews familiar with the Jewish traditions of debate, non-absolutism, humanism, and respect for other religions will recognize it too.

2

The Rabbis Also Have a Resurrection Story

Joshua was shaped by the Roman siege of Jerusalem and the events surrounding its destruction (66–70 C.E.). In this chapter, we'll focus closely on the Talmud's account of these events. The main rabbinic character in this particular story is Joshua's master, Rabbi Yohanan ben Zakkai, and at first glance it may seem that Joshua's part in the story is minor to the point of insignificance. But, as we'll see, the role he plays is important symbolically. Let's get to the Talmud's account itself, which I'll excerpt and paraphrase for the sake of clarity. (There are many translations available for those who would like to read the original. The passage I'm paraphrasing and excerpting is found in the Babylonian Talmud, tractate *Gittin* 56 a-b.)

> The Roman emperor sent his general, Vespasian, who besieged Jerusalem for three years. Three wealthy Jews in Jerusalem offered their personal reserves of food, wood, and other essentials to help the people of Jerusalem endure the siege. They say there were enough provisions to keep the people of the city alive for twenty-one years!
>
> At that time the Zealots were dominating the city. The Rabbis said to them, "Let us go and negotiate peace with the Romans." But the Zealots would not let them, and, on the contrary, said, "No, let us go out and fight them!" The Rabbis responded, "If you do, you will not succeed."
>
> At this point, the Zealots, in order to prevent the Rabbis from attempting to negotiate with Vespasian over their objections, set

fire to the stores of wheat, barley, and the other provisions, in order to force the entire population of Jerusalem to see no option other than fighting the Romans. A horrible famine followed.

After things had worsened severely, the following happened. The head of the Zealot faction, Abba Sikra, happened to be the son of Rabbi Yohanan ben Zakkai's sister. Rabbi Yohanan sent him a message saying "come see me privately." When he came to see him, Rabbi Yohanan said, "How long are you going to carry on in this way and kill all the people with starvation?" Abba Sikra acknowledged that things had gone too far, but he said, "What can I do? If I say anything to the other Zealots they'll kill me!"

Yohanan said to him, "You have to come up with a plan for me to escape the city so I can try to speak with Vespasian. Maybe I can save something of us from total annihilation." Abba Sikra thought about it, and then said, "Here's what you need to do. Pretend that you're seriously ill, and have lots of people come to visit you so that word spreads of your grave condition. Then, have your disciples announce that you've died. Get something really foul smelling and have it placed in your clothing so that you smell like a rotting corpse. Have a couple of your students wrap your body in burial clothes and place it on a bier [a litter that people would use to carry a corpse through the streets during a funeral procession, on the way to the burial site]. The students will ask the Zealots who guard the city gates to let them take your body outside the holy city for burial. Make sure it's your students who are carrying your bier, because if it's just anyone they'll be able to feel that you are not dead weight on the bier."

Rabbi Yohanan ben Zakkai agreed and did as Abba Sikra instructed. When the day came to smuggle him out of the city upon the bier, Yohanan's two students, Rabbi Eliezer ben Hyrcanus and Rabbi Joshua ben Hananiah, stood on either side of the bier and carried it to the city gate as pall bearers. Abba Sikra was there when they arrived.

The Zealot guards, always suspicious of the Rabbis' loyalties to their cause, wanted to pierce the bier with a lance or shake it hard to prove that there really was a dead body inside, but Abba Sikra intervened, telling the guards that the Romans would witness these actions and conclude that the Jews had no respect even for their most important rabbi. The guards finally let Rabbi Joshua and Rabbi Eliezer take the bier outside the city.

[Once the coast was clear, Rabbi Yohanan arose from the bier and headed for the Roman command post.] When Rabbi Yohanan finally reached the Roman general's tent, he approached and asked

The Rabbis Also Have a Resurrection Story

for an audience with Vespasian. It was granted. Upon meeting the Roman general, Rabbi Yohanan said, "Peace to you, O King! Peace to you, O King!"

Vespasian quickly replied: "With those words you've just committed two capital offenses! First, because you call me a king but I am not a king. And second, because if I was a king, then you should have come to pay your respects long ago. Why haven't you?"

Rabbi Yohanan replied: "As for the question of whether or not you are a king, I believe you must be a king, because God would only have Jerusalem delivered into the hands of a king. Our scriptures foretell that our land will fall to a mighty one, and our teaching is that the words 'mighty one' refer only to a king. As for your other question, the reason I could not come to visit you sooner was because the rebellious Zealots wouldn't let me."

Although Vespasian was the one who had asked all the questions so far, the Roman general understood that the rabbi had come to him with questions of his own. Anticipating the rabbi's hoped-for answers, Vespasian posed a riddle to Yohanan. "If there is a jar of honey, around which a serpent is wound, isn't it necessary to break the jar of honey in order to kill the serpent?" It was obvious to Yohanan that Vespasian was referring to Jerusalem as the jar of honey and the Zealots as the serpent, but he could find no words and he fell silent.

Years later, other rabbis came to say that God must have stymied his wits, because Yohanan could have come up with at least some reply, such as suggesting that Vespasian take a pair of tongs and remove the serpent while leaving the jar of honey intact. But in that moment, the great rabbi had no words.

At just that instant, a messenger arrived from Rome bearing the news that the emperor had died, and that Vespasian had been chosen to be the new emperor by Rome's leaders. Vespasian had been putting on his boots when he was given the stunning news. He had one boot on, but suddenly found himself having trouble putting on the second. It was an incredible moment—Vespasian suddenly learning that he was now Caesar, the rabbi in his tent trying to plead for his people, and the new emperor embarrassingly stuck trying to put on an ill-fitting boot. Rabbi Yohanan suggested a folk remedy for getting a difficult boot to slip on. Vespasian tried it, and it worked. The new Roman emperor considered him, this rabbi who was clever enough to escape the Zealots in the city, prophetic enough to be able to foretell his ascension to kingship, and familiar enough with folk wisdom to be able to help a stranger with a troublesome shoe.

"Seeing that you are so wise," Vespasian said, "truly, why did you not come to see me until now?"

"I thought I already gave you an answer," said Rabbi Yohanan.

Vespasian looked at the rabbi. "And I'm afraid that I have also given you mine." After a moment passed, Vespasian said, "I am going now, and I will send someone here to take my place. You can, however, make a request of me and I will grant it."

Rabbi Yohanan spoke. "Give me the coastal town of Yavneh and the sages of the academy there, and permit the family line of Gamaliel to survive, and provide me with a physician for one of my colleagues who is gravely ill in the city."

In later years, the great Rabbi Akiva would say that God must have stripped Yohanan of his senses in this moment, because he should have asked Vespasian to spare Jerusalem and the Jews just this once. As it happened, Yohanan thought of asking for this, but was afraid that it was too great a request, and that if he were to give offense by asking it, he might walk away with nothing at all.[1]

In time, Vespasian sent a new general, Titus, who mocked the Jews and their God. This is the wicked Titus who blasphemed and insulted heaven. When he had sacked Jerusalem and taken over the Temple, he took a prostitute with him into the Holy of Holies. There, he found a Torah scroll and spread it out, and had sex with the woman on top of it. Afterwards, he took a sword and slashed through the curtain that covered the sacred inner chamber of God's dwelling. Miraculously, blood spurted out from the chamber, and Titus thought that he had slain the God of the Jews.

In later generations, notable rabbis commented on God's inaction during Titus' defilements of the Holy of Holies. One credited God for having the incredible strength to show restraint in the face of such violent insults. Another described God as having been struck dumb in the moment.

Titus went on to take the curtain from the Holy of Holies and use it as a basket, in which he looted the Temple of all its sacred vessels. He took everything aboard his ship so he could display it all in triumph back in Rome.

---

1. As is often the case with rabbinic legends, there is more than one version of this story in rabbinic literature. A version of this story appears in a Midrashic collection called *Lamentations Rabbah* in which Yohanan ben Zakkai actually does ask Vespasian to spare Jerusalem, but the request is denied (*Lam. Rab.* 1.31). For a discussion of the different versions of this story found in rabbinic literature, see Saldarini, "Johanan ben Zakkai's Escape from Jerusalem."

The Rabbis Also Have a Resurrection Story

There's more to the story, including a very unusual comeuppance for Titus, but the things I want to discuss relate to the part we've just read above. There were also some sub-plots and details that I omitted in my retelling. For a wonderfully readable and engaging examination of this story, including many of the parts I left out, I recommend a book called *Sage Tales: Wisdom and Wonder from the Rabbis of the Talmud*, by the contemporary rabbi and writer Burton Vizotsky.

There's a lot to explore in this extraordinary and sad story about the Roman siege and the internal dysfunction of the Jewish leadership within the city. What's important to keep in mind is that this story is part of a sacred text—the Talmud—and it forms an important part of the mythology of a new version of Judaism that emerged in the aftermath of the Roman destruction of ancient Israel—rabbinic Judaism. Of course, there was another new religious movement that also emerged in the decades following these events—a movement with its own interpretation of the Roman destruction of Jerusalem, and a movement that also saw itself as the continuation of the religion of biblical Israel: Christianity.

As a foundational mythic story for rabbinic Judaism, the tale of the struggle between the Zealots and the rabbis and the strange meeting between Yohanan ben Zakkai and Vespasian tells us a lot about what the framers of the Talmud (several centuries later) thought about all that had happened in Jerusalem's final months. Many interpreters have commented on the clues this particular story provides to help explain certain aspects of the character and temperament of rabbinic Judaism in the centuries of exile that followed. For example, some have claimed that the story's depiction of the uncontrolled rage and will to war of the Zealots, contrasted with the reasoned and pragmatic pacifism of the rabbis, foreshadows a general leaning in the rabbinic tradition towards distrusting war as a viable means to achieve Jewish liberation. Others have pointed out that, while the Romans certainly come off as oppressive and cruel in the story, the tale definitely highlights internal Jewish factionalism, strife, and extremism as major reasons for the downfall of Jerusalem, making it into a cautionary tale for future Jewish generations.

All of these are important observations. But there's one aspect of this Talmudic text that doesn't get as much discussion as it should, and that is that, in its own way, *this story is a resurrection story*, crafted at a time when Christianity, the main religious movement rivaling rabbinic Judaism, was growing stronger every year. And of course, Christianity certainly had its own resurrection story—one that the rabbis who ultimately framed and edited this Talmudic story knew well.

* * *

Our Talmudic tale is a resurrection story on multiple levels. First, at base, it's a story about a prominent rabbi, Yohanan, whom everyone believed to be dead—in fact, who was seen (and was smelled) by many witnesses to be dead—but who then rose from his place of burial and went on to transform Judaism. (Sound a bit familiar?)

On another level, it's about the collective death and resurrection of the Jews. The Roman armies destroy Jerusalem and the holy Temple, killing hundreds of thousands of Jews and deporting tens of thousands more. Given that the entire Jewish religious system up until that time had revolved around the core concept of the Jews living in their land and worshiping God at the Jerusalem Temple, this story describes to us the last gasps of Jerusalem and then the death of Israel. But, in securing the coastal town of Yavneh[2] for a group of rabbis to have a chance to carry on the religion, Yohanan ben Zakkai's act results in the resurrection of Israel, which will reconstruct itself and redefine itself in new terms suited for exile and diaspora living. To say it more succinctly, in this Talmudic tale Judaism is killed by the Romans, the leader of the Jews puts up no resistance but instead accepts the death as somehow required by God, and then—out of this torture, calamity, and apparent total death—new life.

On still another level, there's the part of the story involving Titus and his shocking desecration of the Holy of Holies within the Temple. It's striking what happens when Titus thrusts his sword through the curtain covering the sacred chamber that the Jews had believed to be, in some mysterious way, the site of God's dwelling place on Earth. God's response is to

---

2. Yavneh is a real town that existed during the period when this Talmudic story is set. But it also fits the mythic power of the story that the word "Yavneh" in Hebrew literally means "He (God) will build." In the Talmud's sacred storytelling, the Jews begin the resurrection of Judaism in a small part of the Holy Land named for rebuilding. Today, in the modern State of Israel, Yavneh is a small city of roughly 30,000—40,000 residents located about 20 km south of Tel Aviv. It includes a tomb dating back to the twelfth century C.E. attributed to be the burial place of Gamaliel II, one of Rabbi Joshua ben Hanaiah's contemporaries, whom we'll read about in the coming chapters. The same tomb is believed to be the resting place not of Gamaliel, but of Abu Hurairah, one of the Islamic prophet Muhammad's companions.

The Rabbis Also Have a Resurrection Story

bleed visibly before him. The narrator tells us that Titus thinks he has just killed the Jews' God. Of course, we know better.

Since we're talking about resurrection stories and religion, I'd like to take a moment to note that there's a curious parallel between this rabbinic text and a key moment in three of the Gospel narratives. Matthew, Mark, and Luke all state that at the time of Jesus's death, the Temple's innermost curtain was torn in two (two of the Gospels specify that it was torn from top to bottom).[3] And yet, just as Titus was wrong to think that he had killed the Jews' God by splitting apart the curtain with his sword, in the Gospel narratives the people who assumed Jesus was dead turned out to be wrong as well. I'm not sure what to make of this literary parallel, except to note that in both the rabbis' story and these early Christian stories, the enemies of God think they have destroyed God/God's son by destroying God's/God's son's physical abode—the Temple in the case of the rabbis and Jesus's body in the case of the Christians—but in fact they've destroyed nothing Divine at all.

Like the Gospel narratives, the rabbinic tale we've been studying here is also a mythic origins story, describing how the rabbinic movement came to replace the Temple and its priesthood as the official religious leadership of Judaism. The rabbis chose a story in which their leader, Yohanan ben Zakkai, personally "resurrects"; the Jewish religion is physically destroyed by Rome but then resurrected at Yavneh; and even God is "slain"—to all appearances at least—but in fact lives on and now accompanies the rabbis in their rebuilding endeavors.

So, both the early rabbis and the early Christians turned to resurrection stories—to mythic sagas of seeming death followed by rebirth in a new religious framework—with new understandings of all that had come before in Israel's religious history.[4] If the rabbis, like their Christian rivals, chose a resurrection story to explain much of their beginnings, the question that then becomes interesting is *what kind of resurrection story is this?*

* * *

---

3. Compare with Matt 27:51, Mark 15:38, and Luke 23:45.

4. Burton Vizotsky writes: "In the annals of Roman history, the Jewish war was but one more provincial rebellion. For Christian theologians, it was oft trotted out as proof of divine punishment of the Jews for rejecting Christ. But for the Jews themselves, especially the rabbis, it was the paradigmatic tragedy of Jewish history." Vizotsky, *Sage Tales*, 105.

The Forgotten Sage

Well, in many ways, it's a weird one, especially in comparison with the Christian resurrection story. At the risk of oversimplifying, while the Gospels' stories of the life, death, and resurrection of Jesus emphasize Jesus's courage, faithfulness, selflessness, determination, and sincerity,[5] the Talmud's story of Yohanan ben Zakkai's "death" and "resurrection" is steeped in irony, questioning, puzzlement, and misdirection. While the Gospels proclaim that Jesus's resurrection was real,[6] the Talmud gives us a story with a fake resurrection carried out by a rabbi and a faked death carried out by God (the blood spurting out of the Holy of Holies when Titus stabs the curtain). And while the New Testament frequently praises having faith in Jesus and reminds readers not to give in to the dark forces of doubt, the Talmud's story stops and interrupts itself more than once to allow various sages to express doubt and even to criticize Yohanan ben Zakkai's decisions. And while the Gospels' hero, Jesus, faces a martyr's death with courage—yes, with painful doubt and questions, but overall with stoic courage and faith—the Talmud's hero in this resurrection story, Yohanan ben Zakkai, arranges safe passage for himself and his colleagues while negotiating with Vespasian, and never even tries to avert the destruction of Jerusalem. Vizotsky candidly writes:

> How shall we understand Rabbi Yohanan's character? Are we meant to see him as the heroic savior of Judaism who risks his life to bring Judaism to its next period, from Temple sacrificial cult to People of the Book? Or is Yohanan ben Zakkai to be read as a traitor who escapes the siege, abandons his fellow Jews, and collaborates with the enemy?[7] . . . [Consider also the way that] Yohanan is silenced by Vespasian's argument [about the serpent coiled around a jar of honey]. In rabbinic narratives, it is the *opponents* of the rabbis who are reduced to silence in arguments,

---

5. I'm not a New Testament expert, and I don't mean to ignore nuances, complexities, doubts, and internally unresolved questions that characterize many of the New Testament writings about the life, death, and resurrection of Jesus. If I am far off the mark in my generalized characterization of the Gospel narratives, I offer apologies.

6. For the accounts of Jesus's resurrection and reappearance in the Gospels, see Matt 28, Mark 16, Luke 24, and John 20. I want to acknowledge that each of these narratives offers different understandings of how Jesus's resurrection was experienced and remembered, and that by no means am I suggesting that there is one simple teaching about the events or meaning of his resurrection in the New Testament. The claim I am making, however, is that each of the canonized Gospels asserts that Jesus *really did* resurrect, and that his resurrection was witnessed in different forms by different people.

7. Vizotsky, *Sage Tales*, 119.

so it is an astonishing assertion our narrator offers. Indeed, Yohanan's helpless silence brings condemnation from other sages. The first to jump is Rabbi Yosef, a prominent Babylonian who lived in the third to fourth centuries, some 250 years and 550 miles distant from the siege. [The critique he offers is given in such a way that it constitutes a] barely polite way of calling Rabbi Yohanan's response to Vespasian idiotic.[8]

Is Yohanan ben Zakkai both courageous and cowardly at once—willing to risk death to get to Vespasian and attempt to save some remnant of the Jewish people, and yet willing to negotiate a post-war arrangement that puts himself and his fellow sages out of harm's way and in charge of the Jews? If the Gospels' attitude towards Jesus is reverence and praise, the Talmud's attitude towards Yohanan ben Zakkai is conflicted and uncertain.

Yohanan himself also never overcomes his own self-doubt about how he handled his encounter with Vespasian. Elsewhere, the Talmud tells the story of his final conversations with his disciples on his deathbed:

> When Rabbi Yohanan ben Zakkai fell ill [and was dying], his disciples went to visit him. When he saw them, he began to weep.
>
> His disciples said to him: "Lamp of Israel, the Right Pillar, the Mighty Hammer—why are you crying?"
>
> He replied: "If I was being taken today before a human king who is here today and tomorrow is in the grave; whose anger—if he is angry with me—is not eternal; who—if he imprisons me—does not imprison me forever; and who—if he puts me to death—does not put me to death forever; and whom I can appease with words and bribe with money—[if I was going to have to be judged by that kind of human king] I would weep. But now that I am [dying and about to be] led before the supreme King of Kings, the Holy One, blessed is He, who lives and endures for ever and ever, whose anger—if He is angry with me—is an eternal anger; who—if He imprisons me—imprisons me forever; who—if He puts me to death—puts me to death forever; and whom I cannot persuade with words or bribe with money . . . [all the more so I have cause to weep]. And not only that, but there are two paths ahead of me,

---

8. Vizotsky, *Sage Tales*, 124.

one leading to Paradise and the other to Gehinnom,[9] and I do not know which way I will be led. Shall I not weep?!"[10]

As we leave poor, tormented Rabbi Yohanan on his deathbed with his devoted students surrounding him, we are now more than ever able to see that it's pretty clear that the early rabbis and the early Christians have two very different kinds of foundational, mythic resurrection stories. And yet, there are important parallels between the two. Let's stick with the scene in which Titus stabs the curtain and God causes blood to gush forth. Both the Jewish and the Christian stories involve a divine being[11] getting slain by the Romans, or appearing to have been slain, only to continue living eternally. Both involve a rabbi/teacher being witnessed as dead, but then shortly afterwards walking the earth and engaging with people again. And most importantly, both tell the story of the establishment of the "new Israel," of a new religious order with a new official leadership and a new layer of mythology added to that of the Hebrew Bible.

For the earliest Christians, the new Israel was to be found among the growing network of churches and in the sacralizing and canonizing of specific accounts of the life, death, and resurrection of Jesus. For the rabbinic Jews, the new Israel was now centered in Yavneh, in the rabbis' houses of study, and soon thereafter in hundreds of similar academies and

---

9. While it is true that, like their Pharisaic predecessors, the early rabbis strongly promoted the belief in the eventual resurrection of the dead at the end of history, it is also true that the ancient rabbis did not have a consistent and coherent doctrine about the afterlife in general. Rather, we find a few different concepts of an afterlife described and debated in the Talmud. One of those several beliefs is the one Rabbi Yohanan expresses in this particular Talmudic text—namely, that after we die we are judged by God and are either sent to heaven (Paradise) or Gehinnom (which in the rabbinic imagination is sometimes depicted as a place of temporary purgatory that ultimately releases one's purified soul to heaven. Of course, there are other rabbis who describe Gehinnom as a permanent place of punishment—more like "hell" as we're familiar with that concept in the Western world). Some readers may be surprised to learn that Judaism has included within its various beliefs about the afterlife concepts of purgatory or hell, given modern liberal Judaism's reputation for having no specific dogma about what happens after we die. Over the course of three thousand years, Judaism has developed, borrowed, and depicted quite a range of ideas and beliefs about the afterlife. For an in-depth study of the subject, see Raphael, *Jewish Views of the Afterlife*.

10. *b. Ber.* 28b. I have adapted for clarity the English translation that comes mainly from *Sefaria*, online at: https://www.sefaria.org/Berakhot.28b.

11. I realize that, during the first decades and even centuries of Christianity, the precise status of Jesus as divinity, or as Son of God, or as Messiah or prophet was a matter that was being debated among various early Christian groups.

The Rabbis Also Have a Resurrection Story

synagogues around the Mediterranean world. The legends and debates of the early rabbis became the "New Testament" of rabbinic Judaism, the newest layer of sacred writing and myth-making defining the religion. To quote the twentieth-century scholar of rabbinic Judaism Louis Finkelstein: after the Roman destruction, "Judea died, but she died in childbirth."[12]

Finally, let me get to the subject of Rabbi Joshua ben Hananiah, the central figure of this book. As you may recall, he appeared in the Talmudic drama we've been examining in a "bit part." He was one of Yohanan ben Zakkai's top students, and he helped carry Yohanan's bier out of Jerusalem. Standing across from him and holding the other side of the bier was another of Yohanan's great disciples, Rabbi Eliezer ben Hyrcanus. This brief moment of storytelling foreshadows much that is yet to come in the larger mythic story of the early rabbis.

You see, in the decades following Jerusalem's sacking by the Romans, Joshua and Eliezer would go on to become legendary rabbinic rivals, engaging in countless debates over matters of Jewish belief, law, ethics, and philosophy. Joshua will carry the banner of the beloved ancient sage, Hillel, who lived before the Roman destruction. Hillel was known for his humanistic and flexible interpretive tendencies. Eliezer will be Joshua's foil, tending towards strictness, attention to detail, rigidity, and impatience with outsiders to the Jewish community. In the narratives of the Talmud, the tensions between them represent some of the great questions facing the early rabbinic movement.

And so we see them here, in the story of Yohanan ben Zakkai's visit with Vespasian, cast in heavily symbolic roles. Carrying Yohanan's body out of Jerusalem together, we visualize them literally upholding the last chance for Judaism's survival. They carry both the possibility of Judaism's death, represented by the bier, and the possibility of its survival, represented by the live body of Yohanan wrapped in burial cloths atop the bier.

Since the editors of the Talmud assumed that the audience for their stories knew who all the major characters were and how their fates would play out, the task that Eliezer and Joshua share in this scene hints to the reader that the Judaism that will survive will be characterized by ongoing tensions, vigorous debates, and multiple viewpoints. Without either one of them, Yohanan's bier could not make its way out of the city. One person alone can't carry a bier.

---

12. Finkelstein, *Akiba: Scholar, Saint and Martyr*, 12.

Together, these two carry Yohanan, representing Judaism, literally into exile, as they deposit their master outside of the Holy City. They carry the chief representative of Judaism into exile, but in doing so they also carry Judaism *forward*, into its new rabbinic form. We know that in the future they will go on to have disagreements that become epic and even tragic; but, even though their respective visions of core aspects of Judaism will fundamentally differ, we also know that they were both marked by this same horrible moment of suspense, of desperation, and of trauma. They are both survivors, escapees haunted by the same terror.

* * *

This book is primarily devoted to Rabbi Joshua's story, but I'd like to close this chapter with a final nod to Yohanan ben Zakkai. There is a midrash that describes a conversation that took place between Yohanan and his pupil Joshua, not long after the destruction of Jerusalem. It goes like this:

> Rabbi Yohanan ben Zakkai was once leaving Jerusalem. Rabbi Joshua was walking behind him and saw the Temple in ruins. Rabbi Joshua said: Woe unto us for the destruction of the Temple, the place of atonement for the sins of Israel.[13] [Yohanan] said to him: My son, do not worry—we have another form of atonement like it. What is it? Acts of lovingkindness. As it is written: "For I desire acts of lovingkindness and not sacrifice." (Hos 6:6)[14]

This rabbinic tale provides, for me personally, Yohanan ben Zakkai's most beautiful and brilliant act of creative religious re-narration.

I say brilliant because, after all, acts of lovingkindness are well suited to a people now in exile. This is an utterly portable religious practice that anyone in the Jewish community can do without the aid of a priest.

---

13. For many centuries, Jews believed that maintaining a good relationship with God required a combination of ritual and ethical atonement for sins. The ethical part of the atonement process generally involved what we moderns would be familiar with as taking time to accept responsibility for the harm, make apologies, make amends, and resolve to not repeat the behavior. The ritual part involved bringing sacred offerings (livestock, grain, money) to the Temple in Jerusalem, where the priests would carefully present the offering. The loss of the Temple caused many surviving Jews to fear that they would never be able to restore their relationship with God to good terms without the ability to present their ritual offerings for atonement. Rabbi Joshua is expressing this fear in this midrash.

14. Translation (slightly adapted) of the midrash from La'u, *The Sages: Character, Context, & Creativity, Vol. 2* (Kindle locations 375–78). The midrash comes from *Avot R. Nat.*, Recension A, chapter 4.

Furthermore, by telling Joshua, "we have another form of atonement like [the Temple sacrifices, and it is] acts of lovingkindness," and then providing a verse from the Hebrew Bible to "prove" his point from Scripture, Yohanan uses well established rabbinic interpretive techniques to proclaim a new Jewish sacred practice that acts as an equivalent to and substitute for the Temple sacrifices. Yohanan models for his aggrieved student an important method for Judaism to navigate the challenges of survival and transformation following the Roman destruction. If I could describe it in a formula, it would go something like this:

1. Rabbi acknowledges the painful loss of *Sacred Practice A* that was based in the Jerusalem Temple.
2. Rabbi announces that the Jews have also received from God an alternative practice, *Sacred Practice B*, which accomplishes the same good as *Sacred Practice A*.
   a. *Sacred Practice B* can be performed in any location—it's a portable practice—so it functions well under conditions of exile.
   b. *Sacred Practice B* also contains a living memory of *Sacred Practice A* embedded within it. When we perform *B*, we also remember its link to *A*.
3. Rabbi offers a "proof text" from the Hebrew Bible, which he has interpreted in a way that confirms his assertions.

I said earlier that I thought Yohanan's statements in this midrash were not only brilliant, but also beautiful. After all, Yohanan could have chosen any number of righteous actions other than acts of lovingkindness as the spiritual substitute for the Temple sacrifices (and other rabbis following him, in fact, would do just that).[15] Other biblical passages make the case that what God desires more than sacrifices is justice,[16] or ending oppression and feeding the hungry,[17] but Yohanan chose the verse from Hosea in which the prophet depicts God desiring acts of lovingkindness more than Temple sacrifices.

---

15. For example, in *b. Sukkah* 49b, Rabbi Elazar ben Azariah states that a person who gives charity is greater than a person who offers all the varieties of sacrifices. In *Deut. Rab.* 5.3, we read that doing acts of righteousness and justice are more desirable to God than sacrifices.
16. Prov 21:3.
17. Isa 1:17.

His choice of lovingkindness is striking on many levels. It's a choice that communicates to his devastated people that the proper antidote to their collective trauma and shattering experience of violent brutality is something soft, gentle, warmhearted, and attentive to the vulnerability of others. This is a remarkable spiritual proclamation.

Hate will not bring victory to those who've suffered the hatred and domination of others. Learning to be brutal will not bring healing to those who have been treated with brutality. No, this amazing quality called "lovingkindness" in ancient Hebrew will bind the wounds of a shattered people. Yohanan tells Joshua, "Let lovingkindness be the new regular spiritual practice that holds the central place in the community's consciousness, as Temple sacrifices once did." And he poignantly tells Joshua this as they are both standing in view of the ruins of the Temple. The pain is still fresh. The destruction is confronting them. And yet, in this very setting of despair, disbelief, and outrage, Yohanan directs a shell-shocked and disoriented, grieving people to rely on frequent acts of deep-hearted compassion and generosity—lovingkindness—as the new glue that will help rebuild the Jewish people.

3

After the Holocaust

From the time when the Second Temple was destroyed, ascetics became numerous in Israel, and they would not eat meat and they would not drink wine.

Rabbi Joshua went to address them. He said to them, "My children, why do you not eat meat?"

They said to him, "How can we eat meat? Every day the daily sacrifice used to be offered upon the altar, and now it is no longer [offered]."

He said to them, "Why do you not drink wine?"

They said to him, "How can we drink wine? Every day it was poured out for libation on the altar, and now it is no longer [poured]."

He said to them, "[In that case] let us not eat even figs and grapes, for [the Jews] used to bring first-fruits from them on the festival of Shavuot. And let us not eat bread, for they used to bring the two loaves and the showbread [used in Temple rituals] from the bread they would bake. Let us not drink water, for they used to offer water libations [at the Temple] on the festival of Sukkot."

They were silent.

Rabbi Joshua said to them, "Not to mourn at all is not feasible, for the Temple is in ruins and we cannot change that.[1] But, to mourn excessively is also not feasible.

---

1. I've altered the literal translation here. More accurately, the text has Rabbi Joshua saying "Not to mourn is not feasible, for the decree has already been decreed." I've changed the wording for clarity of meaning.

Rather, mourn in the way that the sages have advised.² They have taught: A person shall plaster his or her home with plaster and leave over a small bit as a remembrance of Jerusalem.³ A person may prepare all the needs of a meal, but then leave off a little bit as a remembrance of Jerusalem. A woman may prepare all her ornaments, but then leave off a little bit as a remembrance of Jerusalem.

. . . All who mourn over Jerusalem will merit to see her joy, as it is said, "Rejoice with Jerusalem and be glad for her, all who love her, join in her jubilation all who mourn over her" (Isa 66:10).
—*Tosefta Sotah 15.11–15*⁴

Rabbi Joshua lived through the worst national calamity that had ever befallen the Jews.⁵ Their holy city and Temple were destroyed, and their population was decimated. Most Jews no longer lived in the land of Israel, and those survivors who did faced ongoing scrutiny from the Roman authorities.⁶ Per the agreement Vespasian had made with Yohanan ben Zakkai, in the small coastal town of Yavneh, Yohanan succeeded in gathering some of the surviving rabbis and beginning the process of rebuilding Judaism along new lines. The Israeli rabbi and scholar Binyamin La'u writes:

---

2. Again, I've modified the literal translation somewhat for clarity.

3. This is a custom in which, when people repaint their homes with fresh paint, they leave a small corner somewhere unpainted, as a symbol of the grief over the brokenness of the world in which the Temple stands no more.

4. This translation is adapted from a translation by S. Berrin from Lieberman (ed.), *Tosefta, Nashim* 2, 242–44.

5. Shaye Cohen describes the way the authors of one major collection of Midrash thought of the destruction of the Temple as follows: "the temple was more than a building and more than the home of the sacrificial cult. It was the sacred center of the cosmos, the place where heaven and earth meet, the visible symbol of God's love for Israel. The loss of this symbol meant disorientation and despair—did God still love Israel? Has God abandoned his people?" From "The Destruction: From Scripture to Midrash," 24.

6. Lee Levine writes the following to describe Jewish life immediately after the Roman destruction of Jerusalem in 70 C.E.: "[M]uch of Jewish life lay shattered: Jerusalem was totally destroyed; only the three great towers that had once guarded Herod's palace and remnants of the western city wall remained intact. The Temple had been razed and the city's population massacred or exiled. The high priesthood and Jerusalem's aristocratic class, which had dominated Jewish religious and political life for much of the Second Temple period, all but disappeared. Judea had dared rebel against mighty Rome; having failed, she paid the heavy price of revolt." From Shanks (ed.), *Christianity and Rabbinic Judaism*, 126.

After the Holocaust

> The sages in the generation after the destruction of the Temple were seized both by a fierce longing for the Temple and by an intense desire to forge a new way of life that transcended the Temple's absence. It was on this seam between nostalgia and rebirth that Rabbi Yohanan ben Zakkai and his students concentrated their efforts.[7]

As Yohanan grew older and eventually died, Joshua found himself more and more in the position of having to provide leadership to the surviving rabbinic community in the midst of their disorientation, shock, and grief. To borrow an expression from a contemporary writer on the psychology of devastating loss, the Jewish people that Joshua served stood "at the intersection of their greatest fragility and despair."[8]

The ancient rabbinic text that opens this chapter gives us a look at an important part of how Joshua thought the Jewish people could find a healthy way to cope with their calamity. What strikes me about Joshua's advice is not just that it is balanced, good advice—the kind of advice someone would give to a friend whose grieving has been going on for too long. No, the real genius of Joshua's advice is that it charted a path for the Jewish people to shift from the kind of acute grief that is appropriate in the immediate aftermath of a terrible loss to the more contained and limited grief that we engage in through ritualized acts of remembrance.

"Don't become an ascetic," he says, "and don't grieve forever. Instead, *remember*. Remember whenever you are doing something pleasurable. When you're preparing a big meal, set aside a bit of the tastiest dish and pause for a moment of somber reflection. Then go on and eat, drink, live, laugh. Go ahead and repaint your home in that bright, inspiring color—and when you do, go into the living room and find a few inches on the wall near the baseboards to leave unpainted. Engage in remembrance, not endless grief, for the fallen Jerusalem, for the lost sanctuary where our ancestors worshiped, for the dead."

In addition to being psychologically healthy advice, Joshua's instruction is a great example of the kind of creative ritual innovation that the early rabbis developed in response to their trauma and loss. With the Temple in ruins, most of the ritual life of the Jews was lost. Joshua's teaching takes that loss, and the grief that went with it, and soothes it partly by offering the Jews several new ritual practices that weave the mourning for Jerusalem

---

7. Lau, *The Sages: Character, Context, & Creativity, Vol. 2* (Kindle locations 386–88).
8. Lawrence, "Everything Doesn't Happen for a Reason."

into the ceremonial rhythms of a new life that has its own direction and future. Through these ritual practices of remembrance, Joshua helps meet the peoples' need for ritual while re-narrating the sacred story that the people carry with them so that they are not stuck entirely in the destroyed past.

Let me say a word here about the importance of the way Rabbi Joshua's teaching re-narrates the sacred story of the Jews. Before the Temple fell, the Jews' sacred narrative was, in part, one in which they worshiped God by bringing offerings to the Temple and by celebrating the festivals with pilgrimages to Jerusalem. In addition, their sacred story claimed that God kept them secure in their land in part because their Temple offerings pleased God and led God to forgive their sins.

Joshua's teaching in the text we're examining gives the grief-stricken, post-destruction Jews a new sacred narrative. In place of the long-standing Jewish story in which the people bring offerings to the Temple and thus maintain their relationship with God, the new sacred story is this: now the Jews are the people who live among the nations of the world and remember the Temple and Jerusalem. *Their acts of remembrance are sacred acts.* By quoting the Isaiah verse at the end of his teaching, Joshua further tells his students that those who engage in regular acts of remembrance of Jerusalem are helping to bring about the rebuilding of Jerusalem and the Temple in the future. This is an entirely new story—a sacred narrative that holds the previous sacred narrative within itself, accepts the irrevocable loss of the old narrative's ability to function anymore, and moves forward with a new vision and new goals for its subjects.

In one short rabbinic text, Joshua has given the Jews a powerful blueprint for how they will move on. They will have a new religious narrative that incorporates their previous religious narrative but also moves beyond it. They will have goodness and joy in life once again, and they don't have to feel guilty that they are being disloyal to the memory of Jerusalem because incorporated within those moments of joy will be small acts of remembrance.[9]

---

[9]. There's a short midrash in which Rabbi Joshua comments on the moment that Moses calls out to the Hebrew slaves who are trapped at the shore of the Sea of Reeds with Pharaoh's army bearing down on them (Exod 14:9–15). Moses urges them not to panic and to trust that God will battle for them. God responds by chastising Moses for calling out to God in this manner, saying that instead he should be telling the slaves to go forward into the sea. It's a moment in the story of the exodus that Joshua and the other rabbis of his time could relate to, because the Roman destruction also represented a situation that appeared to be a dead end for the religion of Israel. In this midrash, Joshua claims that what God was saying to Moses in this moment was: "There is nothing else

After the Holocaust
Confronting Narrative Wreckage

Arthur W. Frank is a sociology professor at the University of Calgary, and he is the author of *The Wounded Storyteller: Body, Illness, and Ethics*, published in 1995. In the book, Frank discusses the ways that people cope with the disorientation, disruption, and chaos that come with the arrival of a serious illness or disability, with a special focus on how illness affects their life-narratives. I was assigned readings from his book in rabbinical school in some of my pastoral counseling classes.

As a congregational rabbi, Frank's ideas aided me in my efforts to provide people with helpful pastoral counseling during times of crisis and loss. More recently, I began to notice a connection between the issues that faced the Jews who survived the Roman destruction of Jerusalem two thousand years ago and Frank's theories on serious illness and its effects on one's personal life-narrative. There are, in particular, some remarkable parallels between Frank's writing on how individuals cope with the trauma of a major illness and the ways in which Rabbi Joshua urged his fellow Jews to respond to the great Roman destruction, and that's what I'll explore a bit here.

In *The Wounded Storyteller*, Frank claims that when someone discovers that he or she has a serious, life-altering illness, the person becomes a "narrative wreck."[10] (Frank credits this phrase to the American philosopher, Ronald Dworkin.) The idea is that each one of us has an operating narrative that orients our lives. Serious illness interrupts that narrative and, initially, throws its subject into narrative chaos. Here's how Frank describes the way this played out when a friend of his became seriously ill:

> ... like anyone facing a serious illness, [my friend] had lost the central resource that any storyteller depends on: a sense of temporality. The conventional expectation of any narrative, held alike by listeners and storytellers, is for a past that leads into a present that sets in place a foreseeable future. The illness story is wrecked

---

for Israel to do except to go forward. *Go forth*: when their legs go forth from the dry land to the sea, you will see the miracles that I will do for them." (*Exod. Rab.* 21.8, translation from the online *Sefaria* Source Sheet, "Praying with my Feet," by Justus Baird.) Joshua's post-Roman-destruction outlook is that there is nothing else for Israel to do except to go forward. The crucial questions facing the Jewish people revolve around how best to do that, not whether it's possible to go forward. What seems like the end of the road may in fact be the beginning of a new kind of road.

10. Frank, *The Wounded Storyteller*, 54. Frank is referencing Ronald Dworkin's book, *Life's Dominion: An Argument about Abortion, Euthanasia, and Individual Freedom* (New York: Knopf, 1993).

because its present is not what the past was supposed to lead up to, and the future is scarcely thinkable.[11]

I realize that the metaphor of serious illness may not seem, at first glance, like it fits the situation faced by Rabbi Joshua's generation in the immediate aftermath of the Roman destruction. As we saw in the last chapter of this book, we might say that a better metaphor for the task that faced the early rabbis would be "death and resurrection," as opposed to serious illness and an uncertain future.

But I think there's also something to the notion of describing the post-destruction situation of the Jews by means of an illness metaphor. When I consider Frank's words regarding an individual's personal life-narrative, I can't help but apply them to the ancient Jews as a nation, whose national, mythic self-story had also come to be wrecked by devastating and *nearly* fatal injuries to the heart and body of the nation, as it were. The Roman onslaught was fatal to Jerusalem and to Temple-based Judaism, but it was not fatal to the Jewish people, and that's why I think a metaphor of injury or severe illness also works. The Romans destroyed much of what was central to the Jews, but they nevertheless left survivors who were faced with new questions about how to work with a seriously disabled Judaism.

These survivors were given the disorienting task of having to find a way to cope with their national and religious narrative wreckage. The Jews' national-religious story was, in Frank's language, "wrecked because its present [was] not what the past was supposed to lead up to, and the future [was] scarcely thinkable." In a moment, I'd like to draw out the comparison between Frank's ideas and some of Rabbi Joshua's teachings on the question of how the Jews should cope with their loss and their newfound situation as defeated exiles, but before I do that, let's first peer more deeply into *The Wounded Storyteller*.

Elsewhere in his book, Frank describes serious illness in terms of metaphors involving *shipwrecks* and *maps*. He writes:

> Almost every illness story I have read carries some sense of being shipwrecked by the storm of disease, and many use this metaphor explicitly. Extending this metaphor describes storytelling as repair work on the wreck. The repair begins by taking stock of what survives the storm. The old map may now be less than useful, but it has hardly been carbonized. Disease happens in a life that already

---

11. Frank, *The Wounded Storyteller*, 55.

has a story, and this story goes on, changed by illness but also affecting how the illness story is formed.[12]

Frank writes that, having become a narrative wreck because of the shock and disruption of serious disease, the person coping with the illness faces the challenge of having to find a way to re-narrate his or her life going forward. He describes and gives nicknames to three different types of new narratives that people commonly construct in order to face their illnesses: the "Restitution Story," the "Chaos Story," and the "Quest Story."[13]

Before we look at each of these types of narratives, let's pause for a moment and bring Rabbi Joshua and the Jews of his generation back into the conversation. As one of the leading sages in the decades following the Roman destruction—and possibly *the* leading sage in the years following the death of Yohanan ben Zakkai—a big part of Joshua's responsibility to his people was to provide them with a new map and story for a way forward, precisely because of the horrific, massive, and life-altering wounds that they had received. Rabbi Joshua literally was, himself, a "wounded storyteller."

Just how important was it for the survival of Judaism that Rabbi Joshua and other sages of his time develop a workable new story, complete with a new map and new destination? Well, as the contemporary scholar of Islam Reza Aslan writes, "Religion, it must be understood, is not faith. Religion is the *story* of faith."[14] When unexpected events fundamentally wound and disrupt the viability of a religious community's story, a new story needs to emerge if the religion is to avoid dying out in a narrative dead end.

In a few moments, we'll see how Joshua, like the survivors of Frank's metaphorical "shipwreck," identified which parts of the pre-destruction life-story of the Jews were still intact and available for use. We'll also see how they came to identify which parts of that story were now irreversibly gone, and how elements of the mythic Jewish narrative of the past could be incorporated into a new national narrative suited for the kind of precarious future that was brought about by their trauma and loss.

Similarly, Frank describes people facing serious illness as having to assess what has survived "the storm" of their illness. These people still have their old "map" as an available resource, even though the old map can't function anymore as a viable guide in the ill person's life. Nevertheless, the old map also doesn't need to be thrown out. The previous life-narrative

---

12. Frank, *The Wounded Storyteller*, 54.
13. Frank, *The Wounded Storyteller*, multiple locations.
14. Aslan, *No god but God*, xxv.

provides the ill person with a range of salvageable materials, tools, experiences, ideas, and beliefs that are now available to become part of a new map and a reconstructed life story.

Now we're ready to consider Frank's three common types of new narratives that people facing serious illness develop, which are, once again, the Restitution Story, the Chaos Story, and the Quest Story.

The *Restitution Story* treats the illness as something temporary that medicine is going to heal completely. The subject tells himself that the interruption it is causing is only transitory, and that his pre-illness self-narrative will resume shortly. If this in fact is medically true, then the Restitution Story can work well for the subject. But, the Restitution Story can also be an expression of denial, serving only to delay the subject's need for a new life-narrative.

When a seriously ill person embraces what Frank calls a *Chaos Story*, she gets "sucked into the undertow of illness and the disasters that attend to it."[15] Her new story is, in some respects, not even a coherent story—there is no viable narrative, except maybe the expectation of continued chaos or doom. She has no sense of a path towards a viable future meaningful life narrative. Here's the contemporary American Buddhist teacher Sharon Salzberg on this idea:

> In commenting on the power of a story to give our lives cohesion, writer Hannah Arendt says, "The story reveals the meaning of what otherwise would remain an unbearable sequence of sheer happenings." To perceive the events of our lives as "sheer happenings" is indeed unbearable. I was about to explore a story that would take the scattered shards of my life and fit them all together in a new and different way.[16]

The Chaos Story is full of panic and disorientation, and it is painful to witness someone who is living within its brutal and sorrowful grip.

Finally, there is the *Quest Story*, which Frank argues is the healthiest and the noblest kind of new narrative for the person facing severe illness to adopt. "Quest stories meet suffering head on; they accept illness and seek to *use* it. Illness is the occasion of a journey that becomes a quest."[17] When a person facing severe illness develops a quest narrative, she engages in an act of courage and creativity that enables her to tell a new story about her

---

15. Frank, *The Wounded Storyteller*, 115.
16. Salzberg, *Faith: Trusting Your Own Deepest Experience*, 8.
17. Frank, *The Wounded Storyteller*, 115.

After the Holocaust

life that incorporates the disruption of her previous life-narrative, accepts the parts of that narrative that are permanently lost, and designates new meaningful destinations and goals for her life.

For a Quest Story to be successful, Frank writes that it needs to be what he calls a "good story."[18] A "good story" is one that is honest about the past and what's been lost, while also setting forth a new direction in which the subject's goal is to "rise to the occasion" that has been created by the changed reality—including the losses and new challenges. The Quest Story that is also a "good story" "meet[s] suffering head on . . . ," accepting the illness and seeking "to *use* it" so that it propels the subject into a quest to create meaning and goodness within a new and unexpected framework that couldn't have been anticipated before the arrival of the illness.[19]

Now let's bring Rabbi Joshua back into the picture. Let's consider, again, the ancient rabbinic text at the opening of this chapter. It's from a collection of rabbinic teachings known as the Tosefta. (For now, it's enough to say about the Tosefta that its contents developed as oral traditions during the rough timespan of the last two centuries before the Roman destruction and the first two centuries after it.)

This particular Tosefta text presents us with a legend about Rabbi Joshua and his Jewish peers in the decades following the Roman destruction. Joshua sees a growing number of Jews who have embraced what Arthur Frank might call a version of the Chaos Story. Their Chaos Story goes something like this:

> Jerusalem and the Temple are in ruins. But we *need* Jerusalem and the Temple in order to fulfill our mission in life. Since there is no conceivable future that we can orient towards, we have instead redefined our national and religious life story around the Roman destruction. This catastrophic change therefore consumes and defines us within the closed walls of a story that has reached a horrific dead end. The joys and pleasures of this life can have no meaning without the restoration of what was lost, and we don't see any chance of that restoration happening in the imaginable future. We will, therefore, reject the joys and pleasures of this life entirely. We will be ascetics, frozen in a constant state of mourning. To do otherwise is to dishonor the sanctity and essential nature of the national and religious narrative we've lost.

---

18. Frank, *The Wounded Storyteller*, 62.
19. Frank, *The Wounded Storyteller*, 115.

Rabbi Joshua sees these Jewish ascetics carrying on in this manner, and he turns to them with a message that rejects the Chaos Story. Instead, he tells them to opt for a Quest Story. In so many words, what he says is:

> Our loss is truly overwhelming, and it is irreversible. Of course we have to grieve it. But we must not live our lives within the confines of perpetual mourning. We will, instead, forge a new story, and a new set of goals to strive for. This new story will *include* our old story, and it will also incorporate the events that brought that story to an end. Our new story will also include our need to grieve for what we've lost, and we will do so with *new rituals* that will make a small place for that grief and memory to be with us at all times. But, my children, even as we live within the shadow of Jerusalem in ruins, there is a new story for us to discover and use to re-orient ourselves, and it includes living a meaningful life that has room for new joys and pleasures too. And by living in this way—by honoring Jerusalem and the Temple while also moving beyond Jerusalem and the Temple—we will create the possibility of a future in which all of these tragedies are one day made right.

One of the things that's remarkable about this ancient Rabbi Joshua story is the way in which it reflects a lesson that he himself had once had to learn from his master, Yohanan ben Zakkai. If you remember from chapter 1, we read a midrash[20] that told of how one day Joshua and Yohanan ben Zakkai were walking by the ruins of the Temple. In a moment of despair, Joshua broke down and asked his master how the Jewish people could carry on without the Holy Sanctuary and the sacred rites that took place there—rituals that created and maintained the spiritual channel of atonement between the people of Israel and God. In that story, Joshua expresses the despair that the Jewish ascetics in our Tosefta text are expressing.

And just as happens in our Tosefta text, in this midrash Yohanan ben Zakkai redirects Joshua away from a Chaos Story. Instead, Yohanan tells him that while the loss is devastating, there is another way for the Jewish people to receive atonement and maintain their spiritual bond with God, and it is through acts of lovingkindness. In this short midrash, Yohanan ben Zakkai offers a glimpse of what he, as the leader of the rabbinic community, thinks the Jewish peoples' post-destruction Quest Story should look like.

In this midrash and in our Tosefta text, both Yohanan ben Zakkai and Rabbi Joshua offer us quick and partial sketches of elements of the post-destruction Quest Story that the early rabbis came to develop and

20. *Avot R. Nat.*, Recension A, chapter 4.

then teach the Jewish people as a whole. The rabbis' new "map" and new destination still included Jerusalem and the Temple—but the shift was to hold them in memory and in heart, and to include within the new national story a directive to live for today while maintaining the hope of Jerusalem's eventual restoration. This theme of choosing to find a meaningful way to "move on" as a response to the Roman destruction appears again and again in rabbinic literature, and multiple times in connection with Rabbi Joshua.

* * *

I mentioned earlier that Frank wrote about the Restitution Story, in which the person coping with illness tells herself that the illness is only temporary and medicine is going to restore her to her pre-illness life narrative intact. Just like the rabbinic stories that describe Rabbi Joshua rejecting the Chaos Story and encouraging a Quest Story instead, there are also examples in the rabbinic writings of Joshua confronting members of the Jewish community who responded to the Roman destruction by embracing a kind of Restitution Story.

We've discussed how Rabbi Joshua lived through the Roman destruction of 70 C.E., and how, in the years just prior to 70 C.E., the Jewish Zealots had forced the rest of the Jews of Jerusalem to join them in their ill-fated revolt against Rome. After 70 C.E., throughout the rest of Joshua's life, he had to contend with a resurgent Jewish faction of Zealots who wanted to rise up against Rome once again, with the hope of driving the Romans out once and for all and rebuilding Jerusalem and the Temple. Some of these Zealots embraced popular rumors and theologies positing that the Roman destruction of 70 C.E. was merely a "birth-pang" of God's imminent sending of a redeemer—the Messiah—who would lead a Jewish army into victory against Rome and restore all that had been lost.

Not only did Joshua not subscribe to this belief, he thought it was reckless and dangerous. To counter these ideas, in one Talmudic passage, Joshua argued that God would send the Messiah *in God's own time*, and God would do so as an *act of grace* (and not, as some others believed, as a result of collective Jewish action acting as a trigger).[21] This statement, while not directed solely at the Zealots, expressed a belief that Joshua repeated elsewhere in his teachings: that the redemption of the Jews and the restoration of Jerusalem would indeed happen one day, but not in any of their

21. *b. Sanh.* 97b.

lifetimes, and not because of their ability to find the right trigger to initiate those events. (We'll see other examples of Joshua's teachings on this subject later in this book.)

The point I'd like to stress here is that just as Joshua counseled his fellow Jews away from a Chaos Story that would trap them in a narrative cul-de-sac of endless mourning and meaninglessness, he also warned the Jews against embracing the unrealistic fantasies of a Restitution Story. Joshua saw how profoundly wrong the pre-70 C.E. Zealots had been when they launched the first revolt against Rome, and he was enough of a realist to know what would happen to the surviving Jewish community (and the chances of negotiating for the rebuilding of the Temple with a future Roman emperor) if another band of Jewish Zealots was to launch a new attack against Rome. A Restitution Story was a dangerous delusion, and Joshua did what he could to dissuade his rabbinic peers and the Jews at large from buying into the potentially self-destructive fantasy.

* * *

Joshua Podro, a twentieth-century scholar of the ancient rabbinic world, wrote, "[Rabbi Joshua would give the defeated Jews] care rather than frenzied admonition, [and] with consolation aid a return to self-respect . . ."[22] Podro also added, "[Rabbi Joshua's] constant search was for moderation; he rejected the other-worldly movements of those days in which this world counted for next to nothing, regarding [this world] as an important field of action, not without joy . . . Pain and suffering were real and he made it his task to reduce them whenever possible."[23]

What Rabbi Joshua grasped, along with a number of his colleagues, was the power the wounded have to construct a new, meaningful narrative as a means of coping with calamity. Our ability to develop a new guiding story for our lives is one of the most powerful cognitive tools we possess as human beings. Rabbi Joshua's part in developing that coping strategy among the first generation of Jews to survive the Roman destruction helped the Jews of his time adapt quickly and meaningfully to their painful situation, and then go on, for the next nineteen centuries, to use that narrative framework to maintain a distinct Jewish religious and national identity, despite being spread out among many nations. The same basic, renewed

---

22. Podro, *The Last Pharisee*, 53.
23. Podro, *The Last Pharisee*, 47.

narrative that Rabbi Joshua helped develop also helped Jewish communities in the diaspora survive countless persecutions, deportations, libels, and pogroms, and allowed them to continue developing their religious ideas in a way that looked both backwards and forwards in time. As the contemporary theologian Ruby Sales teaches, "I think that one of the things that theologies must have is hindsight, insight, and foresight. That is complete sight."[24]

---

24. Sales, *"Where Does It Hurt?"* Radio interview: *On Being*, with host, Krista Tippett.

4

Clash of the Early Rabbinic Titans —Part I

Spread throughout the various collections of ancient rabbinic writings we find many stories about the leading rabbis of the post-Roman-destruction generation, including their legendary disputes and life dramas. As has been mentioned, these stories aren't organized into one coherent book. They appear here and there throughout the classical rabbinic works, embedded in the semi-chaotic, multiply nested, associative, self-interrupting, "non-linear networking of texts and contexts"[1] that characterizes the Talmud and Midrash.

As we've already learned, after the Temple and Jerusalem fell, Rabbi Yohanan ben Zakkai and his surviving rabbinic colleagues set up shop in the coastal village of Yavneh. From there, Yohanan and the sages focused on preserving and strengthening rabbinic Judaism in the aftermath of the catastrophe.

With Yohanan were two of his most beloved students, Rabbi Joshua ben Hananiah and Rabbi Eliezer ben Hyrcanus, as well as a cast of several prominent disciples who appear throughout the early rabbinic writings. For now, let's meet two more rabbis of the Yavneh crew, each of whom plays a huge role in the key dramas and conflicts that unfold during the first half-century following the Roman destruction.

---

1. Steinmetz, "Agada Unbound," 335.

Clash of the Early Rabbinic Titans—Part I

First, I'll introduce Rabban Gamaliel II, whom I'll just call "Gamaliel" going forward. (By the way, the title "Rabban" was used for rabbis who headed the rabbinic court known as the Sanhedrin—it's an honorific version of the title "rabbi.") Before Jerusalem fell, Gamaliel was part of the social elite of Judean society—wealthy, well-connected, and widely respected. His family was believed to have descended from King David. His father, Shimon ben Gamaliel, was president of the Sanhedrin, as were several of his paternal ancestors, including his great-great-grandfather, the renowned sage, Hillel. (Incidentally, his grandfather, Gamaliel I, was president of the Sanhedrin during the lifetime of Jesus, and he is specifically mentioned by name in the New Testament.[2])

During the Second Temple period, before the Roman destruction, the Sanhedrin served as the highest Jewish religious court of Judea.[3] Rabbinic texts describe it as a council of sages and priests who would meet in a place called the Chamber of Hewn Stones, which was built into one of the walls of the Temple. The Sanhedrin would convene for the purpose of certain serious criminal trials, and it would discuss and debate matters of Jewish law and religious practice. New Testament texts describing the Sanhedrin include stories about the trial of Jesus (Mark 14:53–65, Matt 26:59–68, and Luke 22:66–71) and an account of Paul's appearance before the Sanhedrin (Acts 22:30—23:12).[4]

After the Temple and Jerusalem were destroyed, the bulk of the Jewish population was thrown into exile. Several years after the rabbis led by Yohanan ben Zakkai regrouped and set themselves up in Yavneh, Gamaliel took the reins as president of the Sanhedrin. He had to face some overwhelming

---

2. See, for example, Acts 5:34–42.

3. Historians disagree over questions of how or even whether the Sanhedrin actually functioned during the Second Temple period. Some believe that the descriptions of the Second Temple era Sanhedrin found in rabbinic literature represent a kind of rabbinic fantasy or mythical retrojection. Others argue that there probably was some form of Sanhedrin operating during parts of the Second Temple era, but that it may have been an institution with an erratic history, and that the way it is remembered in the Mishnah and Talmud, for example, is not a reliable record of what actually happened. And of course, still others argue that the Sanhedrin existed and functioned during Second Temple times essentially in the way the rabbinic literature describes it. What interests me in this book is the mythic story-world of the early rabbis, which includes the assertion that the Sanhedrin functioned throughout the Second Temple period, and that prominent sages whom the rabbis regarded as early practitioners of their approach to Judaism, like Hillel and Gamaliel I, were among its leaders.

4. For a short overview about the Sanhedrin, see VanderKam, "Judaism in the Land of Israel," 79.

The Forgotten Sage

questions about how the Jewish people, and the Temple-based religion of Israel, would carry on under such different conditions, and in the immediate aftermath of unprecedented collective loss and trauma.[5]

Some scholars credit Gamaliel with having far-sighted wisdom about the need to establish a standardized *halakhah* across the scattered Jewish communities of exile. Paul Heger writes:

> With the destruction of the Temple, only a unified code of behavior, founded upon the Torah and regulating all aspects of life, could guarantee the future existence of the Jews as a united people. Deviations in the daily routine of rituals, customs, and secular aspects of life would create serious and irreversible splits between the widely dispersed communities. Over time, such gaps would surely widen, and end in the creation of entirely separate communities.[6]

If Gamaliel was a visionary who understood what was needed to ensure a cohesive Jewish identity under the dramatic new conditions of homelessness and exile, the Talmud's stories about him also point out his character flaws. As we'll see shortly, in some of the texts he appears ego-driven and insecure to the point of petty vindictiveness. He also seems insulated by his wealth and privilege from understanding the struggles of many of his impoverished rabbinic peers.

Let's leave Gamaliel for now and briefly meet another sage, Rabbi Elazar ben Azariah. (Watch out for the similarity in the names Elazar and Eliezer—these are two very different individuals.) Elazar was a younger contemporary of our hero, Rabbi Joshua. He was a true genius who was widely respected and liked by his peers. He also had a good sense of the importance of public perceptions in politics, and his astuteness and flexibility would help resolve some of the biggest and most destabilizing conflicts among the rabbinic leadership at Yavneh during the first fragile decades of rabbinic Judaism after the Roman destruction.

So now we've met our starting cast of rabbinic characters.

---

5. Paul Heger, in a lengthy footnote, writes: "Yohanan ben Zakkai, the first leader in the post-70 period, was concerned with . . . mitigating the traumatic impact of the destruction of the central and most holy element of the Jewish people, and strengthening the status of Yavneh and its Sages as the intellectual and cultural center instead of the cultic sanctuary of Jerusalem. He also had the difficult task of placating the understandable opposition of the priests to his perspective and procedures." Heger, *The Pluralistic Halakhah*, 287, n. 161.

6. Heger, *The Pluralistic Halakhah*, 286.

Clash of the Early Rabbinic Titans—Part I

To review: we have Yohanan ben Zakkai, the "dean" and elder of the post-destruction period. This is the same Yohanan who made the agonizing deal with Vespasian that gave up on saving Jerusalem or the Temple, and the same Yohanan who secured Yavneh for the rabbis.

We have our rabbinic sparring partners, Rabbis Joshua and Eliezer, the two disciples of Yohanan who together smuggled his bier out of Jerusalem so he could appeal to Vespasian. As we're about to see, Joshua and Eliezer are going to clash furiously over key questions of how this newly developing, post-destruction, rabbinic approach to Judaism should function. The president of the Sanhedrin, Gamaliel, is going to have struggles with both of them as well. And last but not least, we have Elazar ben Azariah, the youthful rabbinic whiz kid with high emotional intelligence and social savvy. Now we're ready to bring up the curtain on the drama of these rabbis in the first half-century following the Roman destruction.

Except, not quite. At the risk of over-introducing our story, maybe first we need just a little more background for the whole story to make sense...

* * *

Several decades before the Roman destruction in 70 C.E., during the last part of the Second Temple era, two prominent sages famously disputed hundreds of matters of Jewish law. Their names were Hillel and Shammai. Many of their disagreements centered on whether to interpret the laws of the Torah in a more lenient or a more strict way. Hillel tended towards leniency and creative flexibility. Shammai tended towards exactitude and stringency. Both of them headed large academies, though Hillel had more followers than Shammai. After their deaths, their respective schools continued these debates, which ultimately became recorded in the Talmud and in Midrash.

In terms of personalities, the rabbinic literature describing each of them offers a caricature of Shammai as stern, judgmental, impatient, and suspicious of outsiders, in contrast with Hillel, who comes across as humble, welcoming towards outsiders, reasonable, and open-minded—even to Shammai's ideas. These caricatures extend to the schools of each of these sages as well. (Some might say that the fans of Hillel clearly were the "winners who got to write history.")

Probably the best-known bit of rabbinic literature about these two sages is the story of a non-Jewish man who approached Shammai one day and said, "Convert me to Judaism on the condition that you teach me the entire Torah while I stand on one foot." Shammai, who was a builder with a mind for engineering by training, bristled at the silliness and disrespectful audacity of the request. Without saying a word, he shooed the man away with the builder's measuring tool in his hand.

The same man then found Hillel and put the identical challenge to him. Probably to the man's great surprise, Hillel agreed to meet him on his own terms. He converted him and then said simply, "That which is hateful to you, don't do to your fellow. This is the whole Torah, and the rest is commentary. Go and learn it."[7]

Elsewhere in the rabbinic literature, we find this story:

> The [leading sages of the Second Temple period] said: "Raise up many disciples." But the schools of Shammai and Hillel disagreed over [the meaning of] this. The school of Shammai said, "One should teach only someone who is smart, unassuming, of good lineage, and wealthy." But the school of Hillel said: "One should teach anyone, for there were many sinners in Israel who were brought close to the study of Torah, and whose children became righteous, pious, and good people."[8]

Again and again, we find vignettes like these two above in which Shammai seems like a snob, or a joyless stickler, or an inflexible judge, while Hillel comes across as open-minded, welcoming, curious to learn even from Shammai, and compassionate. It's enough to make you think that either Shammai really was an unbearably self-righteous, closed-minded elitist, or that Hillel's disciples were far better at PR and media relations than Shammai's. I say that only half-jokingly.

Anyway, let me get back to describing some of the important elements of the background that the Hillel and Shammai era provide us about the rabbis of Rabbi Joshua's generation. At the time of the Hillel/Shammai debates, the sages had no formal written codes of law apart from the biblical laws in the Torah (Genesis–Deuteronomy). The sages of that time studied the Torah closely and developed a growing body of interpretations of it, including major additions to and interpretive adaptations of its laws and

---

7. I've paraphrased and quoted elements of this well-known Talmudic story, found in *b. Shabb.* 31a.

8. This text comes from a collection of midrash known as *Avot de Rabbi Natan*, as translated by Rabbi Abraham Joshua Heschel in his book, *Heavenly Torah: As Refracted through the Generations*, 44.

Clash of the Early Rabbinic Titans—Part I

ritual practices. But these newer teachings weren't written down; instead, they passed down their debates and Jewish legal (*halakhic*) rulings orally, through their schools and academies. In terms of actual religious practice, different local sages might follow the teachings of Hillel, Shammai, or other sages, and at times they would innovate their own teachings.

From its earliest years, a rabbinic system emerged in Judea in which debate and differing rabbinic opinions were accepted as part of a living interpretive tradition. When disputes needed to be resolved, sometimes the leading sages of the day would convene to hear arguments presented and vote to decide what the normative law would be. However, the teachings of the minority opinions were preserved in the tradition, and local sages sometimes chose to act according to a known minority opinion.

Centuries later, when the early debates of Hillel and Shammai had attained the status of foundational, legendary rabbinic texts, the Talmud records the following:

> For three years the School of Shammai and the School of Hillel disputed. The one side said: The *halakhah* is as we maintain, and the other side said: The *halakhah* is as we maintain. [Then] the "Voice of heaven" [known in Hebrew as the *bat kol*] emerged and said: Both are the words of the living God, but the *halakhah* is [to be decided] according to the School of Hillel.
>
> [The narrating voice of the Talmud then asks: But] since both opinions are "the words of the living God" [that is, equally truthful and authoritative], why is the *halakhah* decided according to the School of Hillel? Because they were kind and humble, and not only did they quote both their own opinions and those of the School of Shammai, they also quoted those of the School of Shammai before their own.[9]

Through this Talmudic text and others, the rabbinic tradition established a principle that Hillel's rulings usually formed the basis of *halakhah*, and Shammai's rulings were preserved as minority viewpoints for the record. It's important to keep in mind two aspects of how the rabbis came to view the opinions of these two great schools.

First, the early rabbis developed[10] the theological belief that both sets of opinions, and even the debates themselves, were all Divinely inspired

---

9 Heger, *The Pluralistic Halakhah*, 60. This is a translation by Heger of a famous passage from *b. Eruv.* 13b. I made a slight adaptation for clarity's sake.

10. As we'll come to explore later in this book, some scholars argue that we don't know whether the early rabbis and their forerunners—sages going as far back as Hillel

"words of the living God." The rabbis' God is a God who sees multiple sides to our questions, and though choices have to be made regarding normative practice, we are meant to study and contemplate the minority as well as the majority opinions in rabbinic debates over *halakhah*.[11]

Second, the reason for why the *bat kol* (the voice from heaven) proclaims that Hillel's views should determine the *halakhah* has nothing to do with the merits of Hillel's powers of biblical interpretation or reasoning. No, Hillel's views will determine the *halakhah*, and not Shammai's, because of how the members of the school of Hillel conducted themselves in the course of their study and debate with the School of Shammai. They were respectful and courteous of Shammai's opposing viewpoints, and on the merit of those qualities of open-mindedness and humility, God intervened in their debates by means of a heavenly voice to proclaim that the *halakhah* always goes according to the School of Hillel.

This is important, and in a way, kind of astonishing. Usually, in Western religious traditions, often people think of God's words as synonymous with The Absolute Truth. The Abrahamic religions, broadly speaking, require us to imagine a God who wants us to know what the truth is, to believe it, and to follow it. Religions, and denominations within the same religion, then get into arguments with one another about what that "Absolute Truth" is, or how we're supposed to interpret it, but tend to all claim that they've got the "correct" understanding.

In contrast, in this particular Talmudic story, a voice straight from heaven tells us that certainty of the truth is less important than personal ethical conduct in the course of debate. And so, this Divine voice says, the *halakhah* will follow the rulings of the school of Hillel.

---

and Shammai and including the Rabbi Joshua who is the subject of this book—were the ones who really developed this belief of Divinely sanctioned pluralism of opinion. Scholars like Daniel Boyarin, for example, argue that because the final versions of the stories that present this take on the early rabbis emerged from the editing of the last generations of rabbis who compiled the Talmud several centuries after the time of these early rabbinic tales, all that we really know is that those later rabbis wanted to promote these stories about the origins of the rabbinic movement. For now, in this chapter, I want to "go with the flow" of the portrait that emerges of a kind of early rabbinic decentralized pluralism in which the dominant belief was that the differing opinions of the sages were all the "words of the living God," despite the contradictions.

11. A thought: it seems to me that this text gives us a portrait of a God who wants us to engage in learning—in study. We are meant to engage the sages' debates, explore the question and figure out the reasoning different sages use, in order to become the kinds of people God wants us to be.

Clash of the Early Rabbinic Titans—Part I

But hold your horses! When we look at the entire body of rabbinic sacred literature, it turns out that the *halakhah doesn't* always go according to the School of Hillel! In other parts of the Talmud, we learn that sometimes the rulings of the House of Shammai won the day and determined the *halakhah*, and that Hillel's views were relegated to minority opinion status in those cases.[12]

How can that be? It's just one of many examples of how the Talmud and Midrash contain contradictory stories and memories, and in the case of Hillel vs. Shammai we find the same tendency.[13] For instance, in one passage we read about three occasions in which the *halakhah* was set according to the views of Shammai because, upon further reflection, the disciples of Hillel realized that the reasoning being used by the School of Shammai for its positions was better than their own. Consequently, they reversed themselves and accepted Shammai's views.[14]

What I hope is coming across in this discussion of Hillel and Shammai is that, from its earliest legendary, mythical beginnings, the rabbinic tradition presents us with a portrait of itself that includes the normative practice of robust debate between scholarly authorities. It also tells us a story about how the great majority of the time, the views of Hillel were adopted by the rabbinic community over the views of Shammai, and that most of the later formulations of Jewish law would base themselves on the opinions of the School of Hillel.

All this is true, and yet, there's one more complicating piece you need to know about this very early period in the recorded stories of the rabbis. You see, there's another contradiction in the early rabbinic literature

---

12. For example, in *y. Ber.* 8.5, Shammai and Hillel argue over the correct order of the rituals and their blessings during the ceremony Jews perform to mark the end of the Sabbath, known as *Havdalah*. The *halakhah* ends up following Shammai.

13. Paul Heger writes, "A ... dilemma was created by the decision in [Yavneh] to establish a general rule that the *halakhah* is always according to Beit Hillel [= the House of Hillel, i.e. Hillel and his disciples]. In some instances, the sages preferred, for legitimate reasons, to establish the *halakhah* contrary to the presumed opinion of Beit Hillel. ... In some cases in which it was deemed advisable to establish the *halakhah* according to Beit Shammai, it was declared that Beit Hillel had changed their minds and accepted the opinion of their opponents. In other instances, the maxim that the *halakhah* was always to follow Beit Hillel was simply ignored, with no justification, and in express conflict with another maxim to the effect that the *halakhah* could never follow Beit Shammai. Occasionally, it seems the Mishnah left matters deliberately vague; [in one instance] we find the ambiguous phrase 'after they conceded,' with no indication of whether Beit Shammai yielded to Beit Hillel or vice-versa." Heger, *The Pluralistic Halakhah*, 359–60.

14. *m. Ed.* 1.12–14.

that is a little difficult to resolve with certainty. On the one hand, these writings describe a system of establishing the normative Jewish legal and ritual practices—the *halakhah*, as defined earlier—that looks pretty simple at first glance: great rabbis establish schools of thought; the various rabbis (or, representatives of their schools) debate matters of *halakhah*; there's a vote by the wider rabbinic leadership; the majority view becomes *halakhah* (law) and everyone is expected to follow it; the minority views get recorded and transmitted because they are also valuable and could be helpful in determining future *halakhah*.[15] And once in a while, when disputes rage on and on and can't seem to get resolved, a Divine voice—a *bat kol*—will show up and announce a winner, though the winners may be selected more for the graciousness with which they pressed their argument than for the correctness of their beliefs.

Except it's even more complicated than that. In some places throughout rabbinic literature, we also read examples of rabbis and local Jewish communities following a *minority* view and rejecting the majority view, as well as examples of individual rabbis setting aside their own halakhic rulings and following those of a colleague when traveling and visiting that colleague's community.[16] Some contemporary scholars of rabbinic Judaism, like Paul Heger, argue that a study of the earliest layer of the Talmud, known as the Mishnah, in contrast with the later historical layers, known as the Gemara, reveals that the earliest generations of rabbis generally accepted that any given sage might choose to practice Judaism according to his own halakhic opinion, even if it was a minority opinion—or, similarly, that ordinary pious Jews might decide to follow a minority viewpoint, especially if it was recognized as an old revered tradition.

---

15. Some examples from early rabbinic legal texts illustrate this principle, such as: *t. Ed.* 1.2—The law is always in accordance with the majority; the only reason the words of a single dissenting voice are mentioned among the majority is in case they are needed in a given hour and can be relied upon; *m. Ed.* 1.5—And why do they record the opinion of a single person among the many, when the *halakhah* must be according to the opinion of the many? So that if a court prefers the opinion of the single person it may depend on that person; and finally, *m. Ed.* 1.6—Rabbi Judah said: why do they record the opinion of a single person among the many, only to set it aside? So that if a person will say, "Thus have I learned the Tradition," it may be said to that person, "According to the [refuted] opinion of that individual did you hear it."

16. For example, see *b. Eruv.* 94a, in which the Talmudic rabbis known as Rav and Shmuel are said to have each refrained from imposing his own opposing view of Jewish law when visiting the other's district.

Clash of the Early Rabbinic Titans—Part I

Heger believes that during the era of Hillel and Shammai—the last of the Second Temple years—rabbinic courts may have tried to standardize *halakhah* for all Jews by majority vote, but that despite their efforts to do that, the entire halakhic system remained fairly ad hoc and localized. He writes that during this era, "there was no aspiration to establish a fixed *halakhah*. The people practiced their religious and civil obligations according to their accustomed traditions; if new problems developed, or there was a lack of information, they approached their local Sage, an erudite person who delivered his decision according to the way he understood the divine precepts of the Torah."[17]

Got all of that? Confused a bit? Don't worry, it gets even more interesting when we return to the ancient texts about the rabbis we were discussing at the beginning of this chapter.

* * *

Let's bring back our focus to the rabbis who lived in the aftermath of the Roman destruction, two to three generations after the era of Hillel and Shammai. If Paul Heger is right, these rabbis inherited a system that was semi-organized and inconsistently followed in practice among the people. It was a system of oral teachings that sometimes conflicted with one another. Sometimes those conflicts were ruled on by a majority vote of the sages. The rabbis who wanted to unify and standardize the *halakhah* sought to publicize these decisions in order to persuade the whole Jewish community, now spread out across the Mediterranean and Middle East, to follow the majority rulings, while respecting and preserving the knowledge of the minority, rejected viewpoints.

But the urge to create a uniform *halakhah* was hampered by the well-established rabbinic belief that *all* of the opinions expressed about the *halakhah* by different rabbis, including the rejected minority viewpoints, were somehow—mysteriously and paradoxically—the words of the same living God.[18] By the time we get to Rabbi Joshua, Rabbi Eliezer, and the rest of the cast of characters I presented at the beginning of this chapter, we find

---

17. Heger, *The Pluralistic Halakhah*, 17–18. Similarly, Jacob Neusner writes, "During the Temple period and the first years after the Destruction, there had been no development of unanimity in the field of *halakha*. Each sage rendered decisions in his town and neighborhood according to the traditions he had received and his *halakhic* speculations." See Neusner, *Eliezer Ben Hyrcanus: The Tradition and the Man*, Vol. 2, 276.

18. *b. Eruv.* 13b.

The Forgotten Sage

Rabban Gamaliel II (remember him?) using his position as president of the Sanhedrin to try to push for a more centralized, less ad hoc system of *halakhah*. Paul Heger writes: "Rabban Gamaliel realized that after the loss of the Temple, the symbol of unity of Israel, only a unitary legal codex could guarantee the people's survival as a single, unified entity."[19]

As the president of the Sanhedrin in the period following the Roman destruction of Jerusalem, Gamaliel was in a profoundly tough spot. He faced an incredibly difficult set of challenges, and his formal position of power situated him as the one surviving Jewish leader who was widely recognized by Jewish and Roman authorities as well. His decisions would play a major role in the post-destruction fate of the Jews, and he knew it.

In addition to the trauma of the Roman devastation, Gamaliel had at least three other worries to contend with. First, there were the Jewish-Christians, who were expanding to include ever more non-Jews and gaining strength and popularity throughout the region. And second, there were communities of Jews who rejected a core theological belief of the rabbinic movement—namely, the claim that God had given Moses "two Torahs" during the revelation at Mt. Sinai—the Written Torah (i.e., the books of Genesis through Deuteronomy) and the Oral Torah (i.e., all the rabbinic debates, stories, and teachings that would ever come to be in the future). These non-rabbinic Jews may in fact have been much larger in number than those who followed the rabbis.[20]

Gamaliel also had a third major worry to contend with. There were still some militant Jewish anti-Roman zealots who had survived the war in the community he oversaw. There were also enough Jews living in various Mediterranean cities of the Roman Empire to potentially cause trouble for the Roman authorities. Going as far back as the Babylonian conquest of Jerusalem and the exiling of many thousands of Jews over six hundred years prior to the Roman destruction, Jewish diaspora communities grew and formed an important minority group in many of the cities and towns of the Middle East and the Mediterranean world. Gamaliel had to deal with the

---

19. Heger, *The Pluralistic Halakhah*, 310.

20. Academic scholarship on the Jews of this period includes many prominent voices who contend that the rabbinic movement did not become a dominant or normative form of Jewish life until several centuries after the Roman destruction. In this book I am not making any claims about the historical evidence for or against the veracity of much of the mythic story that rabbinic Judaism tells about its own origins. I'm interested in exploring the myth.

Clash of the Early Rabbinic Titans—Part I

possibility of new Jewish guerrilla uprisings, and with wary and impatient Roman officials.

In his role as president of the Sanhedrin and recognized Jewish figurehead in the eyes of Rome, Gamaliel tried to find a survival strategy for rabbinic Judaism that could cope with all these challenges: collective exile and disorientation; national PTSD following the Roman destruction; the possibility of new violent rebellion against Rome; rival Jewish and quasi-Jewish religious factions; and a lot of rabbis who valued their ability to pronounce their own opinions on matters of *halakhah*, and, in many cases, who believed that individual rabbis should have the authority to follow and teach their own halakhic viewpoints to their students.

Getting the rabbis to buy in to a standardized, uniform *halakhah*, whether determined by majority vote of the Sanhedrin or by Divine voices from heaven, wasn't going to be easy. These rabbis had their own followers, their own egos, and, some historians claim, a tradition that valued local variation in the *halakhah* based on a decentralized model of individual sages making and enforcing rulings in their own local domains.

Paul Heger writes that Gamaliel opted for a strategy of using his office to try to establish a "unified halakhic system, in contrast to the autonomy and unrestricted liberty of the Sages before 70 [C.E.] to decide *halakhah* according to their personal convictions."[21] Gamaliel figured that if Jews were going to survive for a long time in exile, they would need to establish a much more uniform set of practices in order for Jewish communities spread out across the Roman Empire to have a fighting chance to stay connected to their religion, to their shattered homeland, and to each other.[22] Perhaps Gamaliel reasoned that, with the majority of Jews now living in foreign communities, it was urgently important to assert the Sanhedrin as the one legitimate organ for resolving disputes among rabbis and establishing norms of practice that would unite the exiles with the rabbinic survivors in Yavneh. And of course, Gamaliel was head of the Sanhedrin, so he may have had personal political motivations as well.[23]

In any event, as the first decades following the Roman destruction unfolded, we find in the rabbinic literature a story of a struggle between several great sages to resolve some of these tensions inherent in the system

---

21. Heger, *The Pluralistic Halakhah*, 318-19.

22. I'm basing this assertion on Paul Heger's view that Gamaliel II "initiated the movement towards a fixed *halakhah* . . . ." Heger, *The Pluralistic Halakhah*, 19.

23. Heger, *The Pluralistic Halakhah*, 19.

they had received from their Second Temple era predecessors. Some scholars today argue that Gamaliel hoped that the resistance he might face from rabbis who wanted to maintain independent authority in their local domains could be mollified by preserving minority viewpoints in the official record and declaring that these rejected opinions were also "the words of the living God," to be studied as sacred far into the future and possibly even used to resolve future questions of *halakhah*. In this way, he hoped that a centralized system would create enough uniformity of practice among the spread-out Jewish world that the Jews would avoid splintering themselves beyond the point of being able to function as a cohesive people. Of course, many rabbis resisted Gamaliel's attempted reform, and it's not clear from the rabbinic literature how long it took for Gamaliel's vision to fully become normative.[24]

Some of the rabbis' reluctance to cede authority to Gamaliel's "parliament of rabbis" at the Sanhedrin probably stemmed from the sense many of them had that Gamaliel wasn't actually interested in allowing the full range of rabbinic opinion and debate to flourish in the Sanhedrin. As we'll soon see in this book, there are Talmudic stories that depict Gamaliel as having tried to pack the Sanhedrin with yes-men as much as possible, and as having used bullying and intimidation tactics to suppress rabbis whose views differed from his own. Some sages saw Gamaliel as "an autocratic leader who, as the bearer of authority, attempted to centralize all power in his hands, [in contrast with] the Sages, who believed that *halakhic* authority was grounded in the entire assembly."[25]

---

24. It took a hundred years after the end of Gamaliel II's tenure as president of the Sanhedrin for the first written compilation of ancient rabbinic debates and majority rulings to be published by the Sanhedrin and distributed widely by messengers throughout the exilic Jewish world. Around 220 C.E., the president of the Sanhedrin, Judah ha-Nasi, published this work, known as the Mishnah, the earliest part of what would eventually become the Talmud. He proclaimed it to be the authoritative base text on questions of Jewish law and practice, and over the course of the next centuries the Mishnah came to occupy that status in rabbinic Judaism. But even with the success of the Mishnah, the rabbis who worked with it as a foundational text continued to cite many ancient legal rulings not found in the Mishnah to back up their own arguments. Eventually, many of those non-Mishnaic teachings were compiled, edited, and published in a separate collection of works known as the Tosefta.

25. Heger, *The Pluralistic Halakhah*, 321.

Clash of the Early Rabbinic Titans—Part I

Joshua vs. Eliezer

While Gamaliel was looking for ways to unify and standardize *halakhah* in order to avoid Jewish fragmentation, the two rabbis who had smuggled Yohanan ben Zakkai out of Jerusalem on a bier had now reached their prime and become rabbinic heavyweights. Joshua ben Hananiah and Eliezer ben Hyrcanus came to be known for their many vigorous debates over *halakhah*. The well-known scholar of rabbinic Judaism Jacob Neusner lists sixty-seven head-to-head debates between these two sages in rabbinic literature.[26]

Another scholar, Joshua Gutoff, describes the pair of rabbis as key rivals and "founding fathers" of the new rabbinic model of Judaism, calling them "[t]he Madison and Monroe of the new order . . . ."[27] Gutoff also writes that Joshua "is Eliezer's *bar plugta*, which is a marvelous Aramaic expression meaning 'argument partner,' intellectual adversary, foil."[28]

Both rabbis developed reputations for their differing approaches to *halakhah*. Joshua followed in Hillel's more flexible, liberal approach to Jewish law, while Eliezer tended towards the rigor, precision, and impatience with outsiders characteristic of the school of Shammai.[29] For example, Joshua believed that one of the keys to making rabbinic Judaism a viable and cohesive way forward for the exiled Jews was to make sure that the day-to-day required practices of Judaism did not overwhelm or overburden the ordinary Jew. So, in contrast to other sages who urged Jews to maximize the amount of time they devoted to Torah study,[30] Joshua taught that if a person could just make enough time to study a little of the rabbis' teachings in the morning and in the evening, "it is counted as if one fulfilled the whole of

---

26. Neusner, *Eliezer ben Hyrcanus*, Vol. 1, 4–5.

27. Gutoff, "The Necessary Outlaw: The Catastrophic Excommunication and Paradoxical Rehabilitation of Rabbi Eliezer Ben Hyrcanus," 734.

28. Gutoff, "The Necessary Outlaw," 740.

29. For a similar description of Joshua and Eliezer, see Eisenberg, *Essential Figures in the Talmud*, 135.

30. An early rabbinic text teaches that there is no limit on the amount of time a person might devote to several kinds of positive activities, among them Torah study. The text concludes by asserting that, while all of these activities are worthy, the study of Torah is equal to doing them all (*m. Pe'ah* 1.1). Many rabbinic texts present an ideal of studying Torah day and night. One Talmudic account describes a sage who went to extraordinary lengths to ensure his ability to maximize his Torah study, and then moves on to describe the ways in which all Jews are accountable to making time for Torah study (*b. Yoma* 35b).

the Torah."[31] He also argued that an abbreviated version of the lengthy daily prayers was good enough for the average Jew.[32] In story after story, Joshua comes across as serious about the Torah yet compassionate and pragmatic about its interpretation in terms of peoples' daily religious lives. He was also consistently interested in the views of others, tolerant of a challenge from an approaching outsider,[33] and inclusive towards people, Jewish or not, who might ordinarily be dismissed easily by a great rabbi.

By contrast, the contemporary Talmud scholar Ronald L. Eisenberg writes of Eliezer ben Hyrcanus: "Zealous in his views and remarkably unreceptive to other opinions, Eliezer . . . was incapable of reaching a compromise of any kind."[34] Elsewhere, Eisenberg describes Eliezer as a "conservative traditionalist" who was skeptical of rabbinic colleagues who developed new interpretive strategies for working with the Torah, and who was very reluctant to answer any halakhic question posed to him without being able to cite an established tradition of one of his masters.[35]

Part of what may have accounted for Eliezer's personality was his genius. His master, Yohanan ben Zakkai, taught that Eliezer had a memory like a sealed cistern that never loses a drop of water,[36] and that his greatness was so far beyond that of any other sage's that if you took a scale and placed all the rabbis but Eliezer on one side, and put Eliezer on the other, Eliezer would outweigh them all.[37] In several ancient midrashic texts,[38] there are different versions of a story in which Moses ascends to heaven and, upon his arrival, he finds God studying rabbinic texts discussing a set of biblical

---

31. *Mek. Beshallakh on* 16.4.

32. *m. Ber.* 4.3.

33. There is a Talmudic story about Rabbi Joshua that tells of a time when Joshua expressed contempt for a halakhic ruling that had been made by the School of Shammai on a ritual matter. A student of the School of Shammai then approached Joshua and offered to explain the reasoning for their opinion. Joshua invited him to proceed. After listening to the student's explanation, Joshua admitted to being wrong on the issue, and then felt terribly guilty about having spoken scornfully about the School of Shammai on the matter. The text says that Joshua even went to the graves of Shammai's students and knelt down before them in apology, saying "I humble myself before you, bones of the students of Shammai . . ." (*b. Hag.* 22b).

34. Eisenberg, *Essential Figures in the Talmud*, 59.

35. Eisenberg, *Essential Figures in the Talmud*, 58–59.

36. *m. Avot* 2.8.

37. *m. Avot* 2.8.

38. Versions of this story appear in *Num Rab.* 19.6 and *Midr. Tanh. Hukkat* 8.

Clash of the Early Rabbinic Titans—Part I

verses about a particularly confusing aspect of priestly ritual.[39] (How fitting that the early rabbis imagined God doing what *they* did—studying rabbinic halakhic debates, right?) Moses hears God quoting the halakhic opinion of Rabbi Eliezer[40] aloud to Himself.[41] Amazed to learn that many centuries after his lifetime there will be a Jew like Rabbi Eliezer who is so great a person that God quotes him, Moses asks God if it would be possible for God to arrange (miraculously if need be) for Rabbi Eliezer to be one of Moses's descendants. God consents, and thus we have a rabbinic tradition that valorizes Eliezer to the point of claiming him to be a direct descendant of Moses. That's how special Rabbi Eliezer is in the mythic memory of early rabbinic literature.

So a portrait emerges of Eliezer—a portrait of someone freakishly brilliant, emotionally intense, authoritative, self-righteous, stubborn, and intimidating. His colleagues admire him, but probably don't like him. They find him arrogant and a little scary (we'll see why in a moment). And yet, they recognize the value of his gifts.

In the Mishnah, the Talmud, and in Midrash—three major categories of ancient rabbinic literature—Joshua and Eliezer take different sides on many of the hot-button questions of their day, and often their contrasting approaches to *halakhah* come across in their opinions. For instance, on the subject of the afterlife and heaven (or, as the rabbis sometimes called it, the "Word to Come"), Joshua taught that the righteous of all nations and religions would receive the reward of the World to Come. Eliezer argued that the World to Come was available only to righteous Jews.[42]

Similarly, there's a midrash that tells the story of a Roman convert to Judaism named Aquilas who approaches Eliezer and asks him a challenging textual question. Eliezer gets annoyed with Aquilas and ultimately sends him off without taking him seriously. Aquilas then brings the same

---

39. The biblical passages God was studying were the ones pertaining to the red heifer described in Num 19. The early rabbis puzzled over some of the details of this ritual, which in any case could no longer be carried out following the destruction of the Temple in Jerusalem.

40. The exact rabbinic text God is quoting is from the Mishnah—specifically, *m. Parah* 1.1. Eliezer and other sages offer conflicting opinions on a matter of ritual detail.

41. I use the male pronoun for God here because this particular midrash imagines God being like a studious rabbi, and in the world of the ancient rabbis that role was reserved for men. Elsewhere in rabbinic literature we find a variety of views of God's gender characteristics, including the Kabbalistic notion of God containing masculine and feminine attributes and transcending gender categories as well.

42. *t. Sanh.* 13.2.

question to Joshua, who patiently responds well and with wisdom. The narrator's voice in the midrash tells us that Joshua's patience was better than Eliezer's impatience.[43] Interestingly, in a different rabbinic text, the Jerusalem Talmud, we read that this same convert, Aquilas, is given credit for writing the official translation of the Torah into Aramaic under the supervision of Rabbis Eliezer and Joshua.[44] Joshua's patience made Aquilas's future generativity on behalf of Judaism possible.

Along similar lines, a midrash tells the moving story of a non-Jewish woman who approached Eliezer wishing to convert. Eliezer asked her about her past, and, ashamed, she confessed that her oldest son was the father of her youngest son. Eliezer sent her away. No clarifying questions, no further discussion. He just sent her away. The woman then went to Joshua and he accepted and converted her, saying that the past was dead to her once she embraced Torah.[45]

The Talmud also tells tales of Joshua's humility, tolerance, and open-mindedness in contrast with Eliezer's self-righteousness, impatience, and judgmental nature. Two stories illustrating this point, one about Joshua and one about Eliezer, appear on the same page of the Talmud.

Here's a modified and somewhat paraphrased translation of part of the story about Joshua:

> There is a story about [two of Rabbi Joshua's students] when they went to greet Rabbi Joshua at his home in the town of Peki'in.
>
> Rabbi Joshua said to them, "What new idea was taught today in the House of Study?"
>
> They said to him, "We are your students and we drink from your water." [Meaning, we only learn Torah from you].
>
> He said to them, "Nevertheless, it is impossible for there not to have been some new piece of learning during a session at the House of Study! Tell me, whose turn was it to give the main lecture?"
>
> They replied, "It was Elazar ben Azariah's turn."
>
> [Next, Joshua's students related the interpretation of a particular part of the Torah that Elazar ben Azariah taught that day.]
>
> When they finished telling him what Elazar ben Azariah had taught, Joshua chastised them and said, "You had this precious pearl and tried to withhold it from me!?"

---

43. *Gen. Rab.* 70.
44. *y. Meg.* 10b.
45. *Qoh. Rab.* 1.25.

Clash of the Early Rabbinic Titans—Part I

[Seeing that Joshua didn't feel threatened at all that they had learned Torah from another sage, and that in fact he was eager to learn what they had learned, they continued repeating the rest of Elazar ben Azariah's lecture in detail. They concluded by sharing this teaching of Elazar ben Azariah's:]

"The great masters, who are they? They are the disciples of the wise, who sit in different rabbinic academies and occupy themselves with the Torah. Some of them rule that an item is ritually pure, and others say it's impure. Some prohibit an action, and others permit it. Some disqualify a ritual item for use, and others declare that it's fit for use.

Now, it's reasonable that one might say: *How, then, can I learn Torah, if it contains so many different opinions?*

Therefore, the Torah says: 'All of them are given from one Shepherd' [Eccl 12:11]. Meaning all of these different viewpoints come from one God. One God gave them; and one leader, Moses, uttered them from the mouth of the God of all creation. Remember, the Torah says: 'And God spoke all these words' [Exod 20:1]. The phrase "these words" [emphasizing the plural] teaches that the opposing viewpoints of the sages are all part of God's revelation.

So, do this: make your ear like a storage container that collects all kinds of ideas, and acquire for yourself a perceptive heart, so that you can understand the words of those who pronounce impure and the words of those who pronounce pure, the words of those who prohibit and the words of those who permit, the words of those who disqualify and the words of those who declare fit."

Upon hearing all this, Rabbi Joshua said to his students, "No generation is orphaned that includes Rabbi Elazar ben Azariah in it. [Meaning: Elazar ben Azariah is such a great rabbi that as long as he lives the Jewish people have a good leader.]"[46]

Immediately following this story in the Talmud, the narrating voice of the Talmud asks the following question:

Rabbi Joshua's visiting students should have told him what they had learned at the House of Study without delay. Why did they hesitate to do so?[47]

The Talmud answers its own question with an unflattering anecdote about Eliezer ben Hyrcanus that goes like this:

---

46. *b. Hag.* 3a-b.
47. *b. Hag.* 3b.

[They were hesitant because they had heard a story about a time when] a student of Rabbi Eliezer named Yossi ben Durmaskit went to visit Eliezer at his home in Lod. Rabbi Eliezer asked Yossi, "What new idea was taught today in the House of Study?"[48]

[Yossi explained that the rabbis at the House of Study had taken a vote on a matter of *halakhah* regarding agricultural tithes for the poor, and that they had issued a new legal ruling.] Upon hearing this, Eliezer became upset and said, "Yossi, hold out your hands in front of your face and prepare to catch your eyes!" [Meaning: Eliezer asked for heavenly forces to cause his student's eyes to pop out of his head and into his hands, leaving him blind and terrified.] Yossi held out his hands and caught his eyes as they flew out of his head, leaving him blind.

Eliezer wept aloud, and quoted a line from Psalms [which, in context, implied that the rabbis at the House of Study may have arrived at the correct halakhic decision, but not for the correct reasons]. Eliezer then said to Yossi, "Go back to the House of Study and tell your colleagues to forget about their vote, because they should have known that the ruling they had just proclaimed was a previously settled matter of *halakhah* from many generations ago, . . . [and Eliezer proceeded to explain the details of the long-established Jewish legal reasons for the conclusion that the rabbis in the House of Study reached on their own, in shameful ignorance of the long-established *halakhah*. If their studies had been up to snuff, they would have known that.][49]

Just so you don't think too poorly of Eliezer, he eventually calmed down and asked God for the young man's vision to be restored, and it was. But what we have here, on this single page of the Talmud, is a pair of contrasting portraits of Joshua and Eliezer. And we should keep in mind that it's not just a difference of temperament and attitude that separates Eliezer and Joshua. Eliezer's fervor is so great that we're told that he has supernatural capabilities. In his rage—perhaps a bit like the Incredible Hulk—Eliezer is able to summon destructive miracles. Remember earlier when I said he was a genius but also dangerous—now you know why.

We'll come back to Eliezer again in the chapters to come, but now turn to some of the Talmud's vivid stories about Joshua and Gamaliel.

---

48. In asking this question, Eliezer uses the exact same words that Joshua used in the preceding anecdote, forming a tight literary connection between these two stories.

49. *b. Hag.* 3b.

5

Clash of the Early Rabbinic Titans —Part II

Joshua vs. Gamaliel

While Rabbi Joshua and Rabbi Eliezer spent years as halakhic debate partners, Joshua's great conflict with Gamaliel was of a different nature. Gamaliel, as president of the Sanhedrin, was certain that centralizing halakhic authority through his office was the best way to preserve Judaism in its new state of exile. He accepted the idea of standardizing the *halakhah* according to the majority vote of the rabbis, and the idea of giving respect to minority opinions by continuing to teach them as well. But he wanted that process to be tied to the Sanhedrin and to his office, and he comes across in some of the texts as quick to lash out at threats to his authority, even when no real threat existed.

The Talmud tells a story[1] of how, one year not long after the Roman destruction, Gamaliel used his office to announce the upcoming date for the most important holy day on the Jewish calendar—Yom Kippur (the Day of Atonement). It was standard procedure for the rabbis to make these kinds of calendar-related announcements before the actual holy day occurred, because the calendar was largely lunar and the beginning of each month was traditionally verified by eye-witnesses testifying to their sighting of

1. *m. Rosh Hash.* 2.8–9.

the new moon. Without modern time-keeping technologies, Gamaliel did what the president of the Sanhedrin was supposed to do—use his calculations and observations to send notice to the Jews throughout the diaspora indicating exactly upon which dates the upcoming New Year and Day of Atonement would occur. The Sanhedrin ratified his proclamation and the word went out.

In this particular year, something odd happened. Gamaliel received testimony from witnesses claiming to have sighted the new moon that would begin a new Hebrew month. But something wasn't right. They had testified that they had seen the new moon in a specific part of the sky in the morning and in another specific area in the evening, which anyone skilled in identifying the moon's phases and movements knew was astronomically impossible. One rabbi, named Yohanan ben Nuri, proclaimed that these were "false witnesses." Yet, curiously, Gamaliel validated their testimony.

Some months later, it happened again. Two witnesses testified to a rabbinic court that they had seen the new moon of the Hebrew month of Tishrei, only they claimed to see it on a date when it should not have occurred. Once again, Gamaliel decided to validate sketchy calendrical testimony, and he based his announcement of the formal beginning of the month upon their claim. A colleague of Rabbi Joshua's, Rabbi Dosa ben Harkinas, said that these witnesses were liars, and he traveled to Joshua to discuss the matter.

Joshua looked over the evidence and saw that Dosa was right. Joshua was very upset, because if the first day of the month of Tishrei was off, then the holiest day of the year in the Jewish calendar, Yom Kippur, would also be off. On Yom Kippur, Jews are required to abstain from a great many normal daily activities: eating, drinking, sex, traveling, handling money, work, etc. Joshua didn't want to be observing Yom Kippur on the wrong date, or for the rest of the Jews to be doing so either. Joshua told Dosa that he shared his belief that Gamaliel was wrong.

Perhaps Dosa let word of Joshua's opinion slip, because the next thing we read in the text is that Gamaliel sent word to Joshua ordering him to appear before him, carrying some of his money with him in a sack, on the date that *Joshua* believed to be the real Day of Atonement. In other words, Gamaliel wanted Joshua to violate the restrictions of Yom Kippur in his own mind (by traveling and carrying money), and for him to do so publicly as a show of obedience to Gamaliel's and the Sanhedrin's authority.

Clash of the Early Rabbinic Titans—Part II

Gamaliel could have ignored the gossip he had heard about Rabbi Joshua's dissenting view, and simply carried on with his planned dates for the upcoming holy days. There's nothing in the text that says that Joshua was planning to dispute Gamaliel's dates publicly. But given how well-known and respected Joshua was, Gamaliel may have thought that even if Joshua quietly and privately followed his own judgment in this matter, word would leak out and cast doubt upon the legitimacy and authority of the Sanhedrin and the president's office.

Joshua felt ill at the prospect of violating the Day of Atonement, but his student, Rabbi Akiva, and his colleague, Dosa, both convinced him to give in to Gamaliel's demand. Both sages argued that if Joshua were to disobey Gamaliel in this matter, he would in fact be committing a greater sin. Akiva cited a verse from the Torah[2] making the case that the law requires Jews to observe the holidays on the days that are announced by the rabbinic court of their time, whether or not the court makes an error. Dosa cited another Torah verse[3] to argue that, in essence, acting publicly to undermine the authority of Gamaliel's Sanhedrin would call into question the entire history of rabbinic rulings by rabbinic courts, and would threaten the viability of organized rabbinic authority in Jewish communities throughout the world. That would be worse, Dosa and Akiva claimed, than people observing Yom Kippur on the wrong day. They persuaded Joshua.

So Joshua publicly appeared before Gamaliel, carrying his money bag, on the day he personally believed was Yom Kippur. Gamaliel praised him in front of those who saw it, and if this were the only story about these two sages clashing, there wouldn't be too much more to say other than that this tale may have served as an early rabbinic foundation myth confirming the Sanhedrin's final authority in halakhic debates, even in cases in which it might seem obvious to some that a court had made an error.

And yet, as readers, there's a lot that leaves a bad taste in our mouths about how Gamaliel handled this situation. First of all, the rabbinic texts that tell this story begin by stating that Gamaliel kept a chart with drawings of the phases of the moon on a wall in his home, and that he would use the chart to teach people how to identify the new moon correctly. He should have *known* that these were incorrect testimonies, or at least recognized the mistakes after they were pointed out to him. Why, then, did he approve the errant testimony of the two witnesses? If his initial mistake was the result of

2. Lev 23:4.
3. Exod 24:9.

rushing or too much multi-tasking, why wouldn't he correct himself once he saw the errors? Was he too embarrassed? Was there some other reason—maybe a political reason? Did the two witnesses have some social status that he felt obligated to protect?

In addition, why did Gamaliel assert the authority of the Sanhedrin by unnecessarily publicly embarrassing Joshua?[4] We can't help but feel a little uneasy with the fact that, while Gamaliel may have been right to insist on the entire rabbinic community respecting the duly ratified decision of the Sanhedrin regarding the timing of these holy days, he chose to do so by setting up a public power struggle that required Joshua to abase himself to him and violate his own personal religious beliefs.

This particular text, and the next two we're going to look at, reveal the fragility of Gamaliel's ego. It seems that Gamaliel developed an obsession with subordinating Joshua that would end up creating one of the first major crises of leadership in the young rabbinic movement.[5]

Let's turn to the next Talmudic text.[6] This tale describes a situation in which, once again, Gamaliel had learned second hand that Joshua differed with him, this time not on a calendar question, but on a matter of *halakhah*. One of Joshua's colleagues, Rabbi Tzadok, confidentially asked Joshua for his view on a technical legal matter, and Joshua privately gave it. Tzadok subsequently went to Gamaliel and asked his opinion on the same matter. Gamaliel gave him a contrary answer. Then, Tzadok told Gamaliel how Joshua had answered the same question differently (Tzadok comes across as quite the pot-stirrer in this story, doesn't he? And moreover, why can't any of these rabbis who ask for Joshua's private opinion keep their mouths shut?)

Objectively, Gamaliel had no reason to feel that Joshua's actions were a threat. He already knew from the Yom Kippur/calendar showdown that Joshua had bought in to Gamaliel's vision of a unified *halakhah*, in which the Sanhedrin's official decisions became the operative law. Even though it

---

4. There are several rabbinic texts that treat the sin of publicly embarrassing or humiliating others as one of the worst things a person can do. In one hyperbolic example, one sage even proclaims: "It is better for a person to throw themselves into a fiery furnace than to embarrass someone else in public" (*b. Ketub.* 67b).

5. It's fascinating to me that this kind of ego-driven dysfunction among leaders of the community became the content of rabbinic sacred texts. For the ancient rabbis, the ethics of interpersonal relationships were huge, especially the way people sometimes use and misuse words.

6. *b. Bekh.* 36a.

pained him greatly, Joshua had accepted the authority of the Sanhedrin's Yom Kippur calendar ruling, and he didn't try to convince other rabbis to join him in observing the holy day according to his own calendar calculations.

Given all of that, there was really no cause for Gamaliel to think that Joshua's privately expressing his halakhic view to a colleague on a technical matter would threaten the halakhic system Gamaliel was trying to get rabbis throughout the Jewish world to accept, especially if the matter in question had not even been voted upon yet by the Sanhedrin. One would think that Gamaliel would even encourage rabbis out in the field to state their differing personal opinions on unresolved halakhic questions before the voting began. But Gamaliel seemed really hung up about Joshua, and his desire for personal control seems to have corrupted his commitment to the process of open rabbinic debate and majority rule that he was promoting.

Shortly after Rabbi Tzadok's conversation with Gamaliel, the Sanhedrin met, and after Gamaliel called it into session, he had the agenda set up so that the first question that was put before the rabbis was the same question Tzadok had asked both Joshua and Gamaliel. Joshua, who was aware of Gamaliel's view, didn't want to contradict him publicly, and so, when it was his turn to respond, he lied and pretended to agree with Gamaliel's view. Whatever one thinks of Joshua's decision to lie and avoid a public disagreement with Gamaliel (and there's a case to be made that Joshua should have just owned his real view), Gamaliel pounced on Joshua's words. Ordering Joshua to stand up, he said, "Isn't it true that you told another rabbi you held the opposite view? I can call witnesses to confirm it!"

Blind-sided and humiliated, Joshua said words to the effect that he clearly couldn't defend himself under the circumstances. It was now obvious to everyone in the room that he had lied in order to avoid a confrontation with Gamaliel in public, and that Gamaliel, for his part, was overreaching and trying to disgrace Joshua in front of the rabbis. A tense awkwardness soured the gathering.

Gamaliel then got even nastier. He used the rules of decorum of the Sanhedrin to require Joshua to remain standing while he went on to give a lengthy halakhic lecture. It was a public act of humiliation and abuse of power that would remain vivid in the minds of the rabbis who witnessed it.[7] Gamaliel was showing himself to be a bully who couldn't gracefully handle others differing with him on halakhic matters.

---

7. This story is told in *b. Bekh.* 36a.

The Forgotten Sage

Joshua Podro, who wrote a book about Rabbi Joshua in 1959,[8] said that like Gamaliel, "Joshua, too, sought unity in Israel, but did not believe that Gamaliel's iron discipline would achieve it. Like Hillel he . . . stood for open discussion allowing free play for personal opinion within the framework of Judaism."[9] The irony of Gamaliel's attack on Joshua was that Joshua wasn't really threatening Gamaliel's vision. Joshua sometimes disagreed with Gamaliel's opinions, and Joshua sometimes gave his contrary opinions privately to rabbinic colleagues when asked, but Joshua wasn't gunning for Gamaliel's position or resisting his overall vision for unifying the *halakhah* as a way of preserving Judaism. In fact, later, Gamaliel would find a far more difficult dissenter to the system he was trying to put in place in the person of Joshua's great rival, Eliezer ben Hyrcanus. (We'll see that play out in the next chapter.)

Podro speculates that Gamaliel was insecure about the power he was trying to wield, and that "Joshua's pacifistic principles made him an easy target" for Gamaliel.[10] (In other words, maybe Joshua was a natural target for an insecure leader with tendencies towards bullying.) Given Joshua's very high rank in the Sanhedrin and his status as a sage of the first order, Podro also suspects that Gamaliel may have figured that by making an example out of Joshua, he would frighten the younger rabbis of lesser status into conforming to his will, thus "silencing all opposition."[11]

In any event, sometime after this awkward and awful event, things between Gamaliel and Joshua came to a head in a third, very similar public showdown. Here's my partially paraphrased translation (for clarity's sake) of the Talmud's account of what happened:[12]

> . . . a certain student came before Rabbi Joshua and asked him, "Is the evening prayer compulsory or optional?" [Note to readers: the early rabbis had developed a model of three daily sets of prayers—morning, afternoon, and evening. Joshua's student apparently had heard conflicting views as to whether or not the evening prayers were required or optional, so he turned to Joshua for an answer. Okay, back to the Talmud.]
> Joshua replied: "The evening prayer? It's optional."

---

8. Podro, *The Last Pharisee*.
9. Podro, *The Last Pharisee*, 72.
10. Podro, *The Last Pharisee*, 74.
11. Podro, *The Last Pharisee*, 74.
12. *b. Ber.* 27b–28a.

Clash of the Early Rabbinic Titans—Part II

>The same student then went to Rabban Gamaliel and asked him, "Is the evening prayer compulsory or optional?"
>
>Gamaliel replied: "It's compulsory."
>
>"But," the student said, "Didn't Rabbi Joshua tell me that it's optional?"

Let me interrupt the Talmudic tale for a moment. I know what we're all thinking at this point: "Wait a minute, we've seen this movie before. We know how this is going to turn out!" Well, let's see what happens this time ...

>Gamaliel said to the student, "Wait till the great rabbis enter the central House of Study."
>
>When the rabbis assembled, someone rose and raised the question: "Is the evening prayer compulsory or optional?"
>
>Gamaliel replied: "It is compulsory." Then, Gamaliel turned to the Sages and pointedly asked, "Is there anyone here who disputes this?" Gamaliel specifically directed his gaze at Rabbi Joshua and sought his reply. Joshua then said to him, "No."
>
>Gamaliel then said to Joshua, "Really? Then why did some of the other rabbis report to me that you said you believe it is optional?"
>
>Joshua had no response.
>
>Gamaliel then went on, saying, "Joshua, stand up and let some of your colleagues testify against you!"
>
>Rabbi Joshua stood up and said, "With living witnesses here ready to contradict me, what can I possibly say?"
>
>The decorum of the Sanhedrin required that Joshua remain standing until Gamaliel, the president, gave him permission to be seated. As had happened previously, Gamaliel proceeded to make a show of sitting and lecturing at length on various aspects of the Torah and *halakhah*, forcing Joshua to remain standing as he droned on and on.
>
>But Gamaliel miscalculated. Joshua was deeply respected and loved by his colleagues. The tension in the room swelled, until all the rabbis began to shout and say to one of the officers (a parliamentarian of sorts), "Stop this!" The officer intervened, interrupting Gamaliel's lecture and giving Joshua permission to be seated.
>
>Then the House of Study erupted. Some of the rabbis cried out, "How long is Rabban Gamaliel going to go on insulting Rabbi Joshua? On Yom Kippur last year he insulted him; and he insulted him again in the affair of Rabbi Tzadok; and now he insults him

again! Come, let us depose Gamaliel! Whom shall we appoint as president of the Sanhedrin instead?"

The rabbis moved swiftly to remove Gamaliel from his post, and then started debating who should replace him. Some wanted to appoint Joshua, but as the mood in the room calmed, they said to one another, "We can hardly appoint Rabbi Joshua as president, because he is one of the parties involved in this dispute. It would look too much like he might have planned for things to play out this way."

"There's Rabbi Akiva—he could do it—but we can hardly appoint him because he doesn't have a worthy lineage, and the position needs someone with ancestral merit."

"How about the young prodigy, Rabbi Elazar ben Azariah? He's wise and rich and the tenth in descent from the great Ezra. He is wise enough that if anyone puts a difficult question to him he will be able to answer it. And his being rich is a plus, because if the rabbinic leadership ever needs to receive high Roman officials he will be able to make sure we have the money to host them well. Finally, his ancestral merit is impressive and will make it harder for Gamaliel to damage him."[13]

The rabbis went to Elazar ben Azariah and said to him, "Will you consent to become head of the Academy?"

He replied, "Let me go and consult the members of my family."

He went and consulted his wife. She said to him, "I think you should decline. Look what has happened to Gamaliel. Perhaps things will go badly and they will depose you later on as well."

Elazar replied to her, "You know, there's a proverb: Let a man use a cup of honor for one day even if it be broken the next."

She said to him, "They won't take you seriously at your age. You have no white hair!" In fact, Elazar had just turned eighteen years old that very day. His wife's concern was valid; but then, a miracle was wrought for him, and eighteen rows of hair on his beard turned white! Elazar now looked older and distinguished enough to make a credible president.

---

13. The literal translation states that Elazar ben Azariah's high lineage will protect him from any curses Gamaliel might seek to bring upon him. Throughout the ancient rabbinic literature, we sometimes find accounts of rabbis being able to manifest supernatural powers or summon Divine miracles. I didn't include the literal translation in this instance because I didn't want readers to be distracted by the supernatural content. But one fascinating element of these ancient rabbinic stories is that the way people use and misuse words in community is so powerful that, in the hands of the right (or wrong) person, words can even be used to summon supernatural events.

Clash of the Early Rabbinic Titans — Part II

> On the same day that all of this took place, the rabbis fired the sentry at the doorway of the House of Study. His job had been to limit entry to the rabbis Gamaliel had approved to attend the meetings at the House of Study. They voted to give permission to all the rabbis and their students to enter from now on. Previously, Gamaliel had issued a proclamation saying that only rabbis and students of good character and a matching physical appearance would be allowed entry.

I'm going to interrupt the Talmudic text again to add a bit of my own take on what's going on here. First of all, I'm not sure exactly what Gamaliel's policy about which rabbis and students could or could not gain entry to the House of Study meant. It may have meant that only people with clean, decent clothes could come in, or it might have had to do with the rabbis' and students' physical attractiveness. Scholars like Daniel Boyarin maintain that the text is saying that Gamaliel was only allowing rabbis who were loyalists to him to enter, though of course highly respected figures, like Rabbi Joshua, would have been included nevertheless.[14] Whatever it meant, what it tells us for certain is that Gamaliel had a bouncer at the door to his club, and the power of including or excluding people in his hands.

The text is showing us how Gamaliel tainted his credibility as the promoter of the kind of unified halakhic system of rabbinic majority rule he was trying to get the rabbis as a group to accept. Gamaliel was becoming more and more known for his attempts to use manipulation and intimidation to ensure that the majority view on halakhic questions would correspond to his own views. Let's return to the Talmud's account, picking up the story right after the rabbis fired Gamaliel's bouncer:

> On that day many stools were added to the House of Study to accommodate the great numbers of rabbis and students who wanted to attend. . . . There is a difference of opinion on this matter between one sage[15] and the rest of the rabbis: one says that four hundred stools were added, and the other says seven hundred.
>
> After all these things happened, Rabban Gamaliel became alarmed and said to himself, "Perhaps, God forbid, I was wrong

---

14. Boyarin, "The Yavneh-Cycle of the Stammaim," 259.

15. For those of you who are curious as to who this sage was, the text lists him as Abba Joseph ben Dosetai. I didn't keep his name in my paraphrased translation for clarity's sake in the context of the current discussion in this chapter.

to exclude all those rabbis and students. Maybe I withheld crucial rabbinic teachings from the Jewish people!"[16] . . .

A rabbi of a future generation taught: . . . wherever the expression "on that day" is used in rabbinic writings, it refers to that day that Gamaliel was deposed and Elazar ben Azariah was appointed president of the Sanhedrin. Once Elazar took office, every matter of unconcluded Jewish law that had not previously been fully explored and debated was discussed thoroughly and debated in the House of Study.

To his credit, Rabban Gamaliel accepted his ouster and did not absent himself from the newly expanded House of Study for even a single hour. He even took part in some of the debates, though the other rabbis were no longer afraid to openly oppose him.

For example, we have learned that after Elazar took office, a controversial matter came before the Sanhedrin. An Ammonite who had prepared himself for conversion to Judaism came before them in the House of Study and asked them to decide whether or not he would be accepted as a Jew. (Note to readers: there's a commandment in the Torah prohibiting members of the Ammonite nation from ever being accepted as converts to Judaism—hence this prospective convert's dilemma.)

Rabbi Joshua (in his typically inclusive fashion) said to the man, "Yes, you are permitted to enter the congregation of Israel."

Rabban Gamaliel replied to him, "But isn't it already laid down in the Torah: an Ammonite or a Moabite shall not enter into the assembly of the Eternal One?"[17]

Joshua responded to him, "Do the nations of Ammon and Moab still exist in their ancient homelands? Centuries ago the Ammonites and Moabites were deported and mixed up with many other nations by the Assyrian empire. Isaiah tells us what the Assyrian king did: 'I have removed the national boundaries of the peoples and have robbed their treasures and like a mighty one I have brought down their inhabitants.'[18] We have also learned that

---

16. As I read this part of this story, I see it as the narrator's attempt to avoid a fully black-and-white portrait of the main actors in this drama. Gamaliel is clearly the baddie, and it would have been nobler of him to realize some of the ethical harm he was causing without having to be overthrown in open revolt; however, when the sky finally does fall on his head, we see that he does have some ability to recognize his moral failure. One of my favorite things about rabbinic literature is that it has lots of examples of flawed heroes and villains who aren't all good or all bad.

17. See Deut 23:3 and Neh 13:1.

18. Isa 10:13.

Clash of the Early Rabbinic Titans—Part II

whatever strays from a group is assumed to belong to the larger section of the group."[19]

Rabban Gamaliel retorted by citing a different verse from the Hebrew prophets—this time from Jeremiah: "But has it not been written, '[Sometime after their destruction] I will restore the children of Ammon from their captivity, says the Eternal One,'[20] meaning that the Ammonites have, in fact, reconstituted themselves and remain a distinct, existing nation?"

To which Joshua replied: "But hasn't another prophet said in the name of God: 'And I will restore the captivity of My people Israel,'[21] but have we been restored to our land yet?"[22]

The rabbis immediately voted to allow the Ammonite convert to enter the congregation of Israel.

Rabban Gamaliel realized how thoroughly matters had changed. He said to himself, "Given that this is how things are, I will go and apologize to Rabbi Joshua." When Gamaliel reached Joshua's house he saw that the walls were black. Gamaliel said to Joshua, "From the walls of your house it is apparent that you are a charcoal-burner."

Joshua was put off by Gamaliel's ignorance of his profession and the upper-class insensitivity of the remark. He replied, "Alas for the generation of which you are the leader, Gamaliel, seeing

---

19. Rabbi Joshua is offering a second argument for why they should permit the Ammonite to convert to Judaism. This time he argues from a teaching of well-established rabbinic hermeneutics. In this case, the principle he is invoking is that in many halakhic matters, if something belongs to a group, but it leaves that group and becomes absorbed by a larger kind of group, its status and identity becomes that of the larger group. Since the Isaiah passage states that the Assyrians broke down all the national borders of the ancient biblical peoples, including the Ammonites, and that the Assyrians absorbed these conquered nations and mixed them into their wider population, Joshua reasons that the prospective convert who has appeared before them would have to be considered as a descendent of *the Assyrians*, even if he happened to have Ammonite ancestry. Therefore, there is nothing stopping the rabbis from accepting him as a convert.

20. Jer 49:6.

21. Amos 9:14.

22. This is the Talmud's equivalent of a rabbi winning a verbal smack down and shouting "How you like me *now*, Gamaliel?" Except of course Joshua would never gloat like that. More seriously, Rabbi Joshua's choice to quote this particular verse of Scripture did more than just shut Rabban Gamaliel up. Joshua has also reminded everyone in the room of their condition of exile and distress in the aftermath of the recent Roman destruction. Perhaps it also put the question over the Ammonite's conversion into a larger perspective. Perhaps the other rabbis thought to themselves that, given the current circumstances of the Jewish people, welcoming converts was something they shouldn't be blocking.

The Forgotten Sage

that you know nothing of the troubles of the scholars, their struggles to support and sustain themselves!"

Gamaliel said to him, "I've insulted you. Please forgive me." Joshua ignored him.[23]

"Please, do it," Gamaliel begged, "out of respect for my father."[24]

Joshua then became reconciled to him.

The two of them discussed who would go to inform the rest of the rabbis about their reconciliation. . . . Rabbi Joshua sent a messenger to the House of Study saying, "Let him who is accustomed to wear the robe wear it; it's time to readmit Gamaliel to his proper post." The rabbis at the House of Study suspected that maybe Gamaliel had sent this messenger on his own, as part of a scheme to seize back his power, so they disregarded him.[25] Rabbi Akiva, who was deeply devoted to Rabbi Joshua, even said to his colleagues, "Lock the doors so that the servants of Rabban Gamaliel should not come and disturb us here."

Rabbi Joshua heard what had happened, and he said to himself, "I had better get up and go to them myself." He came and knocked at the door of the House of Study. He said to them (in the form of

---

23. This story isn't the only one in the Talmud depicting Gamaliel's cluelessness about the economic struggles of some of the sages. In *b. Hor.* 10a there's a tale about Gamaliel and Joshua journeying aboard a ship. The journey took longer than expected, and Gamaliel ran out of food. Joshua had brought more than needed and Gamaliel shared Joshua's extra provisions. When Gamaliel asked Joshua how he knew to bring extra food, Joshua explained that he was aware of an astronomical phenomenon that sometimes hampers nautical navigation, and that he brought extra in case this situation arose. In a similar moment of poor social grace, Gamaliel quips that it's surprising that someone as widely knowledgeable as Joshua has to travel by sea to make a living. Joshua responds by telling him that rather than pity him, he should be aware of two other sages who are far more brilliant, but who don't have "bread to eat or a garment to wear." Gamaliel ends up inviting the two sages to take prominent places in the Sanhedrin, though depending on how you read the rest of the story it may be that Gamaliel bungles the social graces of his interaction with the two of them as well.

24. According to some rabbinic texts, Gamaliel's father, Shimon ben Gamaliel, was president of the Sanhedrin during the Jewish revolt against Rome. The Romans arrested him and beheaded him (*Avot. R. Nat.* 38.3). I don't know whether the rabbinic text we're examining now "knows" of the texts claiming that Shimon was beheaded, but it is possible that Gamaliel is invoking his father here because of his martyrdom at the hands of the Romans.

25. The Talmudic text doesn't specifically say that the rabbis disregarded the messenger because they suspected Gamaliel was being deceptive. I've based my interpretive translation on the commentary of the Israeli Talmud scholar, Rabbi Adin Steinsaltz. The Hebrew commentary is available online at https://www.sefaria.org/Berakhot.28a.11?lang=bi&with=Steinsaltz&lang2=en.

a complex metaphor), "Let the one who held the post of president before hold it again. All is reconciled."

Akiva said to him, "Rabbi Joshua, have you been appeased?[26] If you insist, we will readmit Gamaliel. But know that everything we've done here has been out of regard for your honor. Still, explaining this to Rabbi Elazar ben Azariah is going to be difficult. Tomorrow morning you and I should visit him."

The other rabbis said, "How are we going to proceed? Shall we really depose Elazar ben Azariah from the presidency, so soon after we placed him in office? Besides, we have a tradition that once we've promoted someone to a higher rabbinic office, we don't demote them without cause. We could possibly have Elazar and Gamaliel share the office, but then this will cause jealousy between them."

They finally decided to have Gamaliel hold the office of president and give the main rabbinic sermon three Sabbaths of each month, and to have Elazar ben Azariah hold the second highest office, but give the presidential sermon one Sabbath each month.

* * *

In this chapter, we have seen that the aftermath of the Roman destruction of the Temple and Jerusalem didn't stop the already extant culture that the rabbis had developed of engaging in vigorous, public debate over questions of *halakhah*. We have also seen how, once Yohanan ben Zakkai had secured a place for the rabbis to maintain an academy and a Sanhedrin at Yavneh, Rabbis Joshua and Eliezer emerged as the two leading debate partners seeking to settle questions of Jewish law and practice.

And, we saw how Rabban Gamaliel, the heir to a line of presidents of the Sanhedrin going back generations, tried to use his office to centralize and standardize a common *halakhah* for Jews throughout the world. We saw him struggle to win over rabbis far and wide to a system in which all rabbinic opinions would be honored and preserved in the record, but only opinions receiving a majority vote of the rabbis would become normative *halakhah*. And in his conflicts that resulted from his singling out Joshua for

---

26. I want to acknowledge Rabbi Adin Steinsaltz's English translation for this particular phrasing of Akiva's question. The Talmud doesn't have any punctuation marks, so figuring out whether Akiva is making a statement or asking a question to Joshua is a matter of interpretation. Some translations have Akiva saying to Joshua, "Apparently you've been appeased," whereas Steinsaltz has "Have you been appeased?" Steinsaltz makes more sense to me as a reader.

The Forgotten Sage

public showdowns, we saw signs of his tendency towards abuse of power, manipulation, and perhaps even paranoia.

By the time the clashes between Joshua and Gamaliel were resolved, we find Gamaliel a seemingly genuinely more humbled man. He accepts his modified reinstatement to the presidency of the Sanhedrin and the honors he has to share with Elazar ben Azariah. More importantly, he has witnessed firsthand that the rabbis as a group aren't willing to be bullied, and aren't afraid to launch a coup if necessary. Gamaliel is forced to accept an end to his personal control over which rabbis and students can enter the House of Study. As hundreds of new rabbis and students start to participate in the halakhic discussions and debates of the Sanhedrin, Gamaliel is confronted with the true picture of what his vision for a centralized, yet truly inclusive and democratic, halakhic process would look like. He yields, and Joshua emerges stronger than ever.

In the assorted vignettes and longer stories about Gamaliel found throughout rabbinic literature, we see a leader with character flaws and strengths, a genuine mix of sincere concern for his people's survival, and an egotistical desire for personal power and glory. In the same spirit of forgiveness and generosity that Joshua managed to show Gamaliel when they finally resolved their differences, let's close this chapter by highlighting a story that reflects positively on Gamaliel's character. It has to do with what took place in the rabbinic community when Gamaliel died.

At that time, someone of Gamaliel's stature and family wealth would be buried in a very fancy and expensive funeral. A Talmudic tale reports that, in fact, among the general population of Jews at the time, the prevailing custom was for families even of poor means to spare no expense purchasing the finest burial linens for their deceased loved ones. The burden of the social pressure to find the money to bury the dead in finery was so great that the Talmud states that sometimes "the expense of burying the dead would, at first, be a greater disaster for the bereaved relatives than the grief itself," and that there were even cases in which relatives would essentially abandon their dead rather than bankrupt themselves and their families.[27]

Gamaliel's parting gift of good leadership to the Jewish people came when his family members read his will. The Talmud states that in his will, Gamaliel "disregarded his own honor and instructed his family to bury him in plain linen shrouds."[28] Gamaliel's public example established a precedent

27. b. Ketub. 8b.
28. b. Ketub. 8b.

Clash of the Early Rabbinic Titans—Part II

that is still observed in Jewish burial practice to this day—the dead are to be tenderly washed and then wrapped in simple, inexpensive linen shrouds. So perhaps for all his character flaws, which are glaringly exposed in some of the Talmudic texts we've been exploring in this chapter, by the end of his life Gamaliel proved himself to be someone capable of growing in wisdom, humility, and compassion.

* * *

In the introduction to this book, I asked a series of questions about how Judaism came to develop many of its most admired attributes. One of those attributes was Judaism's general suspicion towards the overconcentration of power and authority in any one person or group's hands. Another was Judaism's insistence on the importance of genuine debate and its willingness to respect and teach dissenting viewpoints. The Gamaliel vs. Joshua showdowns recorded in the Talmud are early rabbinic sacred foundational texts giving us a mythic drama that tells the story of how rabbinic debate was affirmed and centralized religious authority in one rabbi's hands rejected.

The big irony about Gamaliel's fixation with Joshua as a rival who needed to be stripped of power is that, if his intention was to remove a threat to his vision for a centralized *halakha* to be determined by the majority vote of the rabbis in the Sanhedrin, he picked the wrong rabbi to attack. Joshua, as I have already noted, had shown that he was willing to buy into the model Gamaliel was promoting. He just wasn't willing to curtail his right to hold a dissenting view from Gamaliel's. No, it wasn't Joshua that Gamaliel should have worried about. As we'll see in the next chapter, it was Joshua's halakhic sparring partner, Eliezer ben Hyrcanus.

6

Boom!

> Jews are a talkative people. Our Torah study, mostly cognitive, is like a wonderful intellectual ping pong game: one person expresses an idea—using his paddle to whack the idea across the table to another, who whacks another idea back! Lots of words, lots of argumentation (which we assert is a *machloket l'shem shamayim*—a controversy for the sake of heaven!). Learning and advancing knowledge in Jewish tradition has always been based on "sacred arguing." Maybe that's why culturally, we are considered such a contentious people!
>
> —Rabbi Leila Gal Berner

This next story helps explain, mythically, how Judaism got to be that way.

One of the best-known stories of the Talmud is known as "The Oven of Akhnai" (Babylonian Talmud, *Bava Metzia* 59b). It has been translated and reprinted many times in different books on Judaism and rabbinic thought. I'll start with a slightly paraphrased translation (for clarity's sake). The story begins with a debate between Rabbi Eliezer ben Hyrcanus and a group of rabbis that included Rabbi Joshua ben Hananiah. The issue: a matter of ritual purity involving certain kinds of communal ovens that were used in ancient times.[1] (I realize that a lot of modern readers might be thinking "why would anyone care," but hang on.)

---

1. As David Luban describes it, "The issue under debate concerns the ritual cleanliness of a baked earthenware stove, sliced horizontally into rings and cemented back

Boom!

Before we get to the story, a piece of important background: as we have discussed already in this book, the early rabbis had developed a tradition of interpretation and debate regarding matters of *halakhah*, and generally their practice was to use majority rule among the rabbis to determine the *halakhah*, while preserving minority opinions in the official record.[2] But rabbinic Judaism's tradition of debate and majority rule was still young, and, as this story will show, it was still open to being challenged as the method that the rabbis would use to decide religious and legal questions.

Now we are ready to jump into this text. The question pitting Eliezer on the one side and Joshua plus all the other rabbis on the other was whether a particular kind of oven, constructed out of several different sections layered one upon another, was susceptible to becoming ritually impure. Rabbi Eliezer ruled that it was not, but all the other rabbis in the debate disagreed with him. Here's where we'll pick up the text itself:

> It was taught: On that day Rabbi Eliezer brought forward every imaginable argument, but the Sages did not accept any of them.
>
> Finally, he said to them: "If the *halakhah* is in accordance with me, let this carob tree prove it!" Sure enough, the carob tree immediately uprooted itself and moved a hundred cubits, and some say four hundred cubits,[3] from its place.
>
> "No proof can be brought from a carob tree," the other rabbis retorted.
>
> So, again, Rabbi Eliezer said to them "If the *halakhah* agrees with me, let this nearby stream of water prove it!" Sure enough, the stream of water miraculously flowed backward.
>
> "No proof can be brought from a channel of water," they rejoined.
>
> Again, Rabbi Eliezer urged, "If the *halakhah* agrees with me, let the walls of the House of Study prove it!" Sure enough, the walls tilted as if to fall.

---

together with unbaked mortar." Luban, "The Coiled Serpent of Argument," 1253.

2. There are key early rabbinic texts, such as *m. Ed.* 1.5 and *t. Ed.* 1.2, that state that the law is determined by the majority opinion, and the minority views are preserved in the record in case they are helpful at some future time. Of course, with rabbinic literature, it's hard to find only one claim about how decisions about the law were made. As discussed earlier in this book, some scholars of the early rabbinic period would say that the early rabbis appear to have had a few different mechanisms by which they would determine which opinion would become the normative *halakhah*.

3. A hundred cubits would approximately equal forty-six meters. Four hundred cubits = 183 meters.

The Forgotten Sage

> But Rabbi Joshua rebuked the walls, saying, "When disciples of the wise are engaged in a Jewish legal dispute, what right have you to interfere?"
>
> In deference to Rabbi Joshua the walls of the House of Study did not fall, and in deference to Rabbi Eliezer they did not resume their upright position; they are still standing aslant.
>
> Rabbi Eliezer then said to the Sages, "If the *halakhah* agrees with me, let it be proved from heaven!" Sure enough, a Divine voice (known in Hebrew as a *bat kol*) cried out, "Why do you dispute with Rabbi Eliezer, with whom the *halakhah* always agrees?"[4]

I'm going to interrupt the text here to comment a bit. At this point, the tension in this tale has reached its peak. Eliezer has not only called for three miracles to back him up and gotten them, but now a voice from *God* has come out of the heavens and told the rabbis not only that Eliezer is right regarding this oven, but that he has always been right in every debate they have ever had.

Given the understanding the rabbis shared, that Judaism is, first and foremost, a religion that commands the Jewish people to obey God's instructions, you would think that this story might go on to tell us that the sages finally conceded the argument to Eliezer, since God had manifested before them and spoken! If this story had played out that way, the moral might have been that majority rule prevails most of the time in rabbinic debate, *unless* there is a great prophetic figure present who is backed up by God in front of witnesses.

If Joshua and the other rabbis had submitted to God's intervention in favor of Eliezer, maybe this story would have gone on to describe the ascension of Rabbi Eliezer to a new position of authority—perhaps even presenting him as *the* redeeming prophet of the Jews of that era and developing a religion entirely along the lines of his teachings. (After all, he was a Jew who argued with rabbis arrayed against him; he summoned indisputable miracles in front of witnesses; and he was claimed by God by means of a heavenly voice. Not exactly an unfamiliar kind of story for first-century or early-second-century Jews, right?)

Before we return to this Talmudic text, let's also remember that over and over again in ancient rabbinic literature, we read that Eliezer was a rabbinic superstar among the rabbis of his generation. (We saw some examples

---

4. Daniel Greenwood describes Eliezer's summoning of miracles to confirm his viewpoint as follows: "Logic having failed, Rabbi Eliezer appeals—directly to the Legislator." Greenwood, "Akhnai: Legal Responsibility in the World of the Silent God," 313.

of this in chapter 4.) And yet, this same Eliezer—who is actually referred to as "Eliezer the Great" in much of rabbinic literature—is threatening to kill the debate-oriented, majority-rule-based rabbinic Judaism of Joshua and the rest of the sages just as it is being born. When Eliezer calls on the walls of the House of Study to support him by doing something miraculous, the walls start to fall inward. The contemporary commentator, Joshua Gutoff, writes:

> ... indeed, the stakes have been raised, for Eliezer is not just offering proof, he is literally threatening to tear down the institution to prove his point.
> It is not enough now, for the Sages to ignore Eliezer's [earlier supernatural] "proofs." They must see to the stability of the Academy. And so it falls to Rabbi Joshua to address the walls—Rabbi Joshua being the only one there with the stature equivalent to Rabbi Eliezer's.[5]

In a similar vein, David Luban writes:

> In his growing anger and frustration, Eliezer resorts to physical threats; like the blind Samson, he prepares to bring the building down on the rabbis' heads. Symbolically, he attempts to demolish the entire practice of dialectic and argument, or give and take within the culture.[6]

* * *

So that we can reenter the Talmudic text itself, let's review what has happened so far and then return to it. When we left our cast of characters, Eliezer had just asked for three different miracles to testify to his being right about the ritual purity status of Akhnai's oven. In front of all the sages who were disputing with Eliezer, each of these miracles occurred, but Rabbi Joshua and the others rejected the miracles as a valid form of argument. The third of these "miracle proofs" that Eliezer summoned led to the walls of the House of Study beginning to tilt inward as if to collapse, but then Joshua rebuked the walls in the name of the rabbis' right to debate matters of Jewish law, and the walls froze in place at an angle. Then Eliezer essentially called on God to back him up even more emphatically, and sure enough, a *bat kol* told the whole crew of debating sages that Eliezer was

---

5. Gutoff, "The Necessary Outlaw," 740.
6. Luban, "The Coiled Serpent of Argument," 1262.

right about this matter and about every other matter as well. Let's find out how Joshua responds (please pay attention here, because this is where the text really gets brilliant!)

> Rabbi Joshua stood up upon his feet and protested to the *bat kol*, quoting a passage from the Torah: "It is not in heaven!" (Deut 30:12) he cried.

Sorry to be annoying, but I have to hit pause on this Talmudic narrative once again in order to unpack the remarkable thing that has just happened. In this one sentence of Talmudic text, Joshua has done several important things. First, he has now taken his argument (and that of the rabbinic majority he represents) to God as well as to Eliezer. Echoing biblical figures who also argued with God successfully (think Abraham or Moses, for instance), Joshua rejects the "God-said-it / I-believe-it / That-settles-it" bumper-sticker form of religion.[7] And how he does this is just as important as the fact that he has the courage to do it.

He presents a rabbinic interpretation of a very small bit of Scripture, using the Torah's own words to make his case. Joshua quotes a fragment of a passage in which Moses is explaining to the Israelites that they are fully capable of following the laws of the Torah and that they shouldn't doubt their ability to do so. Here is the wider context of the bit that Joshua quotes. In this passage from Deuteronomy, Moses is speaking to the Israelites on behalf of God:

> Now what I am commanding you today is not too difficult for you or beyond your reach. *It is not in heaven,* so that you have to ask, "Who will ascend into heaven to get it and proclaim it to us so we may obey it?" Nor is it beyond the sea, so that you have to ask, "Who will cross the sea to get it and proclaim it to us so we may obey it?" No, the word is very near you; it is in your mouth and in your heart so you may obey it. (Deut 30:11–14)[8]

I've italicized the bit that Joshua has quoted. As you can see, the passage in Deuteronomy that he has referenced does not say *anything* about using majority rule to determine matters of religious practice. But by Joshua's time the rabbinic tradition had already established that the rabbis could read parts of Scripture out of context and reveal hidden or counter-intuitive

---

7. If Joshua had had a bumper sticker, it might have read instead, "God-said-it / too-bad / the-rabbis-already-voted-and-settled-it." Sorry. I couldn't resist.
8. NIV.

meanings. Joshua argues that these three little Hebrew words (*lo bashamayim hi*)—"it [the Torah] is not in heaven" are there to teach a different point than the one Moses himself was aiming for in the original passage. Moses was trying to encourage the Israelites that the Torah's laws were not so difficult to understand or hard to follow that only experts or exceptional people could fathom their meaning and successfully follow them. Knowing that he would die soon, Moses wanted the Israelites to trust that they could follow God's teachings without his personal presence.

But Joshua lifts this one phrase from the biblical passage and argues that it *is* actually saying that a group of experts—the rabbis—are needed to determine what the laws are, at least in difficult cases, and that the method of debate and majority voting by the rabbis is how the law is to be decided. He is saying that that's what Moses's words actually mean, at least for his generation of Jews.

It is hard to see Joshua's interpretation in the plain reading of the original verses from Deuteronomy, though it is also not an implausible interpretation within the well-established interpretive methods of the rabbinic tradition of Joshua's time. It is, however, an interpretation that took a lot of chutzpah for Joshua to assert in the moment right after a Divine voice from heaven just told everyone to knock it off and follow Eliezer's view. It is a brave and brilliant counter on Joshua's part. The only thing that could possibly help Eliezer at this point in the story would be another Divine intervention—perhaps the *bat kol* speaking again and rebuking Joshua, or an angel descending and directly instructing the entire group not to listen to Joshua's bold claim for rabbinic independence from heavenly interference in matters of religious interpretation.

But there are no more miracles or Divine voices in the story. Joshua's statement ends the argument, and the rabbis affirm and enact their majority decision regarding the oven. The Talmud adds more to this story, however, so let's rejoin the text. The narrating voice in the Talmud (known in rabbinic terminology as the *stam*—rhymes with "bomb") wants to make sure we understand the full meaning and import of Joshua's "it is not in heaven" argument, so it tells us about a later rabbi who explained what Joshua meant as follows:

> What is the meaning of "It is not in heaven?" Rabbi Jeremiah explained: Since the Torah was already given long ago at Mount Sinai, we pay no attention to a Divine voice, as the Torah states, "Incline after the majority." (Exod 23:2)

The *stam* has just brought in an even more audacious example of rabbinic license in interpreting Scripture than Joshua's "it is not in heaven" from Deuteronomy. Rabbi Jeremiah, who lived generations after Joshua, follows Joshua's lead, and rips another phrase out of its original scriptural context to make the argument that God has actually already decreed in the Torah that the majority of the rabbis should be the final authority on questions of Jewish law. He excerpts from Exodus 23:2, which in its fullness reads, "Do not follow a majority to do evil; nor shall you bear witness in a cause to *incline after the majority* to pervert justice."[9]

As you can see from my italics within the translation of Exodus 23:2, Rabbi Jeremiah has lifted the Hebrew words "incline after the majority" out of their original context, and he has argued that that sentence fragment actually was intended to teach us that, in later times, the rabbis *should* incline after the majority in their rulings.

The irony of the *stam* inserting Rabbi Jeremiah's radical interpretation of this particular verse fragment from the Torah is that it is possible that in the course of calling forth the miracles that Eliezer called forth to "prove" his point, he may have been telling himself he was obligated to do so because of this very same verse from Exodus. He may have been telling himself, "I know that we are supposedly deciding what the Torah means by rabbinic majority rule nowadays, but I just know these guys are wrong, and as Exodus 23:2 states, I must not incline after this majority that is trying to do wrong." Rabbi Jeremiah—and the *stam*—have doubled down on Joshua's side here, saying that not only will the rabbis disregard miracles and Divine voices in debating *halakhah*, but that they are free to even go so far as to interpret parts of the Torah in a way that seems impossibly contrary to the plain meaning of the Torah text.[10] In defense of Rabbi Jeremiah, David Luban writes:

> Jeremiah's interpretive method—plucking words out of context regardless of its meaning and spinning law out of them—is a traditional technique of Jewish hermeneutics. . . . In effect, the rabbis treated the words and phrases of the Torah not as a text demanding a sympathetic reading, but rather as a repository of

---

9. *OJPS* (adapted).

10. David Luban writes: "The trouble is that Jeremiah's argument rips the words 'follow the majority' out of a context that in fact says exactly the opposite. . . . It appears, then, as though Jeremiah has not defeated the Master of the World with an ingenious point of logic, but rather that he has prevailed by cheating." Luban, "The Coiled Serpent of Argument," 1266.

language-fragments, a kind of lexicon or even alphabet providing the raw material for legal rulings. Perhaps a better metaphor would be that the phrases of the Torah resemble a set of musical motifs that interpreters weave into their compositions....

[Luban also acknowledges] ... the rabbis' peculiar hermeneutic practice of wrenching verbal fragments of the Torah (such as "follow the majority") out of their context.[11]

If this seems shockingly irreverent of the Talmud and of Joshua and his colleagues—after all, the Talmud is a Jewish sacred text, and ordinarily we expect such texts to tell the humans what God wants and for the humans to thankfully agree to comply—hold on, there's still more. The next thing the Talmud adds to the Akhnai's oven story is another vignette that reassures its readers that in the end, God accepted Rabbi Joshua and the other rabbis' claim about who has the authority to interpret Scripture. Here is how that part of the story reads:

> At another time, Rabbi Nathan met the prophet Elijah [in rabbinic tradition, Elijah would sometimes emerge from heaven and appear to various rabbis to offer guidance]. [Rabbi Nathan] asked him, "What did the Holy One do at the moment that Rabbi Joshua said 'It is not in heaven" and defeated Rabbi Eliezer in the dispute? Elijah responded: "God laughed with joy, saying, 'My children have defeated Me, My children have defeated Me.'"[12]

David Luban writes, "God's amusement as He admits defeat is certainly one of the most startling images in any monotheistic religious text I am aware of."[13]

* * *

I think of this Talmudic story as the (sort of) Declaration of Independence of Rabbinic Judaism. It is a mythic tale that shares a lot in common with

---

11. Luban, "The Coiled Serpent of Argument," 1267. Rabbi Akiva, the student of both Rabbis Joshua and Eliezer, would go on to champion this "language-fragments" interpretive method, but he faced opposition from his contemporary Rabbi Ishmael, whose interpretive method was more inclined to give weight to the plain meaning of verses of Torah than Akiva's. I mention this difference of approach to illustrate that some of the disagreements that seem to be settled in the Akhnai's oven story in Rabbi Joshua's favor actually continue forward in different ways through the subsequent generations of sages.

12. Bialik and Ravnitzky, eds., *Sefer Ha-Aggadah* (The Book of Legends), 223 (translation adapted).

13. Luban, "The Coiled Serpent of Argument," 1257.

other classic heroic sagas. The hero, Rabbi Joshua, strives with beings mortal and Divine in a quest to secure and establish something foundational and enduring for his community. In Joshua's case, what he wins for his people is God's approval and acceptance of the rabbinic interpretive method as we know it as the basis for the Jewish religion going forward. This messy, multi-vocal, argumentative, creative, and at times errant process, ending in majority rule and minority opinions preserved for the record, had formed during the first generations of rabbinic Judaism, but in this story it was challenged by Eliezer, a rabbinic heavyweight so amazing that even God would quote his opinions. Eliezer represented the possibility of establishing rabbinic Judaism on a basis of prophetic certainty and other-worldly authority. (In fairness to Eliezer, he might have argued that all he wanted was to establish rabbinic Judaism on a basis of Truth—hold on to that thought, as we'll explore it later.)

In overruling Eliezer (and God), Joshua and the other rabbis cemented in place the rabbinic method we recognize to this day; moreover, the story tells us, God accepted it that way—God even accepts that the rabbis who will henceforth be in charge of determining Jewish law, custom, and ethics, will sometimes be wrong. It's an imperfect religion, this rabbinic Judaism that God endorses, and the rabbis' central self-descriptive sacred text, the Talmud, tells us so!

To put it another way, David Luban writes that this story raises questions of the relationship between truth, authority, and interpretation, and Joshua's victory ends up affirming that the authority of the majority of the rabbis to interpret the Torah supersedes Truth (even if Truth can be miraculously proven in front of everyone involved in a debate).[14] Of course, in democracies that rely on majority rule and impartial courts to interpret the laws, there are no heavenly voices that suddenly cry out the Truth in the middle of the judges' deliberations, so they rely on a social contract in which their authority is accepted as final even though it is understood that they are imperfect humans and their judgments may be wrong. To emphasize the relevance of the Akhnai's oven story on the larger philosophy of law question about where societal authority resides, Luban quotes Yale Law Professor Scott J. Shapiro from his article, "Authority," in the *Oxford Handbook of Jurisprudence and Philosophy of Law*:

> Authorities claim the right to impose their will on others regardless of whether their judgments are correct. In doing so, they appear

---

14. Luban, "The Coiled Serpent of Argument," 1256–57 and elsewhere.

to place themselves above the truth—their right does not seem to depend on their being right.[15]

Shapiro's article, written for a Western legal audience and not a rabbinic one, begins with a discussion of the Akhnai's oven story.

If you keep reading this Talmudic story, you will see that Eliezer, the formidable figure representing a path not taken by rabbinic Judaism, ends up excluded by the rabbis from participating in *any* future rabbinic decision-making because of his unwillingness to accept majority rule and human (rabbinic collective) authority as the basis of the religion.

In taking the stand he took, Rabbi Joshua evokes the biblical Jacob of Genesis, who wrestles all night with God (or some kind of angel) and prevails, winning God's blessing in the end.[16] Joshua's victory, and the ideals it represents, offer us a lot to chew on as postmodern Westerners in the midst of cultural confusion and uncertainty about the future of our major religions.

The Sacred Value of Doubt

"Questions, I've found, can bring us together, while answers can tear us apart."[17]

—Letty Cottin Pogrebin

In rejecting Rabbi Eliezer's certainty and God's public intervention backing Eliezer up, Rabbi Joshua and his colleagues won an important place for doubt in the very structure of rabbinic Judaism from that moment forward. Had they conceded to the *bat kol*, they would not only have dismissed their own majority ruling on the case of the ritual status of the oven they had been debating; they would also have had to consider dismissing every previous rabbinic ruling in which the majority had ruled against Eliezer. Remember, the *bat kol* said to them, "Why do you dispute with Rabbi Eliezer, with whom the *halakhah* always agrees?"

If claims of possessing absolute Truth and certainty were the goals of the new rabbinic system of Judaism, then Joshua and his rabbinic colleagues

---

15. Luban, "The Coiled Serpent of Argument," 1254. See footnote 3 at the bottom of the page for Luban's full citation of Shapiro's quote.

16. Gen 32:22–32.

17. Pogrebin, "The Many Gradations of #MeToo," 20.

would have embraced Eliezer as their prophet or chief rabbi and, from that day forward, simply brought every question of Jewish law, belief, and ethics to him. But in asserting the rabbis' determination to use their debate + majority vote method, even though it had just been shown by a Divine voice to be wrong at times, Joshua and his supporters won the day for doubt's place in the religion.

Many students of Talmud are thunderstruck when they first learn this story and its amazing implication: it tells us not only that the majority of the rabbis voted on the matter of the clay oven and got it wrong; but that the majority of the rabbis had ruled incorrectly many, many other times too (every time they overruled Eliezer at the very least). One of the messages of this story for its Jewish readers of future generations is that the rulings of the rabbis throughout the Talmud are subject to doubt. Any one of them—even all of them—might be wrong, this text within the Talmud itself tells us. That's quite an unusually self-undermining religious mythic story about the rabbis, who regarded themselves as religious authorities, don't you think? *Unless* you value doubt as a religious asset, and want your religion's followers to bear in mind that their leaders—the rabbis—sometimes get it wrong.

Of course, even without the Akhnai's oven story, the Talmud acknowledges that its majority rulings could be wrong simply by preserving and presenting dissenting minority opinions within itself as a sacred text. But that multi-opinionated Talmudic format might have disappeared if Judaism had taken the path offered by the *bat kol* and simply followed Eliezer in all of his rulings. In that case, why would the Talmud keep any of the opinions of the rabbis who differed with Eliezer, since a Divine voice said they were all wrong? If *being right* was more important to the Talmud's final editors than the rabbinic process of discussion, debate, and struggle to try to figure out what is right, the Talmud would have emerged as a much different kind of sacred literature (and, it would have been a lot shorter).

David Luban points out that the Akhnai's oven story cleverly casts doubt upon another kind of certainty that religious texts often lay claim to—their stories of miracles. Eliezer is able to manifest several miracles in succession, and even though the rest of the rabbis reject the validity of using miracles as proof in a debate over *halakhah*, the authenticity of those miracles is not questioned in the story. But Luban draws our attention to an easily overlooked part of the way the text presents Eliezer's miracles.

Boom!

Consider the way the text describes the first miracle that Eliezer summons forth:

> It was taught: On that day Rabbi Eliezer brought forward every imaginable argument, but the Sages did not accept any of them.
>
> Finally, he said to them: "If the *halakhah* is in accordance with me, let this carob tree prove it!" Sure enough the carob tree immediately uprooted itself and moved a hundred cubits, and some say four hundred cubits, from its place.

Luban writes:

> ... not only does the Oven of Akhnai story explicitly state that miracles don't prove points of law, it subtly casts doubt on the power of miracles to prove anything. Consider the peculiar aside that appears, almost tongue in cheek, when the Talmud recounts Eliezer's first miracle. "The carob [tree] jumped a hundred cubits. (Some say: four hundred cubits.)" Why the second sentence? One answer is surely that by means of this literary device the narrator of the story ... makes it clear that he wasn't there, and that the story has come down to us in multiple versions.... In addition, though, the disagreement over how far the carob tree jumped suggests that the perceptions of the eye-witnesses diverged. It reminds us that tales of miracles are themselves infected by human fallibility in perception and memory.[18]

* * *

The contemporary commentator Burton Vizotsky describes rabbinic literature, particularly the stories and debates of the early rabbis, as "a rhetoric of identity-formation for rabbinic Jews," adding, "The stories we tell teach us who we are and to what we aspire."[19] Using Vizotsky's understanding of rabbinic literature, what can we learn from this story in which Rabbi Joshua leads a crucial fight to preserve doubt as a permanent part of the Talmudic process of decision making? One possible takeaway is that the Talmud represents a body of religious literature that proclaims to the Jewish people that doubt is sacred.[20] More than that, I think this story teaches that doubt is a permanent part of the human attempt to discern God's will. That it is

---

18. Luban, "The Coiled Serpent of Argument," 1269–70.
19. Vizotsky, *Sage Tales*, 197.
20. Or does it? See chapter 9 of this book, "Don't Trust this Book, It Could Be Wrong," for a discussion of why I may be overstating the case.

our duty to debate the moral and spiritual questions that come before us and then struggle to find a way forward, but no decision is beyond doubt.

This is an important religious idea, one that is often counter-intuitive for practitioners of Western religions. (Buddhists may have a leg up on this one.) Sometimes the monotheistic religions in particular get practiced in such a way that certainty, about the beliefs of the religion or its sacred texts is constantly being reinforced. The fear that creeps into these kinds of religious communities is that if someone could disprove any one part of the sacred teachings, the whole system will come crashing down like a house of cards.

What Rabbi Joshua gives us is an alternative model for our relationship to our sacred texts. We start with the assumption that there are different possible interpretations and opinions about everything in the texts, and that when our religious leaders make religious decisions, they might be wrong. We don't need to worry about our getting it wrong angering God, because God is depicted in this story as lovingly laughing at how God's children—humanity—have grown up and reached a point in which it is important for them to try to use the texts and interpretive tools they've been given as best they can on their own. This is a God who values the sincere effort to find the truth and live by it, whether or not we get it right. God values the doubting mind.

The antidote to the discomfort we may feel about living with constant doubt is not to replace that doubt with rigid certainty, as Eliezer and the *bat kol* tried to get the rabbis to do. The antidote to the fear of doubt is the acceptance of doubt and the trust that God means for us to live with such doubts and do our best. To put it differently, the spiritually mature response to doubt is to cultivate faith that the doubts are okay (as opposed to cultivating rigid beliefs and a habit of trying to banish all doubts).

The Symbolism of the Oven in the Story

At the beginning of this chapter, I mentioned that at first glance the subject of the halakhic debate in this story—the ritual purity status of a particular kind of ancient communal oven—may strike us as trivial and obscure. Daniel J. H. Greenwood points out, however, that there's more than meets the eye with Akhnai's oven. He writes, "It appears that the oven was made of broken pieces [possibly of another oven] cemented together around an inner core of sand to form an entirely new object."[21] The question the rab-

---

21. Greenwood, "Akhnai: Legal Responsibility in the World of the Silent God," 312.

bis are debating has to do with their belief that broken or unfinished objects have a different capacity to transmit ritual impurity than wholly intact objects. Eliezer rules that Akhnai's oven falls into the category of a broken/unfinished object, and Joshua and the rest of the rabbis argue the opposite.

The Talmud's most famous epic story presenting a battle establishing the legitimacy of rabbinic majoritarianism could have centered on a different question of Jewish law. But, as Greenwood points out:

> Akhnai's oven itself is not just the subject of a debate about other matters, but important in its own right. A vessel has been shattered and the remnants gathered and rebuilt.... The question is whether the rebuilt oven has the same mystical significance as the original.
> ... But now, the Biblical world, like the oven, has been shattered. The Temple is no more. God has withdrawn his Presence.
> ... The purity laws themselves are largely meaningless in this new world.... The entire system of sanctity has been shattered and is no more.
> But just as Akhnai's oven has been created from the shards of destruction, so too the rabbis have recreated their legal world. Prayer, acts of loving-kindness, and Torah study will replace sacrifice; kashrut[22] will replace purity. The issue before Eliezer and the rest of the first post-Destruction generation is the status of this world made up of broken pieces cemented together over a core of sand, a world without the comforting absolutes of Temple sacrifice, divine revelation, and the certain knowledge that the Good and the True will prevail.
> In this context, Eliezer's position is the nihilism of the fundamentalist: all or nothing. A reconstructed oven of broken pieces is no oven at all, just broken, meaningless shards.
> ... The rabbis, in contrast, are struggling to find meaning in a world without the perfection that Eliezer demands, one in which all we have to work with is broken vessels, without absolute truths, divine commands, or the rest. Astonishingly, they do this even while acknowledging that Eliezer, at least, still has access to the Truth that has been withdrawn from the rest. Seeking to build meaning in a world from which God has partially withdrawn, they respond to His withdrawal [by ordering God to exit the scene of rabbinic debate and interpretation]. And He laughs.[23]

---

22. *Kashrut* is the Hebrew word for the laws and practices regarding the preparation and consumption of food—"keeping kosher."

23. Greenwood, "Akhnai: Legal Responsibility in the World of the Silent God," 347–48.

7

Eliezer's Gaze Burns Everything It Touches

To understand the place of Joshua's great rival, Eliezer, in rabbinic literature, we should look at the story arc of his life as told—of course in sometimes inconsistent fragments here and there—in the vast literature of Talmud and Midrash. It bears repeating that the narrative I'm about to sketch is a fractured composite, found in rabbinic texts, some of which may have originated as long ago as the first century C.E., and some of which may not have been fully developed until the eighth century C.E. or later. The "Rabbi Eliezer" who emerges from these many story bits and pieces over seven centuries is a literary and mythic mosaic figure based on many different stories that evolved in different parts of the world. The same can be said of the "Rabbi Joshua" portrait I've been painting in this book, as well as the other great characters of these stories.

* * *

Eliezer was born around 40 C.E. and was the son of a wealthy Jewish landowner named Hyrcanus. Against his father's wishes and to the dismay of his brothers, Eliezer left the family estate behind for Jerusalem, the center of rabbinic Torah study, hoping to learn with the rabbis.

If you're puzzled as to why Eliezer's decision would be so upsetting to his family, consider some of the context. His father, Hyrcanus, is a member of the Jewish land-owning class during a time of great political instability.

Eliezer's Gaze Burns Everything It Touches

The Romans are suppressing Jewish groups seeking independence, and the Jews themselves have split into several passionate factions.

The Temple and the priestly upper echelon are regarded by many ordinary Jews as sell-outs to the Romans. Whatever a wealthy landowner like Hyrcanus may have thought of the priestly elites, he probably would have sought to maintain good relationships with them. Maybe he even shared their mixed feelings about the rabbinic movement. These rabbis, with their academies and their innovative approaches to Jewish religious life and thought, may have looked to Hyrcanus like a counter-cultural movement drawing young men from far and wide to leave their duties to their families in order to pursue a potentially impoverished life of rigorous religious practice and endless Torah study. The rabbis were less "establishment" and less predictable than the leaders of the Temple priesthood and their upper-class patrons. The priestly leadership and the Romans both would have been keeping an eye on them.

Eliezer, who maybe has never quite fit in with his brothers, and who seems miserable with his lot in life at home, is probably the sensitive misfit of the family. When he takes off to join up with the rabbis, his oddball reputation in the family is sealed. In leaving home, Eliezer has also deprived his farming family of an able-bodied grown son, leaving his brothers more of the work. And by defying his father's wishes, he has embarrassed Hyrcanus in front of his other sons. So, it makes sense that the family is upset with Eliezer, and as readers we're meant to understand the impacts of his decision.

Anyway, after arriving in Jerusalem, Eliezer became a student of Yohanan ben Zakkai. As we discussed earlier, Eliezer would eventually live through the Roman siege and destruction of Jerusalem, along with our hero, Rabbi Joshua.

One mythic origins story about Eliezer goes like this:[1]

> When Eliezer arrived at Yohanan ben Zakkai's academy, he sat down and began to weep. Yohanan asked him why he was crying, and Eliezer said, "I'm crying because I want to learn Torah." Yohanan asked him whose son he was, but Eliezer evaded the question.
>
> Yohanan then asked Eliezer if he knew some of the basic Hebrew prayers, and Eliezer replied, "No."

---

1. My paraphrased translation, with modifications for clarity, is based primarily on the translation and notes of Gerald Friedlander's *Pirke de Rabbi Eliezer*, especially chapters 1 and 2.

The Forgotten Sage

> So Yohanan taught them to him. Sometime soon afterwards, once again, Yohanan found Eliezer crying alone, and asked him what was wrong.
>
> "I'm crying because I want to learn Torah, and not just the prayers."

Let me interrupt the story a moment to note that, while this midrash presents this back-and-forth between Yohanan and Eliezer in a style that infantilizes Eliezer,[2] in one version of this story we're told that Eliezer was twenty-eight at the time he left his father's house for Jerusalem, and in another he is twenty-two. Either way, the idea these stories are trying to convey about Eliezer's age is that he is much older than the typical initiate in a rabbinic academy—possibly even too old, in many people's estimation, to begin.

Okay, back to the story:

> Rabbi Yohanan ben Zakkai began teaching Eliezer two rabbinic legal concepts each day (two *halakhot*—the plural of *halakhah*). Eliezer memorized and integrated everything he learned. He put in long hours of uninterrupted study. So intense was his study that at one point he went over a week without eating. Then, one day in the House of Study, Eliezer's bad breath from prolonged fasting hit his teacher, Yohanan, squarely in the face, causing Yohanan to flinch and ask Eliezer to back away. Once again, Eliezer sat down and started to weep.
>
> "My son," Yohanan said to him, "Why are you crying?"
>
> "Because you sent me away the way people do with lepers!" said Eliezer.
>
> Yohanan considered this strange, intense new student, who had thus far been unwilling to say who he is or where he came from. Then Yohanan said, "My son, just as the odor from your mouth has ascended before me, so may the savor of the laws of Torah ascend from your mouth to heaven."[3]

---

2. This story puts Yohanan ben Zakkai in the symbolic role of being like a nurturing mother to a weeping and helpless Eliezer. This is similar to other mythic origins stories about some of the great rabbis, who get "adopted" by their rabbinic master and "reborn" into a new kind of Jewish identity.

3. In a different version of this story, Yohanan says to Eliezer, "My son, just as the odor from your mouth has ascended before me, so may the teachings of your mouth go forth from one end of the world to the other." Friedlander, *Pirke de Rabbi Eliezer*, 3 (fn 11). Also, in her 2011 book, *The Aroma of Righteousness: Scent and Seduction in Rabbinic Life and Literature*, Deborah A. Green writes, "To accomplish its goal, [this] narrative relies on our personal experience . . . the climax and resolution of the vignette depend

Eliezer's Gaze Burns Everything It Touches

Yohanan then looked his student in the eye and asked, "Whose son are you?"

Eliezer finally told him. "I am the son of Hyrcanus."

Recognizing the famous name, Yohanan exclaimed, "You are the son of one of the great men of Israel, and you kept that from me? By my life, you need to join me for a meal at my table today!"[4]

Eliezer, for reasons not explained in the text, declines the invitation, claiming that he has already eaten that day at the home of the rabbis who are hosting him. Perhaps this is just the kind of public recognition that Eliezer has feared would bring his family of origin back into his life, potentially thwarting his escape and his adoption into this new "family of choice" at Yohanan's academy. Let's return to our text:

"Who is hosting you?" Yohanan demanded, and Eliezer replied that he had been staying with Joshua ben Hananiah and another rabbi known as Yossi the priest. Yohanan then summoned Joshua and Yossi and asked them if in fact Eliezer had eaten anything at their home. They both told Yohanan that he had not, and that he had been fasting for the past eight days.

What the text doesn't specifically tell us is why Eliezer has been fasting, or why he made up the story about having been fed by Joshua and Yossi the priest. Perhaps the fasting was an attempt to purify himself in some way. Or, perhaps in his intense determination to catch up to the other students in Yohanan's academy, Eliezer decided that taking time to eat, bathe, or even do the first-century equivalent of brushing his teeth were all wastes of precious time.

In any event, in this particular text, the narrative now jumps forward in time. Eliezer has advanced from desperate novice to brilliant and

---

upon our firsthand knowledge of bad breath. . . . [T]he narrator relies on our personal experience so that we will empathize with the students, for we all know how repulsive bad breath in others can be. At the same time, because we know how difficult it is to perceive bad breath in oneself, we might also have sympathy for [Rabbi Eliezer]. . . . More intriguing, however, is [Rabbi] Yohanan ben Zakkai's response, which turns bad odor into a positive—even worthy—attribute. [Rabbi] Eliezer may emit an offensive odor in pursuit of Torah, but once he has acquired knowledge and begins the teaching of Torah he will emit a perfumed fragrance to which people will be drawn." Green, *The Aroma of Righteousness*, 1.

4. For an excellent translation and discussion of an alternate version of this story from a different rabbinic text known as *Avot de Rabbi Natan*, see chapter 1 of Susan Handelman's *Make Yourself a Teacher*.

The Forgotten Sage

promising student. Meanwhile, back at the ranch (meaning his father, Hyrcanus's, estate), Eliezer's father and his brothers have been nursing a grudge against him for leaving to pursue his Torah-study dreams.

"Dad, you should go to Jerusalem, find Eliezer, and formally disinherit him for what he's done," the brothers say.

So Hyrcanus journeys to Jerusalem intent on doing just that. When he arrives at Yohanan's academy, it just so happens that it is the day of a religious festival. He walks in to find Yohanan ben Zakkai celebrating and feasting with his students, and he recognizes some of the wealthy and prominent leading citizens of Jerusalem sitting near Yohanan at his table.

Some of the Jerusalem bigwigs in attendance also notice the arrival of the well-known landowner, Hyrcanus, and word travels to Yohanan that he is in the room. Yohanan sizes up the situation and acts swiftly.

He invites Hyrcanus to take a place of prominence at his table. Then, he finds Eliezer and, in front of everyone, asks him to share a teaching about the Torah. Eliezer initially declines, saying that all that he knows he has learned from his master, Yohanan, and that it wouldn't be seemly for him to lecture at a gathering when his far more learned master was present.

But Yohanan wasn't going to be evaded by Eliezer's clever dodges this time. He responds by saying that Eliezer has worthy new insights of his own to share, and that if it would make him feel more comfortable, he would be willing to leave the room so that Eliezer could offer a teaching without worrying about violating any proprieties.

And then before Eliezer can respond, Yohanan slips out of the room, leaving all eyes on Eliezer. Resigned to the situation, Eliezer sits down and begins giving a discourse on Torah. As he speaks, the text tells us that the room brightened as a Divine light radiated from Eliezer's face.[5]

Seeing this, Rabbi Joshua and another colleague rush to find Yohanan, and they tell him, "Master, Eliezer is offering up insights more profound than the ones God gave to Moses to tell the people at Mount Sinai!"[6] Let's return to the text:

---

5. The original rabbinic texts describe Eliezer's face shining in the same way that the book of Exodus describes Moses's face shining (Exod 34:29–35). Gerald Friedlander's 1916 translation of one of the original midrashic accounts reads, "[Eliezer's] face shone like that of the sun and his effulgence beamed forth like that of Moses, so that no one knows whether it be day or night." Friedlander, *Pirke de Rabbi Eliezer*, 7.

6. In the main midrashic text I'm referencing, the rabbis who run out of the room to find Yohanan and tell him how amazing Eliezer's teaching is are not named specifically.

Eliezer's Gaze Burns Everything It Touches

Rabbi Yohanan slips back into the room and moves in just behind Eliezer, who is still speaking. Yohanan leans over and kisses Eliezer on the head and says, "Our founding ancestors, Abraham, Isaac, and Jacob, are happy because *you* have descended from them."

Now remember, Hyrcanus is in the room, but apparently he has not recognized that the astounding speaker is the son he has come to disinherit.

"Who is this person that Rabbi Yohanan is praising?" Hyrcanus asks the people standing near him, and they reply, "It is Eliezer, your son!"

Hyrcanus replies, "Oh . . . well, instead of saying that Abraham, Isaac, and Jacob should be happy that Eliezer descends from them, Yohanan should have said that *I* should be happy that he descends from me."[7]

Eliezer then notices his father standing, and he falls silent for a moment. Then he says, "Father, please, let us offer you a chair, for it is not proper for me to continue speaking while you are standing."

Hyrcanus replies, "My son, . . . I have to admit that I did not come here to celebrate the festival, to learn Torah, or to hear you speak. I came here to disinherit you and give your portion to your brothers. But, now that I have seen you receive all this praise, I'm going to disinherit *them* and give all their portions of my estate to you!"

Eliezer replies, "Father. I am not equal to even one of my brothers. If I had prayed for land or money, I believe God would have provided me with those things. But that is not what I asked God for. I asked God to be allowed to study Torah, and here I am."

Eliezer ends up asking his father not to disinherit any of them.[8]

But Gerald Friedlander notes that in a different midrashic account of this story, Rabbi Joshua ben Hananiah is one of the rabbis who finds Yohanan and alerts him to the astonishing discourse that Eliezer is giving. Friedlander cites the midrashic collection, *Avot de Rabbi Natan*. Friedlander, *Pirke de Rabbi Eliezer*, 7 (fn 5).

7. I read this statement from Hyrcanus as intending to tell us how self-important Hyrcanus tends to be. I suppose it's possible, however, to read it differently. Perhaps this moment in the story is depicting the change of heart Hyrcanus has regarding his wayward son, and the point is that he is revealing how happy he now is to have sired this gifted scholar.

8. Just a thought to share: this mythic-origins story about Rabbi Eliezer has some thematic similarities to the biblical story of Joseph and his brothers in Genesis. Joseph is disliked by his brothers and betrayed by them. He ends up far away from home, in Egypt. He enters the new cultural world of Egypt at the lowest social status level, but is recognized for his gifts and rises to a place of great leadership. He ultimately gets reunited with

The Forgotten Sage

* * *

From these stories about Eliezer's beginnings as a rabbi, the rabbinic legends about Eliezer then shift to depictions of his unparalleled gift for precise memorization of everything he ever learned at Yohanan's academy. Following the Roman destruction of Jerusalem (complete with the story of Eliezer and Joshua helping to smuggle Yohanan out of the city in a coffin), Eliezer joins Yohanan at the academy of surviving rabbis in the coastal town of Yavneh.

> Rabbi Yohanan ben Zakkai had five students: Rabbi Eliezer ben Hyrcanus, Rabbi Joshua ben Hananiah, Rabbi Yossi the priest, Rabbi Shimon ben Netanel, and Rabbi Elazar ben Arakh. Yohanan would recount their praises: "Rabbi Eliezer ben Hyrcanus is a cistern covered in plaster that does not lose a single drop of water."
> ... [Yohanan ben Zakkai] used to say: "If all the sages of Israel were on one side of a balance scale, and Rabbi Eliezer ben Hyrcanus was on the other side, he [Rabbi Eliezer] would outweigh them all."[9]

Repeatedly in rabbinic literature, we hear about Eliezer's encyclopedic and accurate knowledge of the laws and teachings that came from the sages before him. In the debates over *halakhah* found in the Mishnah, the earliest written work of rabbinic literature, Eliezer's opinions are quoted more often than those of any of his contemporaries. His tendency was towards conservative interpretations of Jewish law, and he became known for his insistence on sticking with received teachings in the face of proposed innovations in interpretation.

As we've seen in previous chapters of this book, Eliezer and Joshua battled each other dozens of times, with Joshua often advocating for lenient or liberal interpretations of *halakhah* and Eliezer favoring tradition and strictness. Eventually, after the famous debate between Eliezer and all the other rabbis over Akhnai's oven, the rabbis voted to ban him from participating in further rabbinic debates.

This was the ancient rabbinic penalty called *niddui* in Hebrew, which is often translated as "excommunication," a word I hesitate a bit to use

---

his father and foregoes any retribution against his brothers. Like Joseph, Eliezer doesn't fit in with his brothers, but unlike Joseph, Eliezer freely chooses to leave home and enter into a new, foreign culture. He then moves from the lowest possible status in the rabbinic community of students to become "Eliezer the Great," a leading light among the rabbis of his generation.

9. *m. Avot* 2.8.

because it conjures up associations with the way that word has been historically used in Catholicism, and here it means something different. For the ancient rabbis, *niddui* meant that a rabbi could no longer take part in the debates and voting on matters of *halakhah*. Also, none of the other rabbis and students could get within a few meters distance of the person who had come under this decree. Apparently,[10] however, people could learn Torah from a rabbi placed under the decree of *niddui*, so long as they kept the proper physical distance—a detail that we'll see will play an important role in the story of Eliezer's death. Finally, someone who died without having this ban of excommunication lifted by the rabbinic leadership would also be denied the usual funeral honors due to a great sage—in fact, the rule was that his coffin would have to be publicly dishonored (the Sanhedrin would place a stone upon it, signaling that the person died while still under the ban of excommunication).

Let's return to the text of the Talmud that narrates what took place immediately following Rabbi Joshua's and the rest of the rabbis' defeat of Rabbi Eliezer in the debate over the ritual purity of Akhnai's oven, so we can see how Eliezer's excommunication played out. We pick up the story right after the stunning scene in which Rabbi Joshua declared that despite the miracles that Eliezer could summon to support his argument, and despite the *bat kol*—the voice from heaven—announcing that Eliezer was right in this matter and in all other debates he had ever had, nevertheless the rabbis would retain the authority to determine the *halakhah* through their process of debate and majority vote. The text[11] continues:

> On that day, the rabbis took all of the things that Eliezer had previously declared to be in a state of purity and they burned them.

This one line of the story is crucial. The Israeli Talmud scholar Adin Steinsaltz, in his running interpretive translation of the Talmud, writes:

---

10. The reason I've started this sentence with the word "apparently" is because I am hedging a bit on making this claim about the specific rules that governed *niddui* or other ancient rabbinic forms of excommunication. There are different rabbinic texts that appear to be describing somewhat different rules regarding excommunication, and moreover, we don't know whether these texts are describing a penalty that was actually practiced or whether they are an exercise in imaginative rabbinic discussion. For the purpose of understanding the essential drama taking place in the stories we are exploring here, my less nuanced presentation of *niddui* can suffice. I'm grateful to Rabbi Mira Wasserman, Ph.D., for her insights into this subject.

11. *b. B. Metz.* 59b.

The Forgotten Sage

That day, Rabbi Eliezer would not accept the Sages' decision. They, therefore, decided to make a public demonstration of their decision. They brought all the foodstuffs that had been prepared in an Akhnai oven and which Rabbi Eliezer had declared ritually pure, and burned them in a fire, to show that Rabbi Eliezer's position was rejected by the *Halakhah*.[12]

Then the text tells us that Eliezer's rabbinic colleagues voted to excommunicate him (place him under the ban of *niddui*). Here's what happens next:

> The rabbis asked one another, "Who will go and inform Eliezer that we have excommunicated him?"
> Rabbi Akiva said, "I will do it, so that someone without understanding does not end up telling him the news [in an unskillful way], which could cause the entire world to be destroyed."

Rabbi Akiva was Eliezer's and Joshua's student, and in the future he will become the greatest sage of his generation (and some would argue, the most important ancient rabbi of all). This Talmudic tale, with its focus on Eliezer and Joshua, also serves to help establish Akiva's character as someone who has wisdom, sensitivity, and courage. So, why would Akiva say that the entire world might be destroyed if this news wasn't conveyed to Eliezer in a very careful manner? Was he exaggerating? In a word, no.

In the world of mythic rabbinic stories, the great rabbis are sometimes depicted as having supernatural influence on the forces of nature. Eliezer is one of these giants among the rabbis. Remember, in the debate over Akhnai's oven, Eliezer was able to summon miracles that violated the laws of nature. So Akiva's concern is literal. He doesn't know what kinds of cosmic forces might be unleashed if Eliezer is brought down hard.

> What did Akiva do? He dressed in black garments, went to Eliezer's home, and then sat down at a distance from Eliezer of four *amot*.[13]
> Eliezer said to him, "Akiva, what's special about today?"
> Akiva said, "My Master, it appears to me that your colleagues have distanced themselves from you."

---

12. Steinsaltz, *The Talmud, Vol. 3: Tractate Bava Metzia, Part 3*, 237.

13. Roughly two meters. *Amot* is the Hebrew plural for the word *amah*, a unit of measure roughly equal to the distance from one's elbow to one's fingertips. This was the distance that everyone was supposed to keep from anyone who was placed under this form of excommunication by the rabbis.

Eliezer's Gaze Burns Everything It Touches

>Rabbi Eliezer then tore his clothes, removed his shoes, and sat down on the ground.[14] His eyes flowed with tears.[15]
>
>At that instant, a third of the harvests of the earth were spoiled—a third of the olive crops, a third of the wheat, and a third of the barley. And some say that even the dough in the hands of women abruptly spoiled.
>
>It was taught by the ancient sages: what happened was so significant that on that same day, everywhere that Rabbi Eliezer cast his gaze was burnt up.

So Akiva's fears were justified, though his foresight about the potential impact of Eliezer's reaction to the news may have limited the damage. There's still more to this particular Talmudic story, but for it to make sense we need an important piece of background information.

Eliezer was married to a woman known as Ima Shalom, which in Hebrew means "Mother of Peace." She is one of the few women who is named and quoted as a halakhic authority in the Talmud. She was also the sister of Gamaliel—yes, *that* Gamaliel, the one who was the president of the Sanhedrin and who got ousted from the job for publicly humiliating Joshua ben Hananiah, and who then later got his job back after everyone patched things up.

Gamaliel had to ratify the vote of the rabbis to excommunicate Eliezer, which he did, very reluctantly. Perhaps before his disastrous showdown with Rabbi Joshua, Gamaliel might have refused to honor the majority vote of the rabbis who excommunicated Eliezer, but by now he had probably learned to respect the limits of his authority in the emerging "democracy of the rabbis" that we have been talking about throughout much of this book.

Anyway, our Talmudic story goes on to say:

>At the time Akiva delivered the news to Eliezer, Rabban Gamaliel was journeying on a ship at sea. When Eliezer received the news, a massive wave approached the ship and threatened to drown him.
>
>Gamaliel said to himself, "This must be happening because Rabbi Eliezer ben Hyrcanus has been told the news."
>
>Gamaliel then stood up and prayed, "Master of the universe, it is revealed and known before You that I did not ratify the excommunication of Eliezer for selfish reasons, nor did I do it in order

---

14. These are the traditional actions of a mourner.

15. Note that the text we examined describing the very beginning of Eliezer's career in the rabbinic community describes him sitting and weeping at Yohanan's academy, and here, in a story about the end of his rabbinic career, he is again sitting and weeping.

The Forgotten Sage

to benefit my father's house.[16] I did what I did for Your honor, in order to prevent endless controversies from multiplying in Israel."

The sea then rested from its fury.

I'd like to unpack a couple important elements of this short vignette. First, if this story about Gamaliel facing Divine wrath aboard a tempest-tossed ship caused you to think about the biblical book of Jonah,[17] that's no accident. The last sentence of the Talmudic text reads *nach ha-yam mi-za-ah-poh*, which literally translates as "The sea rested from its fury." In Jonah 1:15, after the sailors aboard the ship reluctantly throw Jonah overboard, the text reads *va-ya-ah-mod ha-yam mi-za-ah-poh*. Translation: "And the sea arose from its fury." The Talmud's use of this very similar phrasing and vocabulary evokes this vivid biblical text. Gamaliel doesn't want to throw Eliezer under the bus (or, in this case, overboard), but he feels he has been left with no alternative. As the storm rages, he prays to God and protests his innocence, like the conscience-stricken and panicked sailors in the book of Jonah.

And what is Gamaliel's plea of justification for why he agreed to ratify the vote to excommunicate Eliezer? He says he did it in order to avoid endless controversies from multiplying among the Jews. What exactly does that mean?

Remember, this entire drama involving Eliezer's excommunication is the result of Eliezer's attempt to overrule the majority vote of the rabbis by using his ability to summon miracles and a heavenly voice to back up his interpretation. In that story, Joshua and the other rabbis prevail, turning back Eliezer and God as well, setting a key precedent that will guide rabbinic Judaism for centuries to come. That precedent guaranteed that there would be *many* debates—multiple controversies, if you will—among the rabbis for the foreseeable future, and that this was seen, by the editors of the Talmud at least, as a good thing. When the rabbis voted to excommunicate Eliezer and Gamaliel ratified their vote, we might think that this decision would *support* "controversies multiplying in Israel" and prevent a model in

---

16. What Gamaliel means is that he didn't act in order to preserve or add prestige or power to his family line. Why would he say this? Remember, Gamaliel was part of a very prominent and prestigious rabbinic family that claimed to be direct descendants of King David. His father and several of their fathers had served as president of the Sanhedrin. After the incidents involving his public humiliation of Rabbi Joshua and his removal from office, Gamaliel had to face increased scrutiny regarding his motives.

17. Jonah 1:4–15.

which special rabbis, like Eliezer, end all controversies by acting like personal spokesmen for God.

Remember, in the Akhnai's oven story, the *bat kol* told the rabbis that Rabbi Eliezer had *always* been right in his opinion in every rabbinic debate. With Eliezer around, the alternative to rabbinic debate and majority rule would be to just do whatever Eliezer says and be good with that. So, what is Gamaliel talking about when he says to God that his motive was to prevent future controversies multiplying in Israel?

Perhaps he is referring to a particular kind of controversy. In the Mishnah (the earliest layer of Talmudic texts), there is a famous passage that reads:

> Every dispute that is for the sake of heaven will endure, but every dispute that is not for the sake of heaven will not endure. What is an example of the kind of dispute that is for the sake of heaven? The disputes between Hillel and Shammai. What is an example of a dispute that is not for the sake of heaven? The dispute between Korakh and his followers [against Moses].[18]

For the sake of brevity, I'm not going to offer my interpretation of what this text is trying to say in offering the examples it does of arguments that are, or are not, "for the sake of heaven." Suffice it to say that in contemporary rabbinic discussions, the concept of a productive, civil, and worthwhile debate that remains unresolved is often referred to as "an argument for the sake of heaven." In contrast, disputes that are petty, ego-driven, or uncivil are called arguments that are *not* for the sake of heaven. So, let's accept that Gamaliel has just pleaded with God to spare him from the cosmic forces threatening to kill him by claiming that if he had not ratified Eliezer's excommunication there would have been endless disputes of a destructive and unproductive nature in the rabbinic community.

His plea works, for now. But what we see in this story is that the forces of nature are ambivalent about Eliezer's excommunication, just as cosmic forces displayed ambivalence during the Akhnai's oven story. Remember, during that showdown, at one point Eliezer proclaims that if he is right, the walls of the House of Study should start collapsing inward. Joshua responds with his one and only act of summoning supernatural forces in the entire story, chastising the walls of the House of Study for tilting inwards and demanding that they stay out of the argument. The *stam* tells us that the walls stopped inclining but also didn't right themselves either, remaining

---

18. *m. Avot* 5.17.

frozen at an angle "to this very day." I bring this up because one of the most worthwhile aspects of these rabbinic stories is the way they give expression to ambivalence, even cosmic or Divine ambivalence, in vivid ways.

Let's get back to Gamaliel, who has survived his brush with death at sea. He continues on in his role as president of the Sanhedrin, but he is probably worrying that the cosmic forces that tried to kill him at sea remain a threat to him. He is not the only one worried about this. The same Talmudic text that describes the entire debate over Akhnai's oven concludes with this anecdote:

> Rabbi Eliezer's wife, Ima Shalom, was Gamaliel's sister. After Akiva told Eliezer that he had been excommunicated, she worried that Divine wrath would be unleashed against the rabbi who was ultimately responsible for ratifying the decree against her husband—namely, her brother. She was certain that this was most likely to occur if Eliezer offered up the daily prayer known as *takhanun* [prayers of sorrow and supplication]. These prayers were believed to evoke deep empathy and compassion in God for the subject offering them, and Ima Shalom feared that if God were to be subjected to hearing these prayers poured out from Eliezer, then Divine indignation on behalf of her husband would lash out and take Gamaliel's life.
>
> So, Ima Shalom paid attention to when Eliezer offered his daily prayers, and when he would get to the *takhanun* section of the liturgy, she would interrupt him and prevent him from saying the prayers. She kept this up for a long time, but one day she was distracted by a poor person who had come to her door seeking food. Attending to his needs, she forgot to stop Eliezer from offering *takhanun* prayers.[19] When she saw him bent over with his face

---

19. The text actually provides two different opinions about what caused Ima Shalom to neglect to interrupt Eliezer's *takhanun* prayers that day. I included the version in which a poor person came to the door seeking aid in my paraphrased translation. But the text offers another opinion about what happened, saying that Ima Shalom misjudged the timing of the new moon (new month). *Takhanun* is not said on the new moon, so she thought Eliezer wouldn't be offering those particular prayers that day, but she was off by a day. This opinion about what caused Ima Shalom to forget to interrupt Eliezer's *takhanun* prayers offers readers an allusion to one of the rabbinic stories we studied back in chapter 5 of this book. It is the story in which Gamaliel had made a mistake about the correct date of the new moon, and when Gamaliel heard that Rabbi Joshua had told another sage that he thought Gamaliel was wrong about the date, he publicly humiliated Joshua by ordering him to visit him with his money sack in hand on the date that Joshua believed to be Yom Kippur (*m. Rosh Hash.* 2.8–9). This calendrical error version of the explanation of Ima Shalom's forgetting to interrupt Eliezer's *takhanun* prayers makes the

Eliezer's Gaze Burns Everything It Touches

in his hands (the posture for *takhanun* prayers), she immediately said to him, "Get up! You've killed my brother!"

Almost immediately, they received word of Gamaliel's sudden death.

Astonished, Eliezer asked her, "How did you know?"

She replied, "I learned a teaching from my father's house, the descendants of King David himself, that after the destruction of the Temple by the Romans, all the gates of heaven were locked, except for the gates of *oh-na-ah*."

I know what many readers are probably asking. What in the world is "*oh-na-ah*," and why didn't I translate it? Hang on, that's what we're going to look at next. You see, the Akhnai's oven story doesn't just appear in the Talmud out of nowhere. It is nested within a structured section of the Talmud that begins with a discussion of a sin known as *oh-na-ah*, and *oh-na-ah* is a word that is hard to translate.

Oh-na-ah means something close to "great personal wounding caused through speech."[20] The section of the Talmud that includes the Akhnai's oven episode begins with several different rabbinic teachings about the seriousness of the sin of *oh-na-ah*. In one part of the discussion, several rabbis state that there are certain kinds of verbal wrongs that elicit an immediate and intense heavenly retribution against the guilty party, particularly if the victim cries out in their suffering. In making this point, one sage uses a metaphor involving gates. He says that since the Roman destruction of the Temple, the "gates of prayer" are locked, but the "gates of tears" remain open. Another sage says that all of the heavenly "gates" are locked, except for the "gates of *oh-na-ah*."[21]

Let's pause for a moment, because I suspect now some readers are wondering what these gates are that these rabbis are talking about, and whether we are hopelessly heading further and further down lines of thought that keep branching off of one another. Hang in there—we are going to make our way through all of these ideas until we come out the other side, I promise!

---

story of Gamaliel's death into a tale of karmic payback for the way he publicly humiliated Joshua. As we'll see in the next part of this chapter, the sin of publicly wounding someone through words is one that the rabbinic tradition viewed as severe and likely to invite divine retribution.

20. *Oh-na-ah* is actually a more complex category of Talmudic ethics and law, and I've simplified the definition here for clarity's sake.

21. b. B. Metz. 59a.

The Forgotten Sage

What's happening with all this talk about gates is that the rabbis are using a poignant metaphor that gives us a glimpse of the sense of spiritual distance and Divine abandonment that they experienced in coming to terms with the devastating loss of their homeland and Temple. In a number of places in rabbinic literature, the sages talk about God as being distant or unavailable. This is connected to a rabbinic tradition that when the Roman destruction took place, in some sense God too was thrown into exile, and an element of God's Self attached Itself to the Jews in exile, accompanying them but also experiencing a sense of incompletion or cosmic fracture.

In various texts, the rabbis refer metaphorically to certain "gates" of heaven. There are the "gates of prayer" and the "gates of repentance." There are the "gates of justice," the "gates of tears," and the "gates of *oh-na-ah*."[22] The idea is that even after the Roman destruction, the God of Israel is still there, dwelling in heaven, observing all that goes on in the world, and responding in the various ways the rabbis believed God to respond to human behavior. But, when the Temple fell, in the rabbinic imagination some of the normally functioning ways Jews could connect to God—or even arouse a powerful response from God—were shut and even locked. Rabbinic Judaism developed, as part of its messianic hopes, the belief that when the Messiah would come, not only would the Jews be restored to their homeland and the Temple rebuilt, but all of the blocked spiritual pathways to God would be re-opened. But for now, during this time of exile and brokenness, only one or two "gates" to the Divine remain "unlocked."

Some rabbis held that the gates of tears remained open—meaning that there is still something in the sincere weeping of someone suffering that finds its way directly into the heart of God, eliciting Divine response. In the part of the Talmud we are looking at, the key line before we get to the Akhnai's oven story comes from a rabbi who says, "God's punishments for wrongdoing are usually meted out to people not by God Himself, but through an angel. The exception is for the sin of *oh-na-ah*, which God punishes directly."[23]

Shortly thereafter, our Talmudic passage launches into the Akhnai's oven story. And that story continues all the way to the closing passage of this section of the Talmud, in which Eliezer's wife, Ima Shalom, tells Eliezer

---

22. A lot of modern synagogues are named for some of these metaphorical gates. There are synagogues called "*Sha'arey Tzedek*" (Gates of Justice) and "*Sha'arey Shamayim*" (Gates of Heaven). One of the prayer books of the Reform Movement of Judaism is called "*Sha'arey Tefilah*" (Gates of Prayer).

23. *b. B. Metz.* 59a. I've paraphrased the exact quote from the Talmud for clarity.

that he has just caused her brother's, Gamaliel's, death, because "after the destruction of the Temple by the Romans, all the gates of heaven were locked, except for the gates of *oh-na-ah*."[24]

So, why is it important that the Akhnai's oven story is bookended by discussions of *oh-na-ah*? Basically, the Talmud is trying to express its conflictedness about the Akhnai's-oven / excommunication-of-Eliezer story and the big issues it addresses. Yes, Joshua's side wins the day and establishes a system of "majoritarian interpretivism"[25] for rabbinic Judaism going forward, but this story also makes clear to us that Joshua and the other rabbis who opposed Eliezer were wrong about the law. Furthermore, as Daniel Greenwood puts it, "the Talmud—even while affirming Joshua's rule—is not afraid to point out that Eliezer remains heaven's favorite."[26] Another scholar of rabbinic literature, Susan Handelman, writes, "even though Rabbi Eliezer's reasoning is sharp and he has heavenly aid, he is overruled by a majority on the legal level. [But, the Akhnai's oven] narrative sympathizes with him on an emotional level."[27]

Greenwood goes further to claim that the Talmud's final editors' decision to nest this story within the framework of discussions of *oh-na-ah* was their way of showing that Joshua and his supporters went too far when they excommunicated Eliezer and publicly humiliated him by taking all of the objects that he had previously declared to be ritually pure and burning them. That sin—the sin of deeply wounding Eliezer and driving him completely out of the rabbinic community—was the sin of *oh-na-ah*.

David Luban's comments on this scene flow in a similar direction:

> Eliezer's pain and humiliation are real, and [the way Joshua and the other rabbis treat him] emphasizes how ruthlessly the rabbis suppress dissent. The story says that they gathered every object that Eliezer has declared pure and burned it—an image uncomfortably like the book-burnings of the Inquisition. The rabbis burn these objects knowing full well that the *bat kol* has declared them pure, so there is no need for the bonfire other than the need to assert their authority and extinguish Eliezer's.[28]

---

24. *b. B. Metz.* 59b.
25. Greenwood, "Akhnai: Legal Responsibility in the World of the Silent God," 343.
26. Greenwood, "Akhnai: Legal Responsibility in the World of the Silent God," 343.
27. Handelman, *Make Yourself a Teacher*, 67.
28. Luban, "The Coiled Serpent of Argument," 1272.

The Talmud has two lessons to offer here: one, that as imperfect as it may be, the *halakhah* will be determined by the rabbis through their procedures of debating and majority voting; and two, that even rabbis who threaten the system cannot be treated with humiliation and expulsion from the community, because that is *oh-na-ah* and God's retributive anger is aroused by the suffering of the victims of that particular sin.[29]

Greenwood writes that in the debate over Akhnai's oven:

> [Rabbi Joshua's and the rabbis'] claim to being right is procedural: the rabbis must use their God-given intelligence to understand their God-given Law to the best of their God-given abilities, and are not entitled to abdicate in favor of carob trees, streams, or even great scholars. But even a majority is not entitled to dishonor the minority: if telling Eliezer that he had been excommunicated in a rude way would have been enough to warrant his destroying the entire world, then the simple act of excommunicating him itself must be enough to warrant [God's punishing Gamaliel with death the moment Eliezer's prayers of suffering reached God].
>
> ... Rabbi Eliezer has been treated with [the disrespect of *oh-na-ah*], and his wife knows that his prayer will be answered and her brother, Rabban Gamaliel, will die because "all the gates of prayer are locked except the gate of *oh-na-ah*."
>
> The majority is wrong ... on a point as fundamental as the one on which it is right. Just as proper procedure requires that the rabbis not suspend their own judgment in the face of higher authority—either Eliezer's or a Higher Authority still—so too proper procedure requires that the majority remember that the losers are also part of the community and must be treated as such.[30]

Greenwood goes further to add that the way things play out for Eliezer in this story—with the sad account of Akiva telling him of his excommunication and Eliezer's subsequent misery—helps us see how important it is for the rabbis to keep those who lose debates within the community, even if they threaten the democratic system of the rabbis itself.

> ... it is Eliezer ... who is known for behavior that makes community impossible. ... Eliezer is the man with special access to truth, and uncompromising truth is incompatible with a democratic society.

---

29. I give credit to Daniel Greenwood for opening my eyes to the insight that both of these lessons are part of this section of Talmud. His 1997 essay, "Akhnai: Legal Responsibility in the World of the Silent God," is a superb discussion of this text.

30. Greenwood, "Akhnai: Legal Responsibility in the World of the Silent God," 352–53.

> Those who know the truth have no reason to bow to the majority—like Eliezer, they can appeal to heaven. Only by excluding his claim to special privilege could the community continue. But only by respecting his claim to truth can the world endure.
>
> ... [This section of the Talmud suggests the] idea of a nation as a community of dialogue. The [excommunication] failed because, in the end, Eliezer is still part of the conversation....
>
> ... The Law ... is not in heaven and does not require heavenly intervention to be understood. So, God's sovereignty itself requires His withdrawal from the system.... We, not the human or divine Authors of the covenant, must take control of it.
>
> ... But ultimately, [the Law] is about living together: neither insisting on the truth when it is unacceptable to others, nor excluding minorities when they are obnoxious, neither abandoning the tradition nor slavishly imitating its forms when their meanings are gone.[31]

Greenwood is a law professor and his essay appears not in a Jewish publication, but in the *Utah Law Review*. His interpretation of the Akhnai's oven section of the Talmud offers crucial insight into the nature of law and democratic societies. A contemporary Israeli rabbi and scholar, Donniel Hartman, argued for similar values in the Israeli newspaper *The Times of Israel*, in a December 2015 op-ed addressing a national controversy over Israeli groups expressing viewpoints hostile to widely accepted ideas about the nature of Israel as a Jewish state. He writes:

> No society that embraces free speech and dissent as essential gets to pick its critics or set the parameters within which they function. The nature of vibrant criticism and ideological dissent is that someone will always violate some line and engage in actions some find reprehensible. In fact, it is precisely by crossing these lines that critics garner the necessary attention to catalyze public debate.
>
> The Jewish people['s] ... boundaries were always porous and vague. Judaism was never a religion of simple black-or-white. The lines between the heretic and the faithful, the insider and the outsider, were always gray. We survived, because we had an almost infinite capacity to tolerate differences, including those we felt to be dangerous. This tolerance gave birth to a society of debate and self-criticism that is the bedrock of our moral aspirations. Today it is precisely this tolerance which is also our most strategic ally,

---

31 Greenwood, "Akhnai: Legal Responsibility in the World of the Silent God," 354–56.

Eliezer's Poignant Death

Let's turn now to one of the Talmud's accounts of the death of Eliezer. As the story begins, Eliezer is still under the ban of excommunication. What follows is a modified translation that includes some paraphrasing and some author's interruptions for clarity's sake:[33]

> When Rabbi Eliezer became gravely ill, Rabbi Akiva and his colleagues [including Rabbi Joshua] visited him. Eliezer was in his bed, while Akiva and the others sat in his salon. It was late Friday afternoon, getting close to the time for lighting the candles that signify the beginning of the Sabbath.
>
> Eliezer's son, who was named Hyrcanus after Eliezer's father, went in to Eliezer's bedroom and tried to remove his father's *tefillin* from his head and his arm.

Tefillin is a Hebrew word that often gets translated as "phylacteries," an English word that is, for most of the general public, just as incomprehensible as the Hebrew word *tefillin*. *Tefillin* refers to a set of ritual objects that are traditionally worn by men on the forehead and on one arm during certain daily prayers and during Torah study.[34] They are not supposed to be worn on the Sabbath, however. In this scene, Eliezer's well-meaning son, Hyrcanus, is worried that his ailing and aged father may be too weak and scatter-brained to remember to take the *tefillin* off before the Sabbath begins. So, Hyrcanus hurries in and tries to gently remove the *tefillin* for him.

> But Eliezer rebuked his son, and Hyrcanus returned to the salon full of gloom.
>
> "It seems to me," Hyrcanus said to the others, "that my father's mind is deranged."
>
> But Rabbi Akiva retorted, "Oh, his mind is clear," and went on to explain that he realized that Eliezer actually had a sound halakhic reason to rebuke his son.

---

32. Hartman, "Getting Serious about BDS and Breaking the Silence."

33. The version of this story I'm translating and paraphrasing is found in *b. Sanh.* 68a.

34. In non-Orthodox modern movements of Judaism, Jews of all gender identities may wear *tefillin*.

Eliezer's Gaze Burns Everything It Touches

> At that point, Akiva and the other sages went into Eliezer's bedroom and, in observance of the ban of excommunication, sat down at a distance of four amot from him.
> "Why have you come?" Eliezer asked them.
> "To study the Torah," they replied.
> "So, why didn't you come to see me before now?" he asked.
> Their response: "We had no time."

If you're sensing the awkwardness in the room as you read this paraphrased translation, your senses are working well. Akiva, Joshua, and the other rabbis have decided that, despite the ban of excommunication, they are determined to see and speak with Eliezer before his imminent death. Because the decree of excommunication is still in place, the visiting rabbis continue to observe the requirement that they not come any closer to Eliezer than four amot. When Eliezer asks them why they have come, they claim they are visiting him because people are allowed to learn Torah from someone under the kind of excommunication ban Eliezer is under (*niddui*). But if that's really the reason, Eliezer asks, why haven't they visited him to learn Torah from him before now?

The nakedness of their lie is exposed.[35] Joshua and his companions won't tell him what everyone in that room, and we the readers, know—that Eliezer is dying, and the others want to see if he will recant his refusal to abide by rabbinic majority rule and thereby have the excommunication decree lifted before he dies. Otherwise, according to *halakhah*, if he dies while excommunicated, he will be publicly dishonored in his burial. When Eliezer asks them why they haven't come to learn Torah with him during all the time he was under the ban of *niddui*, their "we had no time" response is not only unbelievable, it is even insulting. As we return to the text, keep *oh-na-ah* in mind.

> Eliezer then said to them, "I'll be surprised if any of these men die a natural death."

Uh-oh. *Oh-na-ah* evokes heavenly wrath, especially when the victim is a magnificent rabbi whom God adores, and Eliezer knows it.

> Akiva then asked Eliezer, "And what will my death be like?"
> Eliezer answered, "Yours will be more cruel than theirs."

---

35. For a contrary opinion about whether the visiting rabbis' claim that they were too busy to have visited sooner was, in fact, a lie, see Rabbi Dov Linzer's essay, "Rabbi Eliezer vs. Rabbi Akiva: Two Models of Torah."

Ouch. Indeed, Eliezer's prediction will turn out to be true, but we'll look into that in the next chapter of this book. Side note: if you are ever in the presence of a spiritual genius with access to Divine knowledge, I would recommend *against* asking such a person to tell you what your own death is going to be like. Meanwhile, back to our text . . .

> Eliezer then took his two arms and placed them over his heart. He said, "Woe unto you, two arms of mine that are like two scrolls of the Torah being rolled closed. I've studied much Torah and I've taught much Torah. Much Torah have I learned, yet I have only skimmed from the knowledge of my teachers as much as a dog lapping from the sea. Much Torah have I taught, yet my disciples have only drawn from me as much as a mascara stick[36] from its tube. I have even studied hundreds of detailed laws on [esoteric topics like] a certain type of impurity caused by a skin disease, but no student has ever asked me about them. I even studied three hundred laws about the use of magic to plant and grow fields of cucumbers effortlessly, and no man, except Rabbi Akiva, ever once asked me about this subject![37]
>
> I remember, one time, Akiva and I were walking down a road, when he asked me to teach him about this form of magic. I started to utter the first words involved in this practice, when suddenly the whole field surrounding the road was filled with sprouted ripe cucumbers. Then Akiva said, 'Master, now that you have taught me how to use magic to plant them, would you teach me how magic is used to harvest them?' I spoke the words and all the cucumbers were suddenly harvested and collected in one place."

If the sudden appearance of magic and cucumbers seems random to you, it's not. In one of the major rabbinic texts in which this story is told,[38] the story is nested within a previously begun halakhic discussion about sorcery, magic, and the laws in the Torah that prohibit and restrict

---

36. I learned the "mascara stick" translation from Devora Steinmatz's lecture, "The Death of Rabbi Eliezer." Many other translations read "my disciples have only drawn from me as much as a painting stick from its tube" or something similar. The lecture is online at https://www.hadar.org/torah-resource/death-rabbi-eliezer.

37. If the sudden appearance of cucumbers seems oddly comical as an example for Eliezer to bring up in this moment, one thing to keep in mind is that even though "cucumbers" in English is kind of a comical word, it does not have the same humorous quality in rabbinic Hebrew. For what it's worth, this particular Hebrew word may in fact refer not to cucumbers, but to melons or gourds.

38. *b. Sanh.* 68a.

Eliezer's Gaze Burns Everything It Touches

their use. Remember ancient rabbinic literature is very non-linear, and it is common for Talmudic legal discussions to digress into a narrative that includes a related theme, even if that narrative is important for reasons that go way beyond the legal questions under examination at the beginning of the Talmudic discussion. Let's return now to the final moments of the story of Rabbi Eliezer's demise.

> The rabbis gathered in Eliezer's bedroom began to ask him questions regarding the ritual purity status of various objects: specifically, a ball, a shoemaker's shoe-form, an amulet, a pearl-pouch, and a small weight.[39]

Okay, this part involves some complicated technicalities of Talmudic ritual purity law, and it needs a little explaining. Why are these rabbis asking Eliezer, the most brilliant rabbi of his generation, to say what his halakhic ruling would be on the ritual purity status of a bunch of household objects? Well, it's connected back to the Akhnai's oven story that we explored in depth in chapter 6.

Remember, in that narrative, the ritual question the rabbis were debating was whether a particular kind of clay oven that had been constructed out of layered sections of clay and sand was capable of becoming ritually impure, and thus capable of transmitting this impurity to objects that would be baked inside of it. The legal principle that all the rabbis in that debate agreed upon was that if the oven was a single, complete object, then it was susceptible to impurity.

Where they differed was that Eliezer argued that because this type of oven was made up of different sections of clay stacked upon one another, the oven should *not* be considered as a whole, completed object, but rather was still an incompletely constructed object. Therefore, it was not susceptible to ritual impurity and would not convey impurity to objects coming into contact with it. Joshua and all the other rabbis argued that the oven should be considered a whole, complete object, and therefore it could become impure and pass on its impurity to other objects.

In the story we're studying now, the rabbis visiting Eliezer's deathbed are, perhaps in an indirect way, giving Eliezer a chance to reconsider his earlier ruling. The series of objects the rabbis are asking Eliezer about have a connection to the same issue of ritual impurity as Akhnai's oven. As Joshua Gutoff writes, "the sages had established the answers years ago [to

---

39. I'm using Susan Handelman's translation of the assorted objects listed in this part of the text, from her book, *Make Yourself a Teacher*, 64.

these questions], and Rabbi Eliezer had held a minority view. They have come not to learn *the* answers, but to learn *his* answers; what will they be after all these years in isolation?"[40]

Regarding this scene, Susan Handelman observes: "This is a replay of issues which caused [Eliezer's] banning. Is he now willing to recant?"[41] Let's find out how Eliezer answers and how more of the scene plays out:

> Eliezer replied: they are all susceptible to becoming impure. And if any of those objects do become impure, they should be purified just as they are, as whole, complete objects.
>
> The rabbis asked Eliezer another question: "What is the ritual purity status of a shoe that has been made by a cobbler and is finished, except that it is still on the cobbler's shoe-form?"
>
> Eliezer answered, "Pure," and in pronouncing this word his soul left his body in purity.
>
> Then Rabbi Joshua ben Hananiah stood up on his feet[42] and exclaimed, "The ban of excommunication is annulled! It is annulled!"

Confused? It's okay. It's a very difficult passage. For our purposes, don't worry about the details regarding each of the objects they asked him about or the intricate ancient rabbinic rules of how objects could acquire a pure or impure status. What matters here is really just one thing: whether Eliezer's answers show that he a) reversed his previous halakhic opinions about objects thematically connected to Akhnai's oven; b) stuck to his minority views but signaled his acceptance of the authority of the rabbis' majority-rule system; or c) stuck to his minority views and stuck to his rejection of the rabbis' majority-rule system. If the answer is a) or b), we can treat Eliezer as having finally given up his lonely stand against accepting the authority of the rabbis' majoritarian system. Also, if the answer is a) or b), then Joshua's announcement that the ban of excommunication has been

---

40. Gutoff, "The Necessary Outlaw," 733–34. Italics mine.

41. Handelman, *Make Yourself a Teacher*, 86.

42. Note that this specific phrasing, "Joshua stood up on his feet" (in Hebrew, *amad al raglav*), is the same phrasing that is used in the Akhnai's oven story at the moment when Joshua rebuked the heavenly voice—the *bat kol*—and declared "It is not in heaven!" What these two Joshua moments have in common is that they mark moments of tremendous consequence. The first time Joshua stands on his feet it is to prevent what Eliezer is trying to do to the rabbis and their majoritarian halakhic system. The second time, it is to prevent the halakhic system from publicly humiliating Eliezer by requiring that he be dishonored during his burial - the penalty called for in the case of a Jew who dies while in a state of excommunication.

annulled makes sense, since Eliezer would have returned to the rabbinic fold, as it were, just before he died. If, however, the answer is c), then Eliezer has stuck to his guns even unto death. In that case, the puzzling question becomes why Joshua annuls the excommunication.

In Susan Handelman's superb book, *Make for Yourself a Teacher: Rabbinic Tales of Mentors and Disciples*, she writes that Eliezer went with option "c."[43] That is why Joshua waits until *after* Eliezer has died to revoke the ban of excommunication. Given that the *halakhah* required that Jews who died in a state of excommunication had to be publicly dishonored at their funeral, we can understand why Joshua would want to prevent that from happening to his colleague Eliezer. But why does Joshua think he has the authority to annul the ban now that Eliezer has died? The text doesn't tell us.

Perhaps Joshua's reason is grounded in something Handelman points out. This story is crafted in such a way as to leave the reader contemplating the final moment of Eliezer's life:

> "Eliezer answered, 'Pure,' and in pronouncing this word his soul left his body in purity."

Handelman writes that this line of text offers us a double-meaning, telling us not only how Eliezer answered the visiting rabbis' halakhic question, but also telling us that even though the rabbis' will maintain their majority-rule system, "Eliezer and his Torah are also pure."[44]

Joshua and the others seem to have gotten the answer to the question they brought to Eliezer at his deathbed: Eliezer's kind of purity cannot be reconciled with the rabbinic majority-rule system, which must prevail; however, Eliezer's kind of purity is also genuine, and it is the state in which his soul departed his body, as witnessed by the rabbis in the room. A rabbi who has died in a such a way should not be further humiliated by being dishonored at his funeral due to the requirements of *niddui*. In fact, to allow Eliezer's memory to be disgraced in such a way might even violate the grave sin of *oh-na-ah*. Joshua annuls the ban.[45]

---

43. Handelman, *Make for Yourself a Teacher*, 90. Other scholars interpret this difficult text differently.

44. Handelman, *Make for Yourself a Teacher*, 89.

45. Susan Handelman writes, "[Eliezer's] purity was perhaps too much for this world. . . . [The text] reinforces our sense that the last word [Rabbi] Eliezer says about the shoe—is really also about *him*. For someone who is a 'living Torah,' and whose body merges with the Scroll, these legal issues are indeed inseparable from the essence of his

Here's what happens next in the text:

> When the Sabbath ended, Rabbi Akiva joined a funeral processional in which Eliezer's coffin was being carried to Lod, the town where Eliezer's academy was located. Along the road, Akiva beat his own flesh until his blood flowed down upon the earth. He began to eulogize Rabbi Eliezer, [quoting 2 Kgs 2:12]: "My father, my father, the chariot of Israel and its horsemen." [Akiva also said,] "I have many coins, but I do not have a money changer to whom to give them!"[46]

The verse Akiva quotes from 2 Kings is from the biblical story in which God sends a fiery chariot to carry the prophet Elijah up to heaven. Just prior to Elijah's supernatural ascension, Elijah's disciple, Elisha, asks him to give him a double portion of his spirit when he leaves this world—a request that ends up being granted. For Akiva to cry out this particular verse in his grief over Eliezer means not only that he regards Eliezer as just as exceptional a figure as the deathless Elijah, but that he would like to see himself as a kind of Elisha, hoping that he can receive his teacher's spirit.

Akiva's next statement, about having many coins but no money changer he can give them to, is understood by the medieval scholar Rashi to mean that Akiva has many halakhic questions, but that he no longer has anyone who can answer them. Suffice it to say that Akiva is utterly devastated by Eliezer's death. There's a bit more to this Talmudic story that we have yet to examine, and we'll do that in the last chapter of this book. For now, we'll close out this chapter by looking at one more text.

There's a Talmudic discussion that opens with the words, "After the death of Rabbi Eliezer, four sages each refuted one of his opinions."[47] These four were Yossi ha-Gelili, Tarfon, Elazar ben Azariah, and Akiva. One by one, each of the sages presented a challenge to one of the late Eliezer's halakhic rulings. Akiva even provided two different legal objections to Eliezer's ruling. After each of the sages had spoken, Rabbi Joshua responded with a single statement: "One does not refute the lion after his death."[48] We'll leave Eliezer now, mourned by his humble and admiring opponent, Joshua.

---

being." Handelman, *Make for Yourself a Teacher*, 89.

46. *b. Sanh.* 68a.

47. *b. Git.* 83a. I'm indebted to the author of *Who's Who in the Talmud*, Shulamis Frieman, whose entry on Rabbi Joshua included a reference to this Talmudic story.

48. The medieval commentator Rashi explains Joshua's words by adding, "If [Eliezer] was still living, he would respond with answers to all your objections."

8

Diplomacy, War, and Passing the Torch

> ... born in Pontius Pilate's procuratorship, [Rabbi Joshua] lived under thirteen emperors, some crazier than others, but almost all of them gods in their own eyes: Tiberius, Caligula, Claudius, Nero, Galba, Otho, Vitellius, Vespasian, Titus, Domitian, Nerva, Trajan, and Hadrian. He was a competent Greek scholar and knew not only his own people but their enemies.
> —Joshua Podro, *The Last Pharisee*, 11.

Woven into the Talmud's accounts of the century that followed the great Roman destruction, we find tales of the early rabbis delegating Rabbi Joshua to travel to Rome and seek to negotiate on behalf of the Jews. Whether any of these journeys really happened or not is impossible to know. What we do know is that the literature that emerged out of the rabbinic era repeatedly presents stories depicting Joshua as a wise and trusted advocate for the defeated Jews and the rabbinic enterprise.

Some of the best known of these legends involve Joshua meeting with Hadrian,[1] the Roman emperor from 117–38 C.E. In rabbinic literature, Hadrian is an arch-villain:

---

1. For example, see *Lev. Rab.* 18.1 and *Ruth Rab.* 3.2. In her essay, "The Emperor's Daughter's New Skin: Bodily Otherness and Self-Identity in the Dialogues of Rabbi Yehoshua ben Hanania and the Emperor's Daughter," Mira Balberg writes, "there are more than fifteen rabbinic sources that present a dialogue between R. Yehoshua and the Roman emperor. The Babylonian Talmud refers to the Roman figure as Caesar, whereas the

... the Jews did not hold Hadrian's memory in high honor; the Talmud and Midrash follow his name with the curse "Crush his bones." His reign is called the time of persecution and danger, and the blood of many martyrs is charged to his account.[2]

We also find accounts claiming that Hadrian built a new temple in Jerusalem on the site of the one that the Romans had destroyed—only it was dedicated to the Roman high god, Jupiter. It is hard to imagine an offense that Jews would find more horrific and humiliating than that. Hadrian was also emperor when Rome eliminated the name "Judea" from the region and reconfigured and renamed the province "Syria Palaestina." Some scholars say that the renaming was intended as a punishing act of national erasure against the Jews,[3] though that claim is debated.

During Hadrian's reign, the Roman Empire reached as far north as Britain (think of Hadrian's Wall), as far south as Egypt, as far west as Spain, and as far east as the Persian Gulf, where present-day Iran, Iraq, and Kuwait border each other. Rabbinic and Roman literature both describe Hadrian traveling extensively across the empire, taking an interest in other cultures and ideas, and holding discussions with Jews and other conquered peoples about theology, philosophy, and ethics. In Talmudic and Midrashic literature we find multiple stories about conversations between the homely and humble sage, Joshua, and the glorious emperor of Rome, like this one from the Babylonian Talmud:

> ... the Emperor [Hadrian][4] said to Rabbi Joshua ben Hananiah, "I wish to see your God."
> He replied: "You cannot see him."
> "Indeed," said the emperor, "I will see him."

[midrashic texts] narrate several dialogues between R. Yehoshua and 'Hadrian, may his bones rot.'" Note: "R. Yehoshua" is another way of writing "Rabbi Joshua." Balberg, "The Emperor's Daughter's New Skin," 184.

2. Gottheil and Krauss, "Hadrian," 135.

3. According to Shaye Cohen, "To punish the Jews, . . . the Romans renamed the land 'Syria Palaestina,' forbade Jews to dwell in Jerusalem, now a pagan city, and proscribed the practice of Judaism for several years." Cohen, "The Destruction: From Scripture to Midrash," 18.

4. This Talmudic text doesn't use Hadrian's name, but rather uses the Hebrew word for Caesar, meaning emperor. The emperor is presumed to be Hadrian by many later commentators. That said, it's possible that a different emperor was intended, or that as the story was transmitted for many generations before finally being written into the Babylonian Talmud, its ultimate editors decided that the specific identity of the emperor was unimportant.

Diplomacy, War, and Passing the Torch

> [So Joshua] went and placed the emperor facing the sun during the summer solstice and said to him, "Look up at it."
>
> He replied: "I cannot."
>
> Rabbi Joshua said, "If you cannot look directly at the sun, which is but one of the ministers that attend the Holy One, blessed be He, how then can you presume to look upon the Divine presence?"
>
> On another occasion the emperor said to Rabbi Joshua, "I wish to prepare a banquet for your God."
>
> He replied: "You could not possibly do it."
>
> "Why not?"
>
> "Because God's attendants are too numerous."
>
> "Indeed, I will do it," [said Hadrian].
>
> "Then go and prepare it on the spacious banks of great river, Rebitha."
>
> [The emperor] spent the six months of summer in making preparations when a tempest arose and swept everything into the sea. He then spent the six months of winter in making preparations when rain fell and washed everything into the sea.
>
> "What is [the meaning of] this?" asked the emperor.
>
> "[The winds and rains] are but the sweepers and sprinklers[5] that march before God!"
>
> "In that case," said the emperor, "I cannot do it."[6]

Here's another example from Midrash, as quoted by the contemporary scholar Rabbi Binyamin La'u. Before we examine it, I'll just note that in this text Hadrian refers to the Ten Commandments and makes some specific assumptions about them. He observes that the first five commandments include God's name, but the second set of five do not. He also assumes that the first five commandments involve duties that are specific to Jews and their relationship with their God, but that the last five commandments involve proper behavior between all human beings, and are universal in nature. Here's the text itself:

> Hadrian, may his bones crumble to dust, asked Rabbi Joshua ben Hananiah: The Holy One, blessed be He, bestowed a great privilege upon the nations of the world when He gave five commandments to Israel and offered five to the nations of the world. In the

---

5. In ancient times, if an outdoor banquet was being set up, sweepers would be assigned to sweep the grounds before the guests arrived, and sprinklers would be assigned to sprinkle water to help keep the dust down during the event.

6. *b. Hul.* 59b–60a. These two vignettes about Joshua and Hadrian have been retold as legends for children in Jewish religious schools, for example, in the late nineteenth-century American Jewish educational periodical, *The Sabbath Visitor* 16.1 (1886) 234.

first five commandments which the Holy One, blessed be He, gave to Israel, His name is bound up with the commandments, so that if Israel sins, God rebukes them. But in the second five commandments which He offered to the nations of the world, His name is not bound up with the commandments, so that if they sin, He does not rebuke them.

Rabbi Joshua said to him: Come and walk about the city's squares with me.

In each and every place where Rabbi Joshua led him, Hadrian saw a statue of himself standing there.

Rabbi Joshua said to him: This object—what is it?

The emperor replied: It is a statue of me.

He said: And this one here—what is it?

The emperor said: It is a statue of me.

Finally, Rabbi Joshua drew him along and led him to a privy, where he said to him: My lord king, I see that you are a ruler everywhere in this city, but you are not a ruler in this place.

The emperor asked: Why not?

Rabbi Joshua replied: Because in each and every place I saw a statue of you, but there is no statue of you in this place.

Hadrian replied: And you are a sage among the Jews?! Does it befit the honor of a king to have his statue set up in a place that is loathsome, in a place that is repulsive, in a place that is filthy?

Rabbi Joshua said: Your ears have not heard what your mouth says. Would it befit the honor of the Holy One, blessed be He, to have his name mentioned with murderers, adulterers, and thieves?

He dismissed Rabbi Joshua, who went on his way.[7]

These parables have a similar structure to many vignettes found in the ancient Mediterranean world, going well back into biblical times. The high-minded official with power faces off against the humble, spiritually advanced master of lower social station. The high and mighty one challenges one of the core teachings of the humble master, often in front of a crowd, and the humble master volleys right back. There's a moment of suspense before we know how things are going to turn out, and then the humble master defeats the high-minded official, and Mr-High-and-Mighty exits the scene, either admitting defeat, or else stymied, or otherwise completely exposed as a false source of truth and Divine will.

---

7. *Pesikta Rabati* 21, Ish Shalom edition. La'u, *The Sages: Character, Context, & Creativity*, Vol. 2, Kindle location 6088. I've made slight adaptations to the translation for clarity's sake.

Diplomacy, War, and Passing the Torch

Let's look at another story. This one takes place during one of Joshua's visits to Rome.

> Rabbi Hanina bar Idda said, "Why are the words of the Torah compared to water, as it is written [in Isa 55:1], 'Ho! Everyone who thirsts, come for water?' This is to teach you, just as water flows from a higher level to a lower one, so too the words of the Torah endure only with one whose mind is humble."
>
> Rabbi Oshaia said, "Why are the words of the Torah compared to these three liquids: water, wine, and milk [again, citing Isa 55:1]? This is to teach you, just as these three liquids can only be preserved in the most inferior of vessels, so too the words of the Torah endure only with one whose mind is humble.
>
> This [principle] is illustrated by the story of the daughter of the Roman emperor who addressed Rabbi Joshua ben Hananiah. [Commenting on the rabbi's physical appearance, she said to him,] "Can such magnificent wisdom exist within such an ugly vessel?"
>
> He replied, "Doesn't your father keep wine in an earthenware vessel?"
>
> She asked, "Where else would he keep it?"
>
> He said to her, "You who are important nobles should keep it in vessels of gold and silver!"
>
> So, she went and told this to her father, and he had the wine put into vessels of gold and silver, and it all turned sour.
>
> When [the emperor] was informed of this he asked his daughter, "Who gave you this advice?"
>
> She replied, "Rabbi Joshua ben Hananiah."
>
> So, the emperor had [Joshua] summoned before him and asked him, "Why did you give her such advice?"
>
> He replied, "I answered her according to the way that she spoke to me."
>
> [Next, the unnamed narrating voice of the Talmud—the *stam*—asks:] But are there not good-looking people who are also learned?
>
> [The *stam* answers its own question:] If these same people were ugly, they would be even more learned.[8]

This is a really fun text to work with. I especially love the last word that Joshua gets to have when Hadrian calls him on the carpet and demands to know why he gave his daughter this advice, which, considering the size and scope of an emperor's wine cellar, would have caused the loss of a fortune in wine.

---

8. *b. Ta'an.* 7a–b. Another version of this story appears in *b. Ned.* 50b.

But it's also fun because there's so much going on in the space of a few sparse lines of dialog and action. We take pleasure in parables in which the underdog is vindicated, in which the wealthy and good-looking snob is humbled by the poor and homely hero with integrity. And the story's wine/vessels metaphor is perfect for illustrating its moral—that appearances aren't necessarily equal to true value.

The basic drama of this parable could take place in many places and times, and of course there are lots of parables and sayings in the ancient Mediterranean world involving old wine and old or new skins. But part of what's important about this particular story is this specific setting, and this specific rabbi. Rabbi Joshua's ugliness can't help but symbolize how the Jews are perceived by the triumphant, ruling Romans.[9]

In fact, it's worth looking a little more closely at Hadrian's daughter's opening line to Joshua. She greets him with an insult that's packed with information. "Can such magnificent wisdom exist within such an ugly vessel?" In the original Talmudic Aramaic, the two key adjectives in her question to Joshua are *mih-fo-ar-ah,* which means something like magnificent, glorious, or opulent, and *mi-kho-ar,* which means something like ugly or unattractive. The second of these words, *mi-kho-ar,* can also mean something more than just ugly—it can mean "disfigured," as in something that's been caused to become physically misshapen and deformed.

From this one line we learn that Hadrian's daughter has already witnessed, or at least heard about, Rabbi Joshua's astonishing wisdom. And yet, Hadrian's daughter, representing the Roman imperial outsider, the conqueror who now observes the Jewish people from a high perch, describes the representative of the Jews as breathtakingly abhorrent to look upon.

This story gives us a sense of how the rabbis of ancient times may have seen themselves.[10] Their capital city and Temple lay in ruins, their nation

---

9. Mira Balberg writes, "It is difficult to know whether, by referring to an 'ugly vessel,' [Hadrian's daughter] is referring to the homely appearance of R. Yehoshua in particular or to the entire group for which he stands: the rabbis or even Jews in general." Balberg, "The Emperor's Daughter's New Skin," 188.

10. Julia Watts Belser offers an analysis of multiple rabbinic texts depicting Jews captured by Romans as having astonishing physical beauty—the exact opposite of Joshua ben Hananiah in the text we've just examined. The stories Belser analyzes describe high Roman officials as lustful hedonists who eagerly force beautiful Jewish captives into sexually abusive arrangements. Later in this chapter, we'll look into one of these stories that involves Rabbi Joshua rescuing a beautiful captive Jewish boy from the Romans. In any event, Belser makes a convincing case that one of the ways the rabbis symbolically depicted the Jewish people after the Roman destruction was as both spiritually and

Diplomacy, War, and Passing the Torch

was defeated, and their people were mostly scattered all over Europe, North Africa, and the Middle East. Yet they live on, and they remain the custodians and cultivators of Torah—of a wisdom so radiant and beautiful that it is recognized as such even by their arch enemies. But they now make their way in the world in broken and misshapen bodies. They are hard to even look at.

Another wonderful aspect of this story is the way that, in this part of the Talmud, it is nested within a larger discussion of the importance of humility as a character trait. Remember, just before this parable begins, the Talmud tells us about two different rabbis' teachings about the importance of humility among Torah scholars. Let's look at that part of the text again:

> Rabbi Hanina bar Idda said, "Why are the words of the Torah compared to water, as it is written [in Isa 55:1], 'Ho! Everyone who thirsts, come for water'? This is to teach you, just as water flows from a higher level to a lower one, so too *the words of the Torah endure only with one whose mind is humble.*"
>
> Rabbi Oshaia said, "Why are the words of the Torah compared to these three liquids: water, wine, and milk [Isa 55:1]? This is to teach you, just as these three liquids can only be preserved in the most inferior of vessels, so too *the words of the Torah endure only with one whose mind is humble.* [Italics mine.]

The editors of this part of the Talmud then place this parable about Rabbi Joshua right in the middle of this rabbinic discussion about the importance of having a "humble mind" (the original Aramaic could also be translated to mean having a modest, lowly demeanor). Joshua is one of rabbinic literature's exemplars of deep humility.

There are other rabbinic legends about Joshua visiting Rome that help paint a picture for us of how the early rabbis remembered the nature of the suffering of the Jews at the hands of imperial Rome, stories that contribute to the overall portrait of Joshua's character. One of these tales is found in a part of the Talmud that relates painful stories describing the sexual exploitation of captured Jewish women and children by Roman notables. It goes like this:

> Once, when Rabbi Joshua ben Hananiah went to the great city of Rome, people told him, "There is a young Jewish boy being held

---

physically beautiful, in contrast with the assertion I'm making about this particular Talmudic tale, in which I believe Joshua's great ugliness serves as a symbol of how the Jews and their conquerors perceived them. Both symbolic presentations of Jews—as incredibly beautiful and incredibly ugly—apparently resonated for different Talmudic rabbis at different times. Belser, *Rabbinic Tales of Destruction*, 60–76.

in a slave prison. He has beautiful eyes, a pretty appearance, and curly locks of hair."

Joshua stood outside the entrance to the prison, and in anguish he loudly quoted the first part of a verse of Scripture: "Who has given Jacob over to despoilment and Israel to plunderers?!" [Isa 42:24]

The child heard Joshua's exclamation, and answered immediately by quoting the rest of the verse in a loud voice: "Surely it was the Eternal One, against whom we have sinned, and in whose ways our people would not walk, and whose Teaching we would not follow!"

Amazed, Joshua said, "I am certain that this boy will one day teach many Jewish laws in Israel! I swear by the sacred service of the Temple[11] that I will not move from this spot until I have raised whatever ransom they want to get him released."

People say that Joshua did not budge from the spot until the ransom was collected, and a great sum paid for the child's release.

Within a few days, the boy was expounding Jewish law!

And who was this child?

Rabbi Ishmael ben Elisha.[12]

We haven't met Rabbi Ishmael yet in this book, and we won't be diving deeply into his story. I've included this narrative about him here because it offers another look at ancient Jewish attitudes towards Roman domination, and because of what it tells us about Rabbi Joshua. What's important to know about this boy, Ishmael, is that he will go on to be one of the leading rabbis of the next generation. He and another of Joshua's students, Rabbi Akiva, will both eventually develop foundational systems of interpretation of the Hebrew Bible and Jewish law—systems that will influence centuries of rabbinic knowledge and practice. As the twentieth-century rabbi Abraham Joshua Heschel put it: "Rabbi Ishmael and Rabbi Akiva, the two greatest [sages] of [their] generation, were nicknamed the 'Fathers of the World.' Each of them founded new approaches to the exegesis of Torah and established in Israel schools that bear their name."[13]

But apart from Ishmael's future destiny to be a crucially important rabbi, this story is also important because it shows us a side of Joshua's

---

11. In another version of this story, Joshua says, "I call heaven and Earth to witness against me that I will not move from this spot..." (*t. Hor.* 2:6).

12. *b. Git.* 58a. The translation is mine, and I have paraphrased the literal meaning in places for clarity. Another version of this story is found in *t. Hor.* 2.6.

13. Heschel, *Heavenly Torah*, 29.

Diplomacy, War, and Passing the Torch

character that we've encountered earlier in this book—specifically, his concern for people at the margins, people who might easily be given up on, but who Joshua felt deserved to be valued. We saw this side of Joshua in the story of the woman who approached Eliezer with a request to be accepted as a convert to Judaism, but whom Eliezer rejected when she revealed that her oldest son was the father of her youngest son. When she then went to Joshua, he accepted her. And we saw it in the story of the Ammonite who approached the Sanhedrin asking to be accepted as a convert to Judaism, only to be rejected by Gamaliel. But Joshua argued for a more flexible interpretation of the Jewish laws regarding who could be eligible to join the Jewish people, and successfully championed the Ammonite's admission as a proselyte. There's a teaching in the Mishnah that Joshua embodied, and it goes like this: "Don't disdain any person, and don't discard any thing; for there is no person who doesn't have their hour, and there is no thing that does not have its place."[14]

Let's turn now to another text involving Joshua and his dealings with the Roman Empire—a midrash, which I'll quote from Rabbi Binyamin La'u's translation:

> In the days of Rabbi Joshua ben Hananiah, the evil empire ordered the Temple to be rebuilt. Pappas and Lulianus [two Jewish leaders of the time who later would become martyrs] set tables from Acco as far as Antioch. They provided those who came up from exile with all their needs.
>
> Thereupon Samaritans[15] went and warned the emperor: "Be it known now unto the king that if this rebellious city be built and the walls finished, they will not pay tribute, poll-tax, or toll." [The Samaritans' warning is a quote from Ezra 4:13, which recounts an earlier period when, according to the biblical text, Samaritans wrote to the king of Persia in an attempt to thwart the rebuilding of the Temple in those times].
>
> Hadrian said to them: Yet what can I do, seeing as I have already given the order?
>
> They said to him: Send a command to them that they must change its site or add five cubits to it or lessen it by five cubits, and then they will withdraw from it of their own accord.

---

14. *m. Avot* 4:3 (translation mine).

15. The hostility between Jews and Samaritans of antiquity is a complicated subject beyond the scope of this book. Suffice it to say that we see it come up in both rabbinic and New Testament literature.

[Soon thereafter, t]he communities of Israel were assembled in the plain of Beit Rimon.¹⁶ When the royal dispatches arrived, they burst out weeping, and wanted to revolt against the Romans. The sages decided: let a wise man go forth and pacify the congregation. Let us send Rabbi Joshua ben Hananiah, for he is a master of Torah.

So, he went and expounded as follows:

A wild lion killed an animal, and a bone stuck in his throat.

The lion proclaimed: I will reward anyone who removes it.

An Egyptian heron, which has a long beak, came and pulled it out and demanded his reward. The heron said to the lion: Give me my reward.

The lion said: Be content that you are able to boast that you entered the lion's mouth in peace and came out in peace.

So too, [Rabbi Joshua said], let us be satisfied that we entered into dealings with this people in peace, and have emerged in peace. (Gen. Rab. 64)¹⁷

Joshua Podro takes this midrashic tale and others like it and observes:

> Joshua was ready to accept any compromise [with the Romans] that would avoid hostilities, and recorded his opinion that [a Roman offer that Jews could sacrifice in the Temple ruin but that the Temple would not be rebuilt] should be accepted as better than nothing, since it was permissible to sacrifice at the altar, even if it were not enclosed in a sanctuary.¹⁸

* * *

---

16. Located approximately 10 km north of Nazareth.

17. La'u, *The Sages: Character, Context, & Creativity*, Vol. 2, Kindle locations 6103–28. I've made slight adaptations to the translation for clarity's sake. The midrash collection La'u is citing, *Bereshit Raba*, is also knows as *Genesis Rabbah*. It so happens that there's another rabbinic tale, in *Deuteronomy Rabbah* 2.24, in which Rabbi Joshua and two other rabbis have traveled to Rome. While they are there, the emperor issues a decree to exterminate all the world's Jews after thirty days. The Jews' fate is spared thanks to the heroic self-sacrifice of a Roman official who revered God. I can't say whether the midrash that La'u has presented and the *Deuteronomy Rabbah* story "know" each other, but suffice it to say that rabbinic literature is full of stories that depict the Romans as posing an ongoing existential threat to the Jews.

18. Podro is referring to Rabbi Joshua's stated opinion in *m. Ed.* 8:6 that whether the Temple is standing or not, the sacrificial offerings can be made at the sacred sites and are valid. Podro, *The Last Pharisee*, 102–3.

Diplomacy, War, and Passing the Torch

Rabbinic literature includes multiple stories about the rising tensions between the surviving Jewish population and the Roman authorities in the decades following the Roman destruction of 70 C.E. Richard A. Horsley and John S. Hanson describe the times this way:

> Although the land was devastated and the holy city destroyed by the Romans, the passion for freedom did not die among the Jewish peasants. Nor was the apocalyptic spirit dead. Apocalyptic visions were still cultivated and the revelations written down, at least within intellectual circles. Visionaries . . . were clearly still waiting for God's intervention on behalf of the people. But among the peasantry in particular many refused to give up the active pursuit of the ideal of a just society, free of foreign domination and oppression.[19]

And of Rabbi Joshua's role during these years, the Israeli scholar Gedaliah Alon writes:

> Rabbi [Joshua's] moderate political stance, his spiritual, social, and political activity, his worldly wisdom, and his popularity among the people—all suggest that he was the appropriate person to try to persuade the highly emotional masses to control their rage and not break out in rebellion.[20]

Rabbi Joshua lived until just before the outbreak of the second major Jewish revolt against Rome in the Holy Land, the Bar Kokhba revolt (132–35 C.E.). In the last years of his life, he had to contend with the growing prospect of renewed warfare with Rome. The rabbis of his generation faced not only increasing resentment towards Rome, but also the ongoing hope that Roman policy would change and the Jews would be allowed to rebuild the Temple. Rumors swirled at times that Rome had given the go-ahead for construction to begin, but the orders never came.

The rabbis, along with many Jews of the time, also engaged in speculation and rumor-trading about when God planned to send the Messiah to redeem the Jews, defeat the Romans, rebuild the Temple, and begin a new era of justice and peace in the world. Joshua's student, Rabbi Akiva, was among the rabbis who taught that the Messiah would be coming soon,[21]

---

19. Horsley and Hanson, *Bandits, Prophets, and Messiahs*, 44–45.

20. Alon, *The Jews in their Land in the Talmudic Age*, quoted in La'u, *The Sages: Character, Context, & Creativity*, Vol. 2, Kindle location 6139.

21. *b. Sanh.* 97b.

and when he saw the achievements of the charismatic leader of a new rebel faction, Simon Bar Kokhba, he proclaimed Bar Kokhba to be the Messiah.[22]

This is a good moment for a brief recap of how Akiva and Joshua met in the first place. Akiva, who came late in life to the decision to study with the sages, started attending the academies of both Eliezer ben Hyrcanus and Joshua ben Hananiah. According to one story, for thirteen years Eliezer ignored Akiva at his academy, never even acknowledging him. Finally, Akiva got Eliezer's attention by besting him in a halakhic debate involving Akiva, Eliezer, and Joshua. After Akiva's triumph, Joshua turned to Eliezer and quoted a verse from the biblical book of Judges at him: "There is the army you sneered at—now go and fight it" (Judg 9:38). In other words, Joshua more or less said to Eliezer, "You've ignored this remarkable student for years, so it serves you right to be stunned by his awesome rabbinical debate skills. Good luck with your future debates with Akiva."[23] Ultimately, it is Rabbi Joshua who ordains Akiva as a rabbi.[24]

Though Joshua loved Akiva and took pride in his brilliance,[25] and though he would sometimes turn to Akiva to explain certain difficult Jewish legal issues,[26] he differed with Akiva about messianic expectations. Joshua taught that it was impossible to know when God would send the Messiah, and that the Jews were powerless to affect the timing of God's

---

22. *y. Ta'an.* 24a and *Lam. Rab.* 2.4. There's a point that should be made about the longstanding association of Rabbi Akiva with having proclaimed Bar Kokhba to be the Messiah. As Richard G. Marks writes, "R. Akiba's words about Bar Kokhba are few, appear in the form of legend and midrash, . . . and offer no historical references. We cannot even determine whether R. Akiba did in fact proclaim Bar Kokhba the Messiah. Even if we could accept the legends as historical evidence, we would still learn very little from them about the image R. Akiba actually held about Bar Kokhba—although contemporary scholars have tried to do so. The relevant question for us, however, is what the legends themselves mean as literature, as a memory . . ." Marks, *The Image of Bar Kokhba,* 16. This point bears repeating throughout this book. In some cases, longstanding traditional Jewish depictions of elements of the drama of the ancient rabbis are based on very little material from rabbinic texts. Later rabbinic commentators, like the medieval Jewish philosopher Isaac Abarbanel, discuss Akiva's mistaken embrace of Bar Kokhba as Messiah at length. In this book, I'm exploring the ways in which these disparate bits of narrative and legal debate—some long and some very short—have tended to be remembered collectively in rabbinic tradition as it has come to us over the course of two millennia.

23. *y. Pesah.* 6.3. For a translation and great discussion of this Akiva-Eliezer-Joshua story and others in rabbinic literature, see Holtz, *Rabbi Akiva: Sage of the Talmud,* 92–105.

24. *y. Sanh.* 6a.

25. *m. Sotah* 5.2.

26. *m. Pesah.* 9.6.

plan.[27] Not even massive collective repentance and good deeds could speed up the timeline. Interestingly, Joshua makes this claim in the course of a long debate with, you guessed it, Eliezer, who argues that in order to have the Messiah come, the Jews first have to repent fully. Eliezer brings one biblical proof text after another to make his case. Joshua counters with other biblical proof texts and insists that God's commitment to eventually redeem Israel and send the Messiah is unconditional, but that the timing of it is not going to be determined by the moral behavior of the Jews.[28]

Joshua wasn't alone in disagreeing with Akiva's messianic expectations. In a rabbinic text that depicts Akiva proclaiming Bar Kokhba to be the Messiah, another rabbi responds to Akiva as follows: "Akiva, grass will grow up through your cheekbones and still the son of David [the Messiah] will not yet have come."[29] Joshua, for his part, would likely have remembered the misery and insanity of Jerusalem during the Roman siege of 66–70 C.E., with Zealot factions ruling the militarily encircled city, terrorizing their own people into submission—a hopeless situation that became ever more desperate. Now, several decades later, he sought to avoid war. Unfortunately for Joshua, as he neared the end of his life, the prospects of revolt grew ominously strong. Here's how Podro describes the times:

> From the accession of Trajan to the outbreak of the Bar [Kokhba] revolt the Jews were suffering under what many of them mistook for the preliminary "pangs of the Messiah," and therefore tried to bring him to birth. The Yavneh peace party did what it could to restrain the people from armed revolt. . . . Joshua alone remained to preach reasonableness to his desperate people. The most difficult problem he had to face was the constant clamour for the rebuilding of the Temple. The Jews found it inconceivable that, of all the nations in the world, they alone should remain without a national sanctuary, and they regarded its destruction by Titus as a calamity that was by no means irreparable. Its reerection was assumed to be imminent. . . . The war party were convinced the Messiah must necessarily step forward without further delay to lead them, and that one consequence of their victory must be the rebuilding of the Sanctuary without either the consent or the approval of Rome. Joshua, like his disciples, did not doubt the ultimate salvation of Israel, but was convinced that God's hand could not be forced.

27. *b. Sanh.* 97b–98a.
28. *b. Sanh.* 97b–98a.
29. *y. Ta'an.* 24a and *Lam. Rab.* 2.4.

> He opposed the view that the Messiah would come as a result of warlike preparation, or even as a result of national repentance. . . . Many believed that the Great Day had already dawned, that deliverance was now only a matter of weeks or months.[30]

Joshua's memories of the war of 66–70 C.E. gave him plenty of reason to distrust militant, messianic Jewish movements. Let's return for a moment to the subject of that war, and the Roman siege of Jerusalem that Joshua lived through. Remember, during the course of that war, Joshua was a young student of Yohanan ben Zakkai's. He witnessed the rise of militarized, messianic movements among some of the fighting Jewish factions, and the horrific collapse that their zealotry brought upon Jerusalem. According to the post-war writings of the Jewish general-turned-Roman-collaborator, Josephus, during the course of the war, after initial success in driving the Romans out of Jerusalem, several different Jewish factions wrested control of the city and fought each other viciously.

Josephus describes a certain Menachem son of Judas the Galilean, who led an armed faction into Jerusalem and proclaimed himself king. Around the third year of the revolt, however, a largely peasant Jewish army led by a Galilean guerilla fighter, Simon bar Giora, took control of Jerusalem.[31] Like Rabbi Akiva and the followers of Bar Kokhba six decades later, Simon bar Giora's supporters believed that he was fulfilling messianic prophecies, and that through Simon God would not only defeat the Roman legions but also usher in a new social order that would permanently end all corruption and oppression.[32]

For the remainder of the war, Simon and a rival Jewish faction controlled different power centers in Jerusalem. Near the end, the Roman siege of the city ultimately led to the two factions banding together to fight the invaders, as desperation fueled panic and distrust among different Jerusalemites. Richard Horsley and John Hanson write that at this time "members of the high priestly families and other well-to-do citizens attempted to desert or even betray the Jews' cause to the Romans, especially as the prolonged siege brought famine and increased internecine strife."[33]

This was the grim and horrible situation that Joshua had lived through, that gave him the dread and caution he expressed towards Jewish leaders

---

30. Podro, *The Last Pharisee*, 98–100.
31. Horsley and Hanson, *Bandits, Prophets, and Messiahs*, 122–23.
32. Horsley and Hanson, *Bandits, Prophets, and Messiahs*, 122–23.
33. Horsley and Hanson, *Bandits, Prophets, and Messiahs*, 124.

Diplomacy, War, and Passing the Torch

who started generating renewed enthusiasm for another war against Rome several decades later. Horsley and Hanson write, "Rome had suppressed the revolt and the messianic movement led by Simon bar Giora, but Rome could not suppress messianic hopes and expectations. In fact, Jewish eschatological hopes seem now more exclusively focused on expectations of a messianic king as the central eschatological agent."[34] Joshua and many of the other surviving early rabbis knew firsthand that war was an untrustworthy and dangerous option, one that, once unleashed, could lead to many different kinds of chaos and unpredictable forms of tragedy. Unfortunately, Joshua wasn't able to prevent the war that was to come shortly after his death (approximately 131 C.E.). The contemporary scholar Ronald Eisenberg writes, "With Joshua ben Hananiah's death and the loss of his moderating influence, radical forces gained control and precipitated the disastrous Bar Kokhba revolt."[35]

In 132 C.E., sixty-six years after the outbreak of the previous revolt against Rome, Jewish guerilla fighters under the command of Bar Kokhba began attacking the Roman forces. After some early successes, Bar Kokhba's revolt ended in disaster, as Joshua had feared. The historian Lawrence H. Schiffman describes it like this:

> Within a short time [the fighting] had spread throughout the country, and the rebels took Jerusalem, which had not been heavily fortified by the Romans. It is possible that sacrifices were now reinstituted and that work was begun on rebuilding the sanctuary.
> ... Hadrian sent one of his finest generals, and he succeeded in turning the tide by means of a series of sieges, starving out the rebels in their strongholds and places of refuge. Jerusalem was retaken and future Jewish settlement there was prohibited by Hadrian. The last fortress to fall was Betar, not far to the southwest of Jerusalem, which was captured by the Romans during the summer of 136 C.E. By the end of the war many Jews had been massacred, the land had been devastated again, and distinguished rabbis had been martyred.[36]

Here's how the Bar Kokhba revolt was remembered in a midrash:[37]

---

34. Horsley and Hanson, *Bandits, Prophets, and Messiahs*, 127.

35. Eisenberg, *Essential Figures in the Talmud*, 136. I have altered Eisenberg's spelling of Bar Kokhba's name to conform to the spelling I have been using throughout this book.

36. Schiffman, *From Text to Tradition*, 173–74.

37. Most of the translation that follows is based on "Midrash Rabbah Lamentations

The Forgotten Sage

> Eighty thousand trumpeters besieged Betar where Bar Kozeba was located, who had with him 200,000 men, each with an amputated finger.

Let me interrupt the text to explain a couple things that may be puzzling some readers. First of all, this text refers to the rebel leader as "Bar Kozeba" rather than "Bar Kokhba." "Bar Kokhba," meaning "son of a star," was Rabbi Akiva's nickname for him because he believed him to be the Messiah and he connected him to a biblical verse that mentions a star— a verse that early rabbis associated with belief in a future Messiah (Num 24:17).[38] Throughout the Talmud, however, he is referred to by the name "Bar Kozeba," which can translate as "son of falsehood."[39] It's probable that "Bar Kozeba" was the historical real name of this person, as archeological findings seem to bear out. That said, some interpreters believe the name "Bar Kozeba" was the Talmudic editors' way of insulting the failed revolutionary leader and Messiah.

The other thing that may be raising eyebrows in this first bit of this text is the claim that Bar Kozeba had an army of 200,000 men who all had cut off one of their own fingers (the test you had to pass to show that you were tough enough to be one of Bar Kozeba's fighters). As far as the claim to having raised an army of 200,000, just as with numbers cited in some of the stories of the Bible, sometimes these claims in rabbinic literature totally strain credulity. What's important is that the story is asserting that Bar Kozeba's army was large and formidable. Given that in order to suppress the revolt, Hadrian had to send in legions from afar, led by Julius Severus, who had been stationed in Britain, it seems fair to say that however many soldiers Bar Kozeba commanded, it was a serious and initially successful fighting force. Okay, back to the midrash:

> The rabbis sent Bar Kozeba a message: "How long will you continue to make the men of Israel blemished?" [Bodily mutilation was forbidden under Jewish law.]

2.2.4," online at Livius.org at: http://www.livius.org/sources/content/rabbinical-literature/midrash-rabbah-lamentations-2.2.4/. The translation they present is based on that of A. Cohen in *Midrash Rabbah, Vol. 7*. I have made modifications to the translation for clarity and context.

38. The specific part of the verse that Akiva interpreted to refer to Bar Kozeba reads "A star will go forth from Jacob."

39. In fact, in the midrashic text we're examining now, we find an example of a rabbi saying that we should use the Hebrew word "falsehood" rather than the word "star" in reference to Bar Kozeba.

Diplomacy, War, and Passing the Torch

He asked them, "How else should my soldiers be tested?"

They answered, "Let anyone who cannot uproot a cedar from Lebanon [with their bare hands] be refused enrollment in your army."

Bar Kozeba accepted their advice, and began using their test. Another 200,000 men joined up with him, so that he had 200,000 men who had been tested by both methods.

But, at the time when they were going out to battle, they cried, "O God, neither help nor discourage us!" Thus, we find in Scripture [Ps 60:12]: "Isn't it so that You have rejected us, O God? And that God does not march with our armies?"

I'm interrupting the text again because it's a bit complicated, and because there are some strange things going on in it. First, we read that the rabbis voiced some disapproval towards Bar Kozeba's recruitment methods, although the text doesn't present the rabbis as opposed to Bar Kozeba's overall purpose. They warn him that bodily mutilation is contrary to God's laws, and Bar Kozeba accepts their critique and changes his recruitment test to the one they recommend instead. At this point, we might expect that Bar Kozeba and the rabbis had arrived on the same page, but then the very next thing we hear about Bar Kozeba's war cry shatters that fragile moment of seeming alignment with the rabbis.

Their battle cry calls upon God to neither help nor hinder them. If that doesn't sound to you like a typical ancient Israelite war cry, you're right—it isn't. In this midrash, perhaps the first foreshadowing clue that Bar Kozeba's fighters are not going to fare well is the narrating voice of the text stepping in to tell us that the soldiers' hubristic battle cry is a fulfillment of a verse in Psalms—a verse in which King David is lamenting that God does not seem to be fighting on his behalf.

Ancient rabbinic literature, like this midrash, was written for audiences that were assumed to know the Hebrew Bible backwards and forwards, including all the verses of the Psalm that our midrash has just stated is connected to Bar Kozeba's "God, please stay out of it" war cry. And those audiences would know that the verses that immediately follow the one in which David is lamenting that God is not fighting for his troops read like this: "O God, grant us your help against the enemy, for the help of man is worthless. With God we will triumph—God will trample our foes."[40] For Bar Kozeba's warriors to launch into battle with such hubris and lack of

---

40. Ps 60:13–14. Translation based on *Sefaria*, with some modifications by myself. Online at: https://www.sefaria.org/Psalms.60.13?lang=bi&with=all&lang2=en.

reliance on God to help them prevail is not an attitude that plays well in the rabbinic worldview.

There's another thing worth knowing about Bar Kozeba's odd war cry, and that is that it's connected to other Talmudic and Midrashic stories about other individuals who fought the Romans and might have succeeded, but they rejected the idea of asking for God's help and then died in horrifying ways. In one of these texts, the would-be Jewish heroes actually call out the same words as Bar Kozeba's men: "Oh God, neither help nor discourage us!" Their severed heads end up being brought to Hadrian.[41] In another text, a would-be Jewish hero with super-human strength is on the verge of getting the Roman emperor to surrender to him, but at the last moment he shuns the idea that he needs God's help and quotes the passage from Psalm 60:12 about God not taking part in battle on his behalf.[42] He dies when he visits an outhouse, sits on the toilet, and gets rectally attacked by a hidden snake. (Rabbinic literature is not for the faint of heart!)

To return the focus to the midrash we're examining now, the audiences for whom this midrash was intended would likely have been familiar with the trope of bold Jewish military leaders who use these particular words of arrogance ending up slain. Our midrash is signaling that something's not quite kosher about Bar Kozeba, even though he seems to be operating with the support of at least some of the rabbis. Let's get back to the text:

> And what was it that Bar Kozeba would do [that was so amazing]? He would catch the missiles fired from the enemy's catapults on one of his knees and hurl them back, killing many of the foe. And it is because of this superhuman feat that Rabbi Akiva made his remark [that this man was the Messiah].

Just a brief interruption of the text to note that the unnamed narrator of this midrash has just told us that there was a plausible reason for Akiva to have thought that Bar Kozeba was the Messiah. Perhaps the narrator wants to excuse what will come to be seen as Akiva's greatest mistake. Back to the text:

> For three-and-a-half years the emperor, Hadrian, surrounded Betar. In the city was Rabbi Elazar of Mode'in, who continually wore sackcloth and fasted, and used to pray daily: "Master of the universe, please don't sit in judgment today!" [The rabbi's prayers

---

41. *Lam. Rab.* 2.4.
42. *b. Git.* 57a.

Diplomacy, War, and Passing the Torch

were effective,] and on account of the rabbi's ongoing success, Hadrian became discouraged and thought of returning home.

A certain Samaritan went [to the emperor] and found him, and with regards to Rabbi Elazar of Mode'in, said: "My lord, so long as that old cock wallows in ashes, you will not conquer the city. But wait for me, because I will do something that will enable you to subdue it today."

He immediately entered the gate of the city, where he found Rabbi Elazar of Mode'in standing and praying. He pretended to whisper in the rabbi's ear. People went and informed Bar Kozeba: "Your friend, Rabbi Elazar of Mode'in, wishes to surrender the city to Hadrian."

Bar Kozeba ordered the Samaritan brought to him and asked: "What did you say to the rabbi?"

He replied: "If I tell you, the emperor will kill me; and if I don't tell you, you will kill me. It is better that I should kill myself and the secrets of the government be not divulged."

Bar Kozeba became convinced that Rabbi Elazar of Mode'in wanted to surrender the city, so when the rabbi finished his praying, he had him brought to him and asked him: "What did the Samaritan tell you?"

He answered: "I don't know what he whispered in my ear, nor did I hear anything, because I was standing in prayer and am unaware what he said."

Bar Kozeba flew into a rage, kicked him hard with his foot, and killed him.

A *bat kol* [Divine voice from heaven] then came forth and proclaimed these words from Scripture [Zech 11:17]: "Oh, the worthless shepherd who abandons the flock! Let a sword descend upon his arm and upon his right eye! His arm will shrivel up; his right eye will go blind."[43] The *bat kol* then added, "You have paralyzed the arm of Israel and blinded their right eye; therefore, your arm will wither and your right eye will grow dim!"

Immediately afterwards, the sins [of the people] caused Betar to be captured. Bar Kozeba was slain and his head taken to Hadrian.

Hadrian asked: "Who killed him?"

A Samaritan said to him: "I killed him."

"Bring his body to me," he ordered.

He went to do it, and found a snake encircling Bar Kozeba's neck.

---

43. Zech 11:17. Translation is partly mine, but primarily based on *Sefaria*, online at: https://www.sefaria.org/Zechariah.11.17?lang=bi.

So Hadrian, when told of this, exclaimed: "If his God had not slain him, who could have overcome him?"

Just how bad did the battle for Betar go after Bar Kozeba's fatal mistake of losing his temper and killing Rabbi Elazar of Mode'in, whose humility, prayer, and fasting had been the one thing keeping the settlement from being overrun by the Romans? Well, later in this same text, we read:

> The Romans slew the inhabitants of Betar until the horses waded in blood up to the nostrils, and the blood rolled along stones and flowed into the sea, staining it for a great distance.[44]

Shaye Cohen, a scholar of the ancient rabbis, describes a trend in rabbinic literature that depicts "the revolutionary leaders of the Jews," like Bar Kokhba, as "sinners and fools."[45] In her book, *Web of Life: Folklore and Midrash in Rabbinic Literature*, Galit Hasan-Rokem writes that this story of Bar Kokhba's defeat takes Jewish messianic hopes to "a maimed, beheaded despair."[46] For Rabbi Joshua's most famous pupil, Akiva, the worst was yet to come.

* * *

After the Bar Kokhba revolt, Hadrian imposed new humiliating and confining restrictions on the Jews in the land. Things also got dramatically worse for Akiva. You might remember from chapter 7 of this book the story describing the time Joshua and several of the other rabbis visited Eliezer at his deathbed. At one point, Eliezer remarks that he will be surprised if any of the visiting rabbis will die a natural death. Akiva then asks how his own death will be, and Eliezer responds that it will be worse than the others'. It was. The Babylonian Talmud tells the story of Akiva's death like this:

> Our Rabbis taught: Once the wicked Roman government issued a decree forbidding the Jews to study and practice the Torah. Pappus ben Judah came and found Rabbi Akiva publicly bringing gatherings together and occupying himself with the Torah.
> He said to him: "Akiva, are you not afraid of the Government?"
> Akiva replied: "Let me explain with a parable. A fox was once walking alongside of a river, and he saw fishes going in swarms from one place to another. He said to them: From what are you

---

44. I've modified the literal translation for clarity's sake.
45. Cohen, "The Destruction: From Scripture to Midrash," 28.
46. Hasan-Roken, Galit, *Web of Life*, 169.

Diplomacy, War, and Passing the Torch

fleeing? They replied: From the nets cast for us by men. He said to them: Would you like to come up on to the dry land so that you and I can live together in the way that my ancestors lived with your ancestors? They replied: Are you the one that they call the cleverest of animals? You are not clever but foolish. If we are afraid in the element in which we live, how much more in the element in which we would die! So it is with us. If such is our condition when we sit and study the Torah, of which it is written, 'For that is your life and the length of your days' (Deut 30:20),[47] if we go and neglect Torah how much worse off we will be!"

Soon afterwards Rabbi Akiva was arrested and thrown into prison, and Pappus ben Judah was also arrested and imprisoned next to him.

Akiva said to him: "Pappus, who brought you here?"

He replied: "Happy are you, Rabbi Akiva, that you have been seized for busying yourself with the Torah! Alas for Pappus who has been seized for busying himself with idle things!"

When Rabbi Akiva was taken out for execution, it was the hour for the recital of the *Shema*. While the Romans combed his flesh with iron combs, Akiva was accepting upon himself the kingship of heaven.

His disciples said to him: "Our teacher, [do you maintain your faith] even to this point?"

He said to them: "All my days I have been troubled by this verse, 'with all your soul,'[48] which I have understood to mean 'even if God takes your soul.' I would say to myself, 'When will I have the opportunity of fulfilling this duty?' Now that I have the opportunity, shall I not fulfill it?"

Akiva prolonged the last word of the *Shema* prayer[49]—the Hebrew word *ekhad*, meaning "one," until he died while saying it.

---

47. Akiva is quoting part of Deut 30:20. For context, here's more of the passage he's referencing, with Akiva's exact quote in italics: "I call heaven and Earth to witness against you this day: I have put before you life and death, blessing and curse. Choose life—if you and your offspring would live—by loving the Eternal your God, heeding God's commandments, and holding fast to God. *For that is your life and the length of your days* to dwell upon the soil that the Eternal swore to your ancestors, Abraham, Isaac, and Jacob." Deut 30:19–20, translation modified from *Sefaria*, online at: https://www.sefaria.org/Deuteronomy.30?lang=bi&aliyot=0.

48. Akiva is referring to Deut 6:5: "You shall love the Eternal One your God with all your heart, with all your soul, and with all your strength."

49. The *Shema*, which is probably the best-known prayer in Judaism, is based on words from Deut 6:4: "Listen, O Israel, the Eternal is our God, the Eternal is One."

The Forgotten Sage

A *bat kol* then proclaimed: "Happy are you, Akiva, that your soul has departed with the word *ekhad*!"

The ministering angels said before the Holy One, blessed be He: "This is Torah, and this is its reward? Shouldn't Akiva's death have come from Your hand, O God [i.e., a natural death], not at the hands of men?"[50]

God replied to them: "The reward of those who die a natural death is in life [as opposed to in the afterlife]."

A *bat kol* then proclaimed: "Happy are you, Rabbi Akiva, that you are destined for the life of the World to Come."[51]

There's so much going on in this text about Akiva, a giant of the Talmud, a hero of traditional Judaism, and the subject of many books. Like Akiva, Rabbi Ishmael also will go on to be remembered as one of the rabbinic greats. Both rabbis' methods of biblical interpretation and their respective personal stories—Akiva's especially—will go on to reverberate throughout traditional Jewish study and practice to this day. The martyrdom of Akiva will become a central trope of self-understanding and aspirational piety for future generations of Jews, especially during times of severe persecution in medieval Europe and elsewhere.[52] But Rabbi Akiva's story—and for that matter Rabbi Ishmael's—are beyond the scope of this book. One of the reasons I wanted to write this book is because Rabbi Joshua, the discoverer of both men's potential to become great sages, has gotten so much less attention within the tradition.

* * *

50. The ministering angels are quoting and referencing part of Ps 17:14 in the course of their sharp questioning of God over God's permitting Akiva's public torture and execution. The first-person speaker in Ps 17, King David, asks God to intervene to protect him from pitiless and arrogant surrounding enemies. David is presented as righteous and loyal to God's ways, as he calls on God to rescue him from the imminent, brutal danger of his foes. By quoting part of Ps 17, the angels are confronting God not only with their demand for an explanation of God's actions towards Akiva—they are also asking God to be accountable to this part of the Hebrew Bible. This is a good example of how Talmudic and Midrashic literature can pack very short phrases with multiple layers of meaning and allusion to other sacred texts.

51. *b. Ber.* 61b.

52. Modern scholars of early Christianity and rabbinic Judaism have also explored the parallels and differences between the martyrdom stories of Jesus and Akiva, both of whom were publicly tortured and executed by the Romans after refusing to cooperate with decrees banning their continued work teaching their respective understandings of Torah.

Diplomacy, War, and Passing the Torch

In this chapter we've covered some complex ground, so now I'd like to try to sum up. We started by looking at the many stories in rabbinic literature about Rabbi Joshua traveling to Rome and having conversations (and contests of wit) with Hadrian. As a diplomat, Joshua was both an emissary to Rome and a provider of wise and moderating counsel to the Jews as renewed calls for revolt against Roman rule grew louder. As Joshua grew old, the yearning for the arrival of the Messiah and the restoration of Jewish sovereignty and of the Temple intensified. In that context, we explored some of the connections between Joshua and two of his students, Akiva and Ishmael, who would go on to become far more famous and recognized for their impacts on rabbinic Judaism than Joshua.

If there is a moral to the stories of this chapter, or perhaps a running theme I would like to amplify, it is the way Joshua approached the issues of diplomacy and war, oppression and liberation in the decades after the Roman destruction of 70 C.E. Joshua Podro wrote, "Extremism, both during and after the war, was the curse of the nation."[53] It's hard to write gripping narratives about people who warn against extremism. Moderates are harder to romanticize than true believers who are ready to act.

And yet, Joshua's attitude towards the urge to messianic zealotry and violent revolution—his skepticism and his instinct towards caution—reflect a strong recurring trend in much of rabbinic literature.[54] Given that our world is still convulsing with religious sectarian violence, and given that too often throughout history religious zeal turns into organized campaigns of mass murder, Joshua's stance, and its echoes in other rabbinic literature, deserves our attention. The Talmud states, "When Rabbi Joshua died, good

---

53. Podro, *The Last Pharisee*, 48.

54. In his book, *Holy War and Judaism: The Fall and Rise of a Controversial Idea*, Reuven Firestone talks about how the early rabbis were heirs to the Hebrew Bible and its many, many stories depicting wars that God commanded the Israelites to fight, and the valorization of warriors like the biblical Joshua and King David. He uses the term "holy war" to describe any war that is fought by people believing that they are fighting because God wills them to, and he depicts the early rabbis as having to reckon with the horrifying losses and destruction that the Jews experienced in the aftermath of the two religiously inspired, holy wars that Jewish zealots led against Rome in 66 and 132 C.E. He writes: "For the survival of Jews and Judaism, [the ancient rabbis] engaged in certain exegetical strategies to prevent the dangerous wild card of holy war to be easily played. . . . [T]he rabbis of the Talmud . . . responded to the repeated catastrophic failures of military campaigns that were considered holy wars by their protagonists. They agreed that holy war was a genuine and perhaps even eternal divinely authorized institution, but they also made it virtually impossible for holy war to be an *operative* category in Judaism." (Italics are the author's.) Hammer, *Holy War and Judaism*, 3–4.

counsel and deliberate thought ceased."[55] Those are the personal attributes that informed Joshua's attitude towards war as a means of throwing off Roman oppression, and that helped influence rabbinic tradition as a whole.

The rabbinic texts on the ethics of war, unsurprisingly, are full of differing opinions and don't provide a single set of rules that apply clearly to all situations. Rabbinic literature prizes the pursuit of peace as a core value,[56] though the same body of literature also discusses many situations in which people have the right—and sometimes the obligation—to defend themselves by force of arms or even launch a war.[57] Overall, I would describe the sum total of rabbinic teaching about the ethics of war as one that deeply distrusts war but regards it as sometimes necessary. Former President Obama once famously said, "I don't oppose all wars. What I am opposed to is a dumb war. What I am opposed to is a rash war."[58] Over the years, I have come to think of this Obama quote as something Rabbi Joshua could have said, as well as many rabbis who lived after him. When it comes to zealous calls to arms, the overall attitude of the rabbinic tradition is cautious and concerned, for both moral and pragmatic reasons.

For sure, it is possible to cherry pick quotes from the Talmud to make the rabbis look either like warmongers or pacifists, like heartless ethnic chauvinists or altruistic universalists. But cherry-picking quotes violates the very nature of rabbinic literature, which is a literature of debates and multiple takes on the same questions. When we look at the full body of rabbinic sacred literature—the Talmud, Midrash, and even medieval legal codes—what seems to emerge is a general attitude towards questions of war and the use of force, an attitude that is often deeply skeptical of those advocating for war without being ideologically pacifist.

There are others in the mix of the debate, of course—rabbis who are more ready to dehumanize the enemies of the Jews and support violence, and those quite horrified at the loss of even a single human life by means of violence. What I am describing is the broad middle ground that has tended to form the basis of mainstream rabbinic attitudes towards the use of force. (At least, such was the case until the alarming recent growth of radical writings on war and the valorizing of violence-towards-enemies that have

---

55. *b. Sotah* 49b.

56. See, for example, *Num. Rab.* 19.27, *Lev. Rab.* 9.9, *m. Avot* 1.12, *m. Sanh.* 4.5, and many other texts.

57. See, for example, *m. Sotah* 8.7, *b. Sanh.* 20b, and *b. Sotah* 44b.

58. Obama made these remarks in 2002, when he was a state senator in Illinois.

emerged from many rabbis of the religious-nationalist far right in Israel and their supporters abroad.)

For the better part of nineteen centuries, the rabbis were leaders of a nation without an army, a nation thrown into exile and reliant upon the willingness of various host nations (with armies) to tolerate their presence. They witnessed not only the horrible failures of Jewish military campaigns against Rome, but also the misery and cruelty of wars that took place in the many different lands where Jews in the diaspora came to settle. In much rabbinic writing on war—by which I mean rabbinic writing from ancient times to modern—there is a general fear or dread of war, a worry that war rarely works out well for the Jews, and a belief that it desecrates the Divine image within human beings. And yet, as I've said, what you won't find in the ancient rabbinic texts is a full-on anti-war ethical stance. Reticence and caution about war, yes, but straight up pacifism, no.[59]

Rabbi Joshua was among the most important post-Roman-destruction-era rabbis to express this cautious approach. It is possible that had Bar Kokhba's revolt succeeded in establishing a long period of Jewish independence, rabbinic tradition would have validated Akiva's mistaken belief that Bar Kokhba was the Messiah. It is possible that the repeated crushing defeats at the hands of Rome served as the primary reason for the general rabbinic tendency towards pragmatic pacifism. But before history had the chance to prove Joshua's instincts right, he advised his people to be wary of extremism and skeptical of war as a means of liberation.

---

59. In a review of Richard G. Marks's book, *The Image of Bar Kokhba in Traditional Jewish Literature: False Messiah and National Hero*, Joel Kaminsky writes, "Marks' meticulous reading of the Jewish texts that discuss Bar Kokhba leads one to the conclusion that the tradition neither promotes a total rejection of political and military action, nor does it advocate an outright endorsement of Jewish militancy, but rather it counsels the informed reader that political action will only succeed when it is in accord with the divine will. Inasmuch as the divine will is often difficult to discern accurately, one must be wary of being led astray by false prophets and messiahs." Kaminsky, "Reviewed Work: The Image of Bar Kokhba in Traditional Jewish Literature".

9

Don't Trust This Book— It Could Be Wrong

In this book, I've presented a composite portrait of an ancient rabbi, Joshua ben Hananiah, and of a small group of sages who lived roughly within the same hundred years. I have pieced that narrative together out of episodes and story fragments that appear across a wide range of ancient Jewish texts. There is no single ancient rabbinic text, however, that presents the story that I've told as a coherent narrative. As the contemporary scholar, William Scott Green, writes, "The literature of rabbinic Judaism offers no coherent or systematic biographies of its important sages. Indeed, unlike other religious systems of late antiquity, rabbinic Judaism seems to have produced no hagiographies, no lives of 'holy men' and no literary form uniquely suited to that enterprise."[1]

The truth is that scholars of rabbinic Judaism could easily challenge the validity of the biographical portraits I've sketched in this book, and some might object to the very attempt to present *any* biographical sketches of the ancient rabbis. I take seriously the words that Green wrote in the preface to his scholarly work, *The Traditions of Joshua ben Hananiah*:

> When, as a graduate student, I began systematically to study the rabbinic materials about Joshua ben Hananiah, my goal was a critical biographical study of this important first-century master and an historical assessment of his role in the creation of rabbinic

---

1. Green, *The Traditions of Joshua ben Hananiah*, 1–2.

Don't Trust This Book—It Could Be Wrong

Judaism. A reputed disciple of Yohanan ben Zakkai and purveyor of his counterfeit coffin[2] beyond Jerusalem's boundaries; the apparent catalyst, if not agent, of the ouster of Gamaliel II; an alleged emissary of the Jews to Rome; senior colleague and perhaps teacher of [Rabbi Akiva]; Joshua lived at the center of events decisive in Judaism's history, and the study of his life and career seemed an ideal entry into the world of rabbinism's formation....
The project's principal focus was on the discovery and description of the historical Joshua, and that perspective informed my doctoral dissertation, an analysis of Joshua's early legal rulings, which was to be the first stage of the work. Subsequent examination of Joshua's materials and attention to the results of [Green's mentor] Jacob Neusner's research . . . made the assumptions which had shaped my approach to the problem seem naïve and self-serving and forced me to rethink the enterprise of rabbinic biography.[3]

The operating assumption behind this book is that it *is* possible to offer readers a composite biographical sketch of Joshua ben Hananiah, not as an *historical* figure, but as a key *mythic* figure in the best-known Talmudic and Midrashic stories depicting the Roman destruction of the Second Temple and the first decades of rabbinic rebuilding that followed. Another assumption of this book is that it is worthwhile for readers to know about the Rabbi Joshua stories as an important dramatic component of rabbinic literature's mythic landscape, fragmented though the stories may be.

And, in support of this book's premise, I'm happy to report that many Talmud scholars—academics as well as rabbis—agree that the Talmud's scattered tales about Joshua, Eliezer, and the first generations of rabbis at Yavneh *do* represent a genuine mythic origins story of the early rabbis. Daniel Boyarin, for example, argues that the Talmud intentionally offers its readers a coherent epic story about the rabbis of Joshua's generation, comprised of "interlocking Babylonian rabbinic narratives distributed throughout the Talmud...."[4]

Boyarin writes that the Talmud's various Yavneh legends collectively form a grand mythic origins story[5] built into the final, edited and

---

2. I can't resist this aside: I love the phrase "counterfeit coffin," and I think it would make a great alt-rock band name.
3. Green, *The Traditions of Joshua ben Hananiah*, ix.
4. Boyarin, "The Yavneh-Cycle of the Stammaim," 246–47.
5. Boyarin, "The Yavneh-Cycle of the Stammaim," 272. Boyarin uses the phrase "Babylonian talmudic mythopoesis" to describe this phenomenon.

published version of the Babylonian Talmud (Boyarin specifically argues that this claim applies to the Babylonian Talmud, and not the less studied Jerusalem Talmud. For those unfamiliar with the difference between the two Talmuds, see the footnote below).[6] As he sees it, the final editors of the Babylonian Talmud included and shaped these stories in order to cement into Jewish consciousness the great drama of how the rabbis of the Yavneh generation struggled with each other mightily over issues of rabbinic authority and decision-making processes, and how their struggle ended with Divine affirmation of rabbinic pluralism and endless disputation.[7]

Joshua and his supporters defeat Eliezer and even God in the dispute over Akhnai's oven, and in the end, God chuckles with affection and accepts the rabbis' majority-rule, democratic system of deciding sacred matters, and from that point forward rabbinic Judaism becomes a system that welcomes debate, including unresolved debate, and preserves minority opinions. It is important to note that Boyarin is not saying that these stories really took place, nor is he asserting that we can be certain that the rabbis of Joshua's generation actually established the kind of debate-oriented, democratic rabbinic Judaism that these stories claim they did. Rather, he thinks that the final editors of the Babylonian Talmud, around 500 C.E., selected, shaped, and wove these stories into the Talmud because *they* believed in a rabbinic Judaism with an "ideology of endless dispute for its own sake, or a divinely justified *polynoia* (multiple mindedness, as opposed to single minded interpretation of sacred texts and beliefs)."[8]

Here's a bit of Boyarin on this subject in his own words:

---

6. There are two different Talmuds. The lesser known, and less influential, Talmud is known as the Jerusalem Talmud, or sometimes the Palestinian Talmud. It was written and edited by ancient rabbis who lived in different parts of what is now mainly northern and central modern Israel. The far more influential Talmud was compiled in rabbinic academies in Babylon (present-day Iraq). Often when scholars write about "The Talmud" they are really referring to the Babylonian Talmud. Boyarin argues that the Babylonian Talmud was ultimately edited and shaped by rabbis who valued rabbinic argument and unresolved disputation as a sacred foundation of Judaism, whereas the editors of the Jerusalem Talmud seem more interested in presenting rabbinic arguments as being resolved one way or another.

7. Boyarin, "The Yavneh-Cycle of the Stammaim," 281. There Boyarin writes of "the canonized, theologically sanctioned undecidability of the Babylonian Talmud, as symbolized in the legends of 'Yavneh'...."

8. Boyarin, "The Yavneh-Cycle of the Stammaim," 247. Italics are the author's. I added in the parenthetical definition of the word "polynoia."

Don't Trust This Book—It Could Be Wrong

I wish to claim the narrative of the excommunication of Rabbi Eliezer to be a moment of rabbinic mythopoetic historiography, connected via literary allusion to the narrative of Rabbi Joshua, a narrative within which the Babylonian Talmud remembers its own history, producing a diachronic myth of origins, one that not only describes the structure of the present sociocultural system but that narrates its development, as well. . . . [T]exts like this do not represent the "actual" past, but they do represent a mythic memory of change within the cultural system, a cultural memory that is interesting in its own right for presenting the structure of cultural practice. In this case the narrative records, as it were, a historical shift from a regime of orthodoxy/heresy to a regime of control via a defanging of controversy of the power to subvert.[9]

The final compilers and editors of the Babylonian Talmud are known in rabbinic tradition, as well as in academic study, as the *stammaim* (plural of the singular, *stam*, meaning the unnamed narrating and organizing voice of the Talmud, as we have learned in earlier chapters of this book). For Boyarin, the stories surrounding Rabbi Joshua, or the "Yavneh-cycle" as he refers to them, represent the *stammaim* generation's effort to validate *their* own beliefs about how rabbinic Judaism should work and *their* system of practicing it. He writes:

> [The Talmud's depiction of] Yavneh as a "grand coalition" in which everybody in Jewish antiquity who wasn't an outright "heretic" was a Rabbi, and all opinions were equally "Torah" was . . . [a] belated talmudic invention. This late moment of literary crystallization was the juncture at which the "agreement to disagree" was raised to a theological and hermeneutical principle of the highest order, indeed, to a divine institution.[10]

Boyarin offers historical theories for why the *stammaim* in the Babylonian rabbinic academies of the late 400s and early 500s C.E. favored a rabbinic Judaism that "raises ever-unresolved dialectic to the level of a divine principle."[11]

I'm not going to go into those historical reasons here, but I would like to explore further Boyarin's description of the powerful purpose that the stories of the Yavneh cycle achieve—stories that Boyarin refers to as "the

---

9. Boyarin, "The Yavneh-Cycle of the Stammaim," 274.
10. Boyarin, "The Yavneh-Cycle of the Stammaim," 281.
11. Boyarin, "The Yavneh-Cycle of the Stammaim," 281.

talmudic epic before us."[12] Boyarin writes about the struggle that the rabbis of the first five centuries following the Roman destruction faced to win their place as the sole legitimate heirs to the religion of ancient Israel. They had to compete with the increasingly powerful church, to be sure, but they also had to compete with other Jewish, non-rabbinic communities. They had to compete with rabbinic leaders who preferred a version of rabbinic Judaism that strictly followed the rulings and beliefs of specific teachers and left no major questions of law or belief unresolved in debate. And they had to compete with the periodic rise of Jewish figures making messianic claims about themselves and seeking to build a following.

Boyarin claims that the epic drama that we've been examining in this book valorizes the overturning of one post-Roman-destruction rabbinic order and its replacement with a much better rabbinic order.[13] Did these events really take place? Nobody knows. What we have before us in these texts is myth-making and the creation of a sacred memory that provided the *stammaim* "a myth of foundation that represents the bad old days that it displaced and replaced."[14] In the part of the epic story in which Rabban Gamaliel humiliates Rabbi Joshua repeatedly and is finally overthrown by the rabbis of the Sanhedrin, several principles get affirmed as part of the new, more enlightened order that has replaced "the bad old days."

Remember, back in chapter 5 of this book, we read about how Gamaliel had severely restricted who among the rabbis and their students could enter the House of Study, but when he was deposed, they opened up the halls to hundreds more rabbis.[15] Gamaliel had also tried to stamp out dissent against his halakhic rulings, even when such dissent was only privately held and privately discussed among rabbis.[16] That regime was also overthrown. By the time we reach the end of the Akhnai's oven story and the great battle between Joshua and Eliezer, the regime change is complete.

Boyarin writes that Rabbi Joshua's victory in the Akhnai's oven dispute

> represents an instance of that complete take-over of religious life and practice via the Oral Torah [one of rabbinic Judaism's terms for its many opinions and debates]. Not even God, not even the angels can compete with the Rabbis and their Torah. The Torah is

---

12. Boyarin, "The Yavneh-Cycle of the Stammaim," 260.
13. Boyarin, "The Yavneh-Cycle of the Stammaim," 259–60.
14. Boyarin, "The Yavneh-Cycle of the Stammaim," 260.
15. *b. Ber.* 28a.
16. *b. Rosh Hash.* 25a and *b. Bekh.* 36a.

Don't Trust This Book—It Could Be Wrong

no longer in heaven. It is on earth in the possession of the rabbinic institution.... Rabbinic Judaism thus represents a particular episteme[17] of power/knowledge. In the face of the perceived failure of dialectic to produce consensus, it seeks to effect a transfer of authority and of control over discourse from heaven ... to Earth, the allegedly God-given authority of the majority of Rabbis.[18]

So, if scholars like Boyarin are certain that the Rabbi Joshua/Yavneh stories I've presented in this book really do represent a foundational mythic epic story of how rabbinic Judaism came to acquire its character, and that it's legitimate to claim that the "Rabbi Joshua" character found in those scattered Talmudic tales can be discussed as a bona fide literary figure of the mythos of rabbinic Judaism, why am I going out of my way to raise doubts about those basic premises?

Well, partly because there is still an ongoing debate among scholars about how far you can go with the construction of mythic biographies of the figures of the Talmud, given that the Talmud is such a vast collection of centuries worth of legal debates and anecdotes, reflecting more contexts and agendas than can be counted. And partly because I think if I've learned anything from the rabbis who championed debate, majority rule, and open defiance of direct interference from heaven in the messy task of trying to decide the law in community, it is that *to doubt one's own beliefs is a virtue*. To say, "I could be wrong" is a *mitzvah*, a worthy act, even a necessary one. What's more, for a group or community to say, "We're going to discuss a question together, study together, debate what we should do, and then vote on it, understanding that we might be wrong"—to say *that* means needing to always keep some doubt active in your mind.

There's another big reason why I feel I have to question the basic assumption I'm relying on that there really is a literary "Joshua ben Hananiah" who emerges from the various stories and debates in which he appears in rabbinic literature, and that is that there are Rabbi Joshua stories in rabbinic literature that seem disconnected from any kind of coherent narrative about Joshua and the other sages at Yavneh. In some cases these stories even go against the grain of the character portraits I've presented about these rabbis. It may scandalize you to hear that I didn't include any of these potentially "contrarian" texts in the earlier chapters of this book.

---

17. For those not familiar with this term, it more or less means a foundational framework for all knowledge, or a body of ideas that shapes the knowledge of the times.

18. Boyarin, "The Yavneh-Cycle of the Stammaim," 269.

The Forgotten Sage

Why wouldn't I have included them? Several reasons: 1) In some cases, I didn't know about them (the rabbinic literature is so vast I may have missed some relevant texts, particularly texts in lesser known works); 2) some of these texts seemed to me to have no bearing upon what I perceived as an emergent portrait of Joshua in the Talmudic and Midrashic literature, so I may have wrongly dismissed them in a kind of confirmation bias; and, 3) some of these texts may be part of alternative traditions about Rabbi Joshua's character and personality—texts that may have emerged side-by-side with the "humane and humble Joshua" texts I've been presenting in this book. Remember, many rabbinic texts appear to have developed centuries after the eras in which the rabbis depicted in them lived.

There is no getting around the fact that rabbinic literature frequently offers varying or contradictory legal and narrative texts, and I have assumed the role of deciding which bunches of texts together give us as readers some stories and patterns that are "dominant," and others that are outliers and "exceptions." Maybe I've been incorrect in my assessments.

William Scott Green points out another problem in the effort to construct a rabbinic biography from these thousands of texts spanning many centuries of transmission, retransmission, editing, and scribal enhancements. Often in rabbinic debates about *halakhah*—especially in the earliest work of rabbinic literature, the Mishnah—the debates are presented in a format in which an unnamed narrator poses a legal question or simply introduces a legal topic. We'll then be told what Rabbi A and Rabbi B had to say on the matter (and maybe even Rabbis C, D, and E), and then the narrator might say "and the Sages ruled X." Alternatively, there will sometimes be an anonymous opinion presented first, followed by one or more named rabbis expressing dissenting opinions.

Generally speaking, in the Mishnah, the opinion of the majority of the rabbis would simply be presented without the name of the specific rabbi who may have made the argument for that opinion.[19] Unlike a U.S. Supreme Court decision, the Mishnah doesn't present majority opinions with

---

19. The assumption that the unnamed opinion should always be assumed to be the majority view is an oversimplification on my part. While this is generally a reliable operating assumption, there is also a rabbinic tradition that the unnamed opinions are the opinions of specific rabbis. In the case of the earliest written rabbinic work, the Mishnah, there's a tradition that the rabbi credited with being the compiling editor of the Mishnah, Judah ha-Nasi, is actually the *stam*—the anonymous narrating voice—of that text, and that sometimes the Mishnah's anonymously stated opinions represent his personal views and not necessarily the majority view.

Don't Trust This Book—It Could Be Wrong

"Rabbi So-and-So, writing for the majority, says . . ." The named rabbis in these legal-dispute texts typically represented the minority viewpoints that were not established as normative Jewish law, but which were preserved in the record for reasons I've described earlier in this book.

Green attempted to do a study of all of Rabbi Joshua's recorded halakhic opinions, perhaps in the same way that a law student in the U.S. today might write a dissertation seeking to describe the legal philosophy of a Supreme Court justice of the past by reviewing all of their legal opinions and pointing out key patterns. But then he realized that many of Joshua's legal opinions may have been the unnamed, majority opinions presented in rabbinic texts anonymously.[20] The detective work he had planned to do to review the totality of Joshua's legal rulings, and thus provide readers with a compelling portrait of his legal philosophy—his "halakhic personality" if you will—became hopelessly impossible due to the conventions of rabbinic legal literature.

Green also writes that other tendencies in rabbinic literature serve to undermine any certainty we can have that the legal opinions attributed to a particular rabbi actually were that rabbi's opinion:

> [Rabbinic] attributions also are suspect because of the collective character of rabbinic literature and the apparent importance of disciple-circles in the transmission of rabbinic materials. It is not unusual for the disciples of a teacher to perceive in or derive from his teachings and then to attribute to him positions he did not hold but which are consonant with other teachings of his or with their own contemporary concerns. It therefore cannot automatically be supposed that all views assigned to a given master actually originate with him. Specific opinions may be interpretations or inventions of the followers of a particular sage. The names attached to specific sayings consequently may not represent an individual at all, but rather a group or circle which identified itself with a particular master or others who adhered to his teachings.[21]

The same uncertainty about a rabbi's legal opinions applies to narratives featuring specific rabbis. While I honestly believe that the series of stories we have explored in this book really do represent prominent storylines that are foundational to rabbinic Judaism's mythic understanding of its origins, the fact remains that there are also instances in which there are

---

20. Green, *The Traditions of Joshua ben Hananiah*, 11.
21. Green, *The Traditions of Joshua ben Hananiah*, 9.

differing accounts of stories that I have included here, sometimes reflecting very different memories or oral traditions about the personalities and events making up the mythical world of rabbinic Judaism. It's not hard to find a text in Talmud or Midrash that would present a contrary take on the rabbinic personality sketches I've included in these pages.

For example, I've presented readers with a string of stories and halakhic debates in which Rabbi Joshua consistently offers a more flexible, universalist, humanitarian, and pragmatic view than his opponents, most especially Rabbi Eliezer. But if I wanted to present a contrary tradition about Joshua, there are several I could choose from.

For instance, there is a long Talmudic tale[22] in which a Roman emperor and Joshua are arguing about a scientific matter, and the emperor asserts that he must be right because the renowned sages of Athens support his view. Joshua replies, "We [rabbis] are wiser than they." The emperor then challenges Joshua to engage the sages of Athens in debate and defeat them in order to prove which group is wiser.

Joshua accepts the challenge, on the condition that the emperor follow his instructions for setting up the contest. His condition is that the emperor have a ship built, with sixty separate compartments (a detail that is relevant to a complex part of the story I'm skipping over). The emperor agrees and orders the construction of Joshua's peculiar ship.

Then Joshua travels to Athens, where he outwits an ordinary resident in order to find out the highly secret location of where these sages hold their meetings. Next, he outwits the guards who prevent outsiders from accessing the sages (which, unfortunately, results in the guards being put to death for their incompetence—apparently the sages of Athens were pretty tough customers.) When he finally stands face to face with the sages, he proposes a contest of wits. If they win, they can do whatever they want to him (presumably they'll kill him). If he wins, they have to get on board the ship he has had built.

The next phase of the story presents a showdown of riddles. Joshua solves all the riddles the Athenians put towards him, thoroughly confounding them. He even uses his ability to invoke God's supernatural powers to best them in a couple instances. Conceding their defeat, the sages of Athens board the ship and sail to Rome. The emperor meets them and finds them wanting, and he declares that Joshua can do with them as he pleases. Joshua then sets them up so that they think they are setting sail to return to

---

22. *b. Bekh.* 8b–9a.

Don't Trust This Book—It Could Be Wrong

Athens, but he devises a trap that results in all of them dying a drawn-out, excruciating death aboard ship.

This is a strange story, and it seems very out of character for the Joshua who one major scholar of rabbinic literature described as having a reputation that "spoke of his sagacity, his political moderation, and his profound humanity ... coupled with a certain homespun quality ...."[23] It is possible that this story developed initially without any attribution to Joshua, but then as the Talmud's editors were shaping the version we have before us, they may have thought, "Who is a rabbi who traveled a lot to Rome and had lots of conversations with the emperor? We know—Joshua ben Hananiah!" And so the story got attached to his name.

Or, it is possible that the tale is part of a well-established Joshua story tradition that I have not delved into in this book—his public debates and contests of wits with early Jewish-Christians.[24] Some scholars think that the "Sages of Athens" story is actually about early Christians, with the Athenians serving as euphemistic stand-ins for Christians. The stories about Joshua going head to head with "sectarians," as early rabbinic writings often referred to the first generations of Jewish-Christians, share a number of common features. They often involve contests of magic as well as wits. They often depict Joshua and other Jews being threatened with death, but by prevailing in these showdowns Joshua saves the Jews from harm. And they often depict the "sectarians" getting killed.

Here's another example, in a paraphrased translation:

> Rabbi Joshua ben Hananiah was standing in Ceasar's house. A certain apostate made a physical gesture at him whose meaning was that Joshua's people was a people God had turned His face away from. Rabbi Joshua responded with a gesture whose meaning was that God's arm continues to be outstretched over His people.
>
> Then, Ceasar said to Joshua, "What was that all about?"
>
> Joshua replied, "He gestured at me saying that I belong to a people that God has turned His face away from, and I gestured at him saying that God's arm remains outstreched over my people."
>
> About the same time, some of Ceasar's people asked the sectarian, "What did you gesture to him?"

---

23. Alon, *The Jews in Their Land in the Talmudic Age*, 440.

24. For an interesting overview of key rabbinic texts involving the conflicts and complexities of the relationship between the early rabbinic community and some of the various Jewish-Christian groups of the period, see Gedaliah Alon's *The Jews in Their Land in the Age of the Talmud*, chapter 13: "Jewish Christians: The Parting of the Ways."

He answered, "I gestured that he belongs to the people that God has turned His face away from."

They then asked, "And what did he gesture to you?"

He replied, "I don't know."

They said to him, "A person who doesn't know what others' gestures mean dares to make gestures in the presence of the king?!"

Then they took him away and executed him.[25]

Joshua was so strongly associated with being one of the leading sages who could successfully defeat Jewish-Christians in debate that the Talmud tells the following story of a group of rabbis visiting him at his deathbed:

> When Rabbi Joshua ben Hananiah was dying, the sages said to him, "What will become of us because of the threat of the heretics, when there is no scholar like you who can refute them?"
>
> He replied by quoting a verse from Jeremiah: "Has counsel perished from the prudent? Has their wisdom vanished?" (Jer 49:7). He then explained, "Since counsel has perished from the prudent—from the Jewish people—the wisdom of the nations of the world has vanished as well, and there will be no superior scholars among them.[26]

* * *

Talmudic and Midrashic literature is a birds' nest of crisscrossing narratives, narrative fragments, legal debates, technical terms, and other types of literature, compiled over several centuries. It includes extended portrayals of certain sages that are fairly consistent, but it is also riddled with countertraditions and alternative portrayals. Some of these alternative texts may come from ancient rabbinic traditions that were not even aware of the more popular stories and personality portraits of the most famous sages of the Talmud.

Furthermore, in rabbinic literature, attributions of legal opinions or stories to specific rabbis are always subject to some questioning. Rabbis who give one particular legal opinion in one version of a debate sometimes give a different opinion in the same debate as it is represented in another rabbinic text, or else a different text presents the same debate but puts the

---

25. *b. Hag.* 5b—my paraphrased translation, relying in part on *Sefaria's* translation, online at: https://www.sefaria.org/Chagigah.5b.4?lang=bi.

26. *b. Hag.* 5b—translation largely based on *Sefaria*, online at: https://www.sefaria.org/Chagigah.5b?lang=bi. I've modified their translation a bit for clarity's sake.

Don't Trust This Book—It Could Be Wrong

same opinion in the mouth of a different rabbi. Rabbinic literature invites us, as its audience, to follow strong storylines as they develop and emerge out of its thousands of pages, but it also asks us not to hold too firmly to those story lines. So again, I say, please don't trust this book—or perhaps, rather, I should say: please give a fair hearing to those scholars of rabbinic literature who would question or refute the claims contained in these pages.

10

Why This Rabbi Matters Now

There are a lot of reasons that I am fascinated with the rabbinic literary figure of Joshua ben Hananiah. He survived the mass murder and exile of his people and the physical destruction of its homeland and sacred places. He stood up to the likes of Gamaliel, Eliezer, and even God in the course of rabbinic debate, and he defended the messiness and uncertainty of the rabbinic method of sacred argument against claims of absolute certainty, even claims backed up by miracles and a voice from the heavens.

In the years following the Roman destruction, he advocated for an approach to Jewish survival that maintained important ties to the past but chartered a creative and meaningful path forward. He helped craft the Jewish transition from one form of religious worship to another, and was happy to learn from others in the process. He rejected asceticism and endless mourning as a way of coping with national trauma. While he was through and through an ancient rabbi, and therefore he subscribed to traditional rabbinic beliefs about Israel's chosenness, he nevertheless taught that righteous people of other religions also had a share in the World to Come. And in the spirit of the great sage Hillel, he welcomed prospective converts that Eliezer and others rejected out of hand.

Though his people had become the disempowered and oppressed victims of an imperial giant, he pursued an approach to resistance to Roman domination that was simultaneously compassionate, determined, pragmatic, patient, and accepting of that which could not realistically be changed. He rejected messianic and militant zealotry, instead opting for a

Why This Rabbi Matters Now

realistic and religiously creative long-term survival strategy. On top of all that, he was ugly and poor, yet kind-natured, unselfish, and assertive when necessary. I love brave, principled, sympathetic underdogs, and Joshua more than fits the bill.

Fixed, Diminishing Torah vs Generative, Growing Torah

I also love Joshua ben Hananiah because of the role he plays as a proponent of a forward-looking, creative rabbinic Judaism in which human beings play a major role in the ongoing development of the laws and beliefs of their religion. He fends off two rabbinic heavyweights—Gamaliel and Eliezer—who, each for their own reasons, sought to shut down free-flowing rabbinic interpretation and debate.

As we saw in chapter 4 of this book, Gamaliel tried to unify the system of *halakhah* across the newly dispersed global Jewish community. But while he purported to preside over a centralized system of rabbinic debate and majority rule, he also tried to rig the system so that he maintained personal control over which rabbis could take part in the debates, humiliating perceived rivals like Joshua and shutting hundreds of rabbis and students out of the process.

In the story of Akhnai's oven, we saw that Rabbi Eliezer tried to force the rabbinic community to accept the idea that if a rabbi could show beyond doubt that he knew the correct interpretation of the law (like by summoning miracles to back him up), then the debates and majority opinions of the rabbis should be set aside. Eliezer also framed Torah as a closed system of knowledge that begins full and pure, but gets diminished and distorted in each successive generation, as we'll see further on in this chapter in a text we'll explore.

Joshua countered both Gamaliel's and Eliezer's efforts to control or thwart the emerging system of rabbinic debate, majority rule, and the preservation of minority views for possible use by future generations. In the face of their challenges, Joshua held firm in service of an adaptive Judaism that would grow in complexity over time, even though it would be vulnerable to the rabbis making mistakes in their majority opinions.

Joshua wasn't the only rabbi of his time to stand up to Gamaliel's and Eliezer's visions of rabbinic Judaism, and he isn't the rabbi who is most celebrated in rabbinic literature for setting Judaism on the path of endless interpretations, discussions, and debates. That honor belongs to Joshua's and Eliezer's student, Rabbi Akiva. But in the mythic drama of the early rabbis after the Roman destruction of Jerusalem in 70 C.E., Joshua plays a pivotal role that makes Akiva's influence possible.

Let's look at a few rabbinic texts that illustrate these points. First, we'll turn to the earliest layer of rabbinic writing, the Mishnah, where we find this well-known passage:

> Rabbi Yohanan ben Zakkai had five students: Rabbi Eliezer ben Hyrcanus, Rabbi Joshua ben Hananiah, Rabbi Yosi the Priest, Rabbi Shimon ben Netanel, and Rabbi Elazar ben Arakh.
>
> He would recount their praises like this: "Rabbi Eliezer ben Hyrcanus is a cistern sealed with plaster that does not lose a drop. Rabbi Joshua ben Hananiah—happy is the one who gave birth to him! Rabbi Yossi the Priest is pious. Rabbi Shimon ben Netanel fears sin. And Rabbi Elazar ben Arakh is an ever-strengthening spring."
>
> [Yohanan ben Zakkai] used to say: "If all the sages of Israel were on one side of a balance scale, and Rabbi Eliezer ben Hyrcanus were on the other side, [Rabbi Eliezer] would outweigh them all." Abba Shaul said in [Yohanan ben Zakkai's] name that if all the sages of Israel, including Rabbi Eliezer ben Hyrcanus, were on one side of a balance scale, and Rabbi Elazar ben Arakh were on the other side, [Rabbi Elazar ben Arakh] would outweigh them all.[1]

This text starts out by naming five of Yohanan ben Zakkai's students, and it tells us a different compliment that he gave each one of them. But in its second half, the text shifts to its "balance scale" imagery. It offers us two conflicting traditions about what Yohanan ben Zakkai used to say about the "weightiness" of two of these five students. First, the narrator says that Yohanan ben Zakkai used to say that Eliezer would outweigh all the other sages of Israel combined. But then another sage, Abba Shaul, comes along and says that he heard it differently. He heard that Yohanan ben Zakkai used to say that Elazar ben Arakh would outweigh all the other sages, including Eliezer.

The text doesn't tell us which of the two accounts is more accurate, nor does it address the possibility that at different points in time Yohanan ben Zakkai may have said each statement. But the text does leave us with the impression that Elazar ben Arakh is even greater than Eliezer ben Hyrcanus,

---

1. *m. Avot* 2:8. Translation with my adaptations from *Sefaria* online at https://www.sefaria.org/Pirkei_Avot.2.8.

Why This Rabbi Matters Now

because of the way it's written. The editors gave Abba Shaul the last word, and let's note when he says that Yohanan ben Zakkai used to teach that Elazar ben Arakh would outweigh all the other sages of Israel combined, he claims that Yohanan would mention Eliezer by name as one of the many sages on the other side of the balance scale from Elazar ben Arakh.

It's important to keep in mind that what is being compared in the second half of this text is not just these two ancient rabbis, but the metaphors that the first half of the text used to describe both of them. Eliezer is a sealed cistern that doesn't lose a drop of water. Elazar ben Arakh[2] is an ever-strengthening spring.

The contemporary Jewish scholar Devora Steinmetz teaches that what we have here in this comparison of these two metaphors—the sealed cistern and the ever-strengthening spring—is a comparison of two different models of Torah. In a wonderful lecture[3] she gave at a Jewish learning center called Hadar,[4] Steinmetz discusses this text along with several others to explain her sense of how rabbinic Judaism, writ large, ends up viewing Eliezer's understanding of the nature of Torah versus Elazar ben Arakh's understanding.

Steinmetz argues that Eliezer's understanding of Torah is pessimistic. He sees a Torah that is ever-diminishing, ever diluting. The farther we move in time from the earliest, most authentic Torah, the more Torah is lost in transmission. That is why Eliezer works so hard to be a sealed cistern that doesn't lose a drop. Let's consider, briefly, another early rabbinic text that illustrates Eliezer's understanding of an ever-diminishing Torah:

> Rabbi Eliezer the Great says: from the day the Temple was destroyed, the sages began to be like scribes, the scribes like synagogue-attendants, the synagogue-attendants like common people, and the common people became more and more debased. And nobody seeks [the meaning of Torah]. Upon whom shall we depend? Upon our Father who is in heaven.[5]

---

2. And who is this Elazar ben Arakh, you might ask, especially since his name has barely come up in this book? He is not the same person as the young sage we met back in chapter 4, Elazar ben Azariah. This Elazar is a figure who only appears a few times in rabbinic literature, and for our purposes, let's just go with the text's presentation of him as a rabbi so weighty in his value that he may have outweighed Eliezer and the other sages combined.

3. Steinmetz, "The Death of Rabbi Eliezer" (audio recording online).

4. www.hadar.org.

5. *m. Sotah* 9.15.

The Forgotten Sage

We saw another example of Eliezer's attitude towards Torah in chapter 7 of this book, in the text describing the scene at Eliezer's deathbed. In that text, as Eliezer lay dying, he says to Joshua ben Hananiah and the other rabbis who have come to visit him:

> Woe unto you, two arms of mine that are like two scrolls of the Torah being rolled closed. I've studied much Torah and I've taught much Torah. Much Torah have I learned, yet I have only skimmed from the knowledge of my teachers as much as a dog lapping from the sea. Much Torah have I taught, yet my disciples have only drawn from me as much as a mascara stick from its tube.[6]

Eliezer's understanding of Torah is that it is a static body of information that is ever diminishing over time, because from generation to generation students fail to learn everything their masters know, and they make errors in their efforts to receive and transmit the Torah knowledge of their teachers. Steinmetz teaches that Eliezer's is also an understanding of Torah that has no need of collaborative process, because that process is not worth anything if it does not arrive at the correct answer. The Talmud teaches: "Form many groups and study Torah, for the Torah is only acquired through group study,"[7] but it seems like Eliezer doesn't see what the purpose of all this group study would be, unless it was strictly focused on memorizing the teachings of the past. If Torah is like a vast body of water that was given once at Mt. Sinai but has been leaking away through the process of transmission from generation to generation, then what is the point of multiple opinions and innovative insights? That's the view of Torah that leads Eliezer to give up on the rabbinic system of debate and majority rule in the Akhnai's oven story.

Steinmetz teaches that ultimately the understanding of Torah that rabbinic tradition embraces is not the ever-diminishing model of Eliezer, but the ever-strengthening spring of Elazar ben Arakh. Rabbinic Judaism as we know it ends up celebrating an understanding of Torah that is generative, that grows through new debate, interpretation, and innovation. This understanding of Torah also owes a great debt to our hero, Joshua ben Hananiah, who courageously fended off the threats that Eliezer and Gamaliel brought to the rabbinic method of debate and majority rule. And this understanding of Torah gets championed by Akiva.

6. *b. Sanh.* 68a.
7. *b. Ber.* 63b.

Why This Rabbi Matters Now

Back in chapter 7, I wrote that there was a bit more to the Talmudic story of the death of Eliezer that we would examine, so let's do that now. It turns out that this story is framed by a question preceding it and an answer to that question immediately following it. Just before the Talmud launches into this story, the *stam* states that there are two conflicting traditions about who Akiva learned the esoteric laws about sorcery and magically growing cucumbers from (yes—we're back to those magic cucumbers again!). In one place we are told that Akiva learned those laws from Joshua ben Hananiah, but in the story of the death of Eliezer, we are told that Akiva learned those laws from Eliezer. The *stam* asks, "Well, which is it?"

After posing the question, the Talmud then presents the story of Eliezer's death. As you may recall, that story ends with Akiva's dramatic public expressions of grief and his eulogies for the deceased Eliezer. Then, the *stam* answers the question that triggered the sharing of the story as follows:

> [Rabbi Akiva] learned it first from Rabbi Eliezer, but he did not understand it. Later he learned it from Rabbi Joshua, and Rabbi Joshua explained it to him.[8]

Devora Steinmetz teaches that Akiva "learned it—in the sense of to receive a teaching—from Rabbi Eliezer, but he didn't understand it. At a later point in time, Akiva received the teaching from Rabbi Joshua, and Rabbi Joshua was able to make Akiva understand it."[9] Akiva was able to hear the information from Eliezer, but he couldn't really learn it from Eliezer. He needed to learn it from someone who could teach it to him in a different way. The tragedy of this story is that Eliezer really is recognized by the rabbis of his time as an unparalleled receptacle of Torah, but the Torah he contains within himself is inaccessible to others. "He can't teach Torah in a way that other people can receive it."

Steinmetz adds:

> This story is really talking about two different models of what Torah is, how Torah grows, how Torah lives within us and within community. What has to be understood is that the model that our rabbinic tradition celebrates is the model of Rabbi Akiva, not the model of Rabbi Eliezer. That is our past. That is something that we value, but it is not the Torah that we can learn. It is not the Torah of our future. . . . The rabbinic tradition ends up opting instead

---

8. *b. Sanh.* 68a.
9. Steinmetz, "The Death of Rabbi Eliezer" (audio recording online).

for a model of Torah that has to be understood—which means not only that you have to explain it to me technically, but it has to live within me in a way that it makes sense to my experience, which means it's new Torah. When I learn Torah from somebody in a way that it becomes mine, it becomes new Torah, it lives in a new way.[10]

If Akiva is the most visible champion of a generative, growing, living Torah in early rabbinic literature, what stands out for me in this last bit of Talmudic text that we've looked at is that it is Joshua who is able to teach Akiva Torah in a way that he can understand it and make it his own. And maybe that is why the Mishnah mourns Joshua's death with these words:

> When Rabbi Joshua died, goodness ceased from the world.—*m. Sotah* 9.15

---

10. Steinmetz, "The Death of Rabbi Eliezer" (audio recording online).

11

About Joshua Podro

This book began with a question. I was thinking one day about the Akhnai's oven story, and I was trying to remember the name of the rabbi who stood up and argued against the Divine voice from heaven—the *bat kol*—who had just proclaimed that Rabbi Eliezer was right about the oven and about every matter on which he had issued a legal opinion. Who was that rabbi again—the one who got up and said, "It is not in heaven!"?

I looked it up. Rabbi Joshua ben Hananiah. This led to a second question: what other important things did this rabbi say in rabbinic literature? I began looking up every Rabbi Joshua story I could find, in the Talmud, in Midrash, and in other ancient rabbinic texts as well. One by one, the stories I discovered drew me back into the mythic story world depicting the first generation of rabbis who survived the Roman destruction and then carried on after it.

The more I studied, the more I noticed that there seemed to be a lot of stories in which Joshua emerged as a voice of compassion and reason, as a gentle and inclusive thinker, and as an assertive advocate for the newly developing rabbinic system of debate, majority rule, and the preservation of minority opinions in the record. I also noticed that he had both deep compassion and audacious courage—a combination I found magnetic. "Someone has probably written a rabbinic biography of him," I thought, and I began searching for some. I was only able to find one title: a 1959 book called *The Last Pharisee: The Life and Times of Rabbi Joshua ben Hananyah, a First-Century Idealist*, by Joshua Podro (1894–1962).

It wasn't an easy book to get a hold of. I eventually got a copy through interlibrary loan, and it was a bit banged up. In its pages I discovered many more legends and legal decisions attributed to Joshua throughout the wide span of rabbinic literature. I also felt a bit of kinship with Podro, who clearly admired Rabbi Joshua's approach to trauma, ethics, and the meaning of Judaism in a post-destruction world. Like Podro, I identified with many of the rabbinic (and humanistic) values associated with Rabbi Joshua in rabbinic literature.

The renowned British poet, classicist, and writer, Robert Graves, wrote the Foreword to Podro's book. I later learned that Podro, a scholar of Hebrew and Aramaic as well as biblical and rabbinic literature, had collaborated with Graves to write the 1953 work, *The Nazarene Gospel Restored*. The two men had a long and close friendship and scholarly relationship.

Podro was born in Russia as Joshua Podroushnik. A veteran of World War I, he made his way to New York, where he worked as a journalist. Later he moved to England, where he ran a successful press clipping service. In addition to *The Last Pharisee* and *The Nazarene Gospel Restored*, Podro wrote *Nuremberg, The Unholy City: A Chapter in Jewish Martyrology* (1937), and with Graves he co-wrote *Jesus in Rome: A Historical Conjecture* (1957).

Without Joshua Podro, I would not have written this book. I'd like to close this work with gratitude to him for his research and writing, which has influenced me deeply and given me a deepened appreciation of rabbinic literature.

Joshua Podro

Bibliography

Adler, Morris. *The World of the Talmud*. New York: Schocken, 1958.
Alon, Gedaliah. *The Jews in Their Land in the Talmudic Age*. Translated and edited by Gershon Levi. Cambridge: Harvard University Press, 1989.
Antonelli, Judith S. *In the Image of God: A Feminist Commentary on the Torah*. Northvale, NJ: Aronson, 1975.
Aslan, Reza. *No god but God: The Origins, Evolution, and Future of Islam*. New York: Random House, 2005.
Baird, Justus. "Praying with My Feet." Online at: https://www.sefaria.org/sheets/25820.?lang=bi.
Balberg, Mira. "The Emperor's Daughter's New Skin: Bodily Otherness and Self-Identity in the Dialogues of Rabbi Yehoshua ben Hanania and the Emperor's Daughter." *Jewish Studies Quarterly* 19 (2012) 181–206.
Bazzana, Giovanni Battista. "The Bar Kokhba Revolt and Hadrian's Religious Policy." In *Hadrian and the Christians*, edited by Marco Rizzi, 85–110. Berlin: de Gruyter, 2010.
Belser, Julia Watts. *Rabbinic Tales of Destruction: Gender, Sex, and Disability in the Ruins of Jerusalem*. Oxford: Oxford University Press, 2018.
Berman, Samuel A., *Midrash Tanhuma—Yelammedenu: An English Translation of Genesis and Exodus from the Printed Version of Tanhuma-Yelammedenu with an Introduction, Notes, and Indexes*. Hoboken, NJ: KTAV, 1996.
Bialik, H. N., and Y. H. Ravnitzky, eds. *Sefer Ha-Aggadah* (The Book of Legends). Translated by William G. Braude. New York: Schocken, 1992.
Boyarin, Daniel. "The Yavneh-Cycle of the Stammaim and the Invention of the Rabbis." In *Creation and Composition: The Contribution of the Bavli Redactors (Stammaim) to the Aggada*, edited by Jeffrey L. Rubenstein, 237–89. Tübingen: Mohr Siebeck, 2005.
Broyde, Michael. "Pacifism in Jewish Law." Online at: https://www.myjewishlearning.com/article/pacifism-in-jewish-law/.
Cohen, A. *Midrash Rabbah: Vol. 7, Deuteronomy, Lamentations*. New York: Soncino, 1983. Online at: http://www.livius.org/sources/content/rabbinical-literature/midrash-rabbah-lamentations-2.2.4/.
Cohen, Shaye J. D. "The Destruction: From Scripture to Midrash." *Prooftexts* 2.1 (1982) 18–39.
———. "The Significance of Yavneh: Pharisees, Rabbis, and the End of Jewish Sectarianism." *Hebrew Union College Annual* 55 (1984) 27–53.
Eisenberg, Ronald L. *Essential Figures in the Talmud*. Lanham, MD: Aronson, 2013.

Bibliography

Feintuch, Rav Dr. Yonatan. "Shiur #20: The Story of the Death of R. Eliezer—part I." Online at: https://www.etzion.org.il/en/shiur-20-story-death-r-eliezer-%E2%80%93-part-i.

———. "Shiur #21: The Story of the Death of R. Eliezer—part I." Online at: https://www.etzion.org.il/en/shiur-20-story-death-r-eliezer-%E2%80%93-part-ii.

Finkelstein, Louis. *Akiba: Scholar, Saint and Martyr*. Philadelphia: Jewish Publication Society, 1936.

Firestone, Reuven. *Holy War and Judaism: The Fall and Rise of a Controversial Idea*. Oxford: Oxford University Press, 2012.

Frank, Arthur W. *The Wounded Storyteller: Body, Illness, and Ethics*. Chicago: University of Chicago Press, 1995.

Fraenkel, Jonah. "Time and Its Role in the Aggadic Story." *Binah: Studies in Jewish Thought*, Vol. 2, edited by Joseph Dan, 31–56. New York: Praeger, 1989.

Friedlander, Gerald, trans. and annotator. *Pirke de Rabbi Eliezer (The Chapters of Rabbi Eliezer the Great) according to the Text of the Manuscript Belonging to Abraham Epstein of Vienna*. London: Kegan Paul, Trench, Trubner & Co., 1916.

Frieman, Shulamis. *Who's Who in the Talmud*. Jerusalem: Aronson, 1995.

Gottheil, Richard, and Samuel Krauss. "Hadrian." In *The Jewish Encyclopedia*, edited by Isidore Singer, 6:134–35. New York: Funk & Wagnalls, 1906.

Green, Deborah A. *The Aroma of Righteousness: Scent and Seduction in Rabbinic Life and Literature*. University Park, PA: Penn State University Press, 2011.

Green, William Scott. *The Traditions of Joshua ben Hananiah: Part One: The Early Legal Traditions*. Leiden: Brill, 1981.

Greenwood, Daniel J. H. "Akhnai: Legal Responsibility in the World of the Silent God." *Utah L. Rev.* 309 (1997) 309–58.

Gutoff, Joshua. "The Necessary Outlaw: The Catastrophic Excommunication & Paradoxical Rehabilitation of Rabbi Eliezer Ben Hyrcanus." *Journal of Law and Religion* 11.2 (1994–95) 733–48.

Hammer, Reuven. *Akiva: Life, Legend, Legacy*. Lincoln, NE: Published by the University of Nebraska (Jewish Publication Society), 2015.

Handelman, Susan A. *Make Yourself a Teacher: Rabbinic Tales of Mentors and Disciples*. Seattle: University of Washington Press, 2011.

———. *Slayers of Moses: The Emergence of Rabbinic Interpretation in Modern Literary Theory*. Albany, NY: State University of New York Press, 1983.

Hartman, David. *A Heart of Many Rooms: Celebrating the Many Voices within Judaism*. Woodstock, VT: Jewish Publication Society, 1999.

Hartman, Donniel. "Getting Serious about BDS and Breaking the Silence." *The Times of Israel*, Dec 24, 2015.

Hasan-Rokem, Galit. *Web of Life: Folklore and Midrash in Rabbinic Literature*. Translated by Batya Stein. Stanford, CA: Stanford University Press, 2000.

Hayes, Christine. "Rabbinic Contestations of Authority." *The Cardozo Law Review* 28.1 (2006) 123–41.

Heger, Paul. *The Pluralistic Halakhah: Legal Innovations in the Late Second Commonwealth and Rabbinic Periods*. Berlin: de Gruyter, 2003.

Heschel, Abraham Joshua. *Heavenly Torah: As Refracted through the Generations—Edited and translated from the Hebrew with commentary by Gordon Tucker, with Leonard Levin*. New York: Continuum, 2006.

Bibliography

Holtz, Barry W. *Rabbi Akiva: Sage of the Talmud*. New Haven, CT: Yale University Press, 2017.

Horsley, Richard A., and John S. Hanson. *Bandits, Prophets, and Messiahs: Popular Movements at the Time of Jesus*. San Francisco: Harper San Francisco, 1985.

Jaffee, Martin S. *Early Judaism*. Upper Saddle River, NJ: Prentice-Hall, 1997.

Kamenetz, Rodger. *The Jew in the Lotus: A Poet's Rediscovery of Jewish Identity in India*. New York: HarperCollins, 1994.

Kaminsky, Joel S. "Reviewed Work: The Image of Bar Kokhba in Traditional Jewish Literature: False Messiah and National Hero." *Jewish Political Studies Review* 9.1/2 (1997) 123–24.

LaGrone, Matthew. "Judaism and Religious Freedom in the Rabbinic Period (70 CE–1000 CE)." Online at: https://berkleycenter.georgetown.edu/essays/judaism-and-religious-freedom-in-the-rabbinic-period-70-ce-1000-ce.

La'u, Binyamin. *The Sages: Character, Context, & Creativity, Vol. 2: From Yavneh to the Bar Kokhba Revolt*. Jerusalem: Koren—Translation Edition, 2012. Kindle edition.

Lawrence, Tim. "Everything Doesn't Happen for a Reason." Online at: http://www.timjlawrence.com/blog/2015/10/19/everything-doesnt-happen-for-a-reason.

Lieberman, S., ed. *Tosefta, Nashim 2*. Translated by S. Berrin. New York: Jewish Theological Seminary of America, 1973.

Linzer, Rabbi Dov. "Rabbi Eliezer vs. Rabbi Akiva: Two Models of Torah." Online at: https://library.yctorah.org/2010/04/rabbi-eliezer-vs-rabbi-akiva-two-models-of-torah/.

Luban, David. "The Coiled Serpent of Argument: Reason, Authority, and Law in a Talmudic Tale: Epilogue: Law and Fable." *Chicago-Kent Law Review* 79 (2004) 1253–88.

Marks, Richard G. *The Image of Bar Kokhba in Traditional Jewish Literature: False Messiah and National Jewish Hero*. University Park, PA: Penn State University Press, 1994.

Meszler, Rabbi Josheph B. *Witnesses to the One: The Spiritual History of the Sh'ma*. Woodstock, VT: Jewish Lights, 2006.

Neusner, Jacob. *Eliezer ben Hyrcanus: The Tradition and the Man, Vol. 1*. Reprint, Eugene, OR: Wipf & Stock, 2003.

———. *Eliezer ben Hyrcanus: The Tradition and the Man, Vol. 2*. Leiden: Brill Academic, 1973.

———. *Lamentations Rabbah: An Analytical Translation*. Neusner Titles in Brown Judaic Studies—Book 193. Atlanta: Scholars, 1989.

Ouaknin, Marc-Alain. *The Burnt Book: Reading the Talmud*. Translated by Llewellyn Brown. Princeton, NJ: Princeton University Press, 1995.

Podro, Joshua. "A 1st-Century Jewish Sage: The Life and Teachings of Rabbi Joshua ben Hananiah." *Commentary*, July 1958. Online: https://www.commentarymagazine.com/articles/a-1st-century-jewish-sagethe-life-and-teachings-of-rabbi-joshua-ben-hananiah/.

———. *The Last Pharisee: The Life and Times of Rabbi Joshua Ben Hananyah—A First Century Idealist*. London: Vallentine, Mitchell, 1959.

Pogrebin, Letty Cottin. "The Many Gradations of #MeToo." *Moment Magazine* 43.6, 2018, 20.

Raphael, Simcha Paull. *Jewish Views of the Afterlife: Second Edition*. Lanham, MD: Rowman & Littlefield, 2009.

Rich, Tracy R. "Halakhah." Online at: http://www.jewfaq.org/defs/halakhah.htm.

Bibliography

Roller, Duane W. *The Building Program of Herod the Great.* Berkeley: Regents of University of California Berkeley, 1998.

Rubenstein, Jeffrey L. *Rabbinic Stories.* Mahwah, NJ: Paulist, 2002.

Saldarini, Anthony J. "Johanan ben Zakkai's Escape from Jerusalem: Origin and Development of a Rabbinic Story." *Journal for the Study of Judaism in the Persian, Hellenistic, and Roman Period* 6.2 (1975) 189–204.

Sales, Ruby. *"Where Does It Hurt?"* Radio interview: *On Being*, with host, Krista Tippett. Online at: https://onbeing.org/programs/ruby-sales-where-does-it-hurt/.

Salzberg, Sharon. *Faith: Trusting Your Own Deepest Experience.* New York: Riverhead, 2002.

Schiffman, Lawrence H. *From Text to Tradition: A History of Second Temple & Rabbinic Judaism.* Brooklyn, NY: KTAV, 1991.

Shanks, Herschel, ed. *Christianity and Rabbinic Judaism: A Parallel History of Their Origins and Early Development.* Washington, DC: Biblical Archeological Society, 1992.

Steinmetz, Devora. "Agada Unbound." In *Creation and Composition: The Contribution of the Bavli Redactors (Stammaim) to the Aggada*, edited by Jeffrey L. Rubenstein, 293–337. Tübingen: Mohr Siebeck, 2005.

———. "The Death of Rabbi Eliezer." Audio recording of a lecture given at Hadar, online at: https://www.hadar.org/torah-resource/death-rabbi-eliezer.

Steinsaltz, Rabbi Adin. *The Talmud, Vol. 3: Tractate Bava Metzia, Part 3, the Steinsaltz Editon (English and Hebrew Edition).* Edited and translated by Berman, Rabbi Israel V. New York: Random House, 1990.

Thiede, Barbara. "Is Modern Rabbinic Judaism Based on a Myth?" *Scribe: The Forward's Contributor Network.* Online at: https://forward.com/scribe/392170/is-rabbinic-judaism-based-on-a-myth/.

VanderKam, James C. "Judaism in the Land of Israel." In *Early Judaism: A Comprehensive Overview,* edited by John J. Collins and Daniel C. Harlow, 70–94. Grand Rapids: Eerdmans, 2012.

Vizotsky, Burton L. *Sage Tales: Wisdom and Wonder from the Rabbis of the Talmud.* Woodstock, VT: Jewish Lights, 2011.